New American Review

810.8
Vol. 14

A Touchstone Book
Published by
Simon and Schuster

NEW AMERICAN REVIEW
Editor: Theodore Solotaroff
Managing Editor: Rhoma Paul
Poetry Editor: Richard Howard
Associate Editors: Alice Mayhew, Daniel Moses, Carol Saltus
Assistant to the Editor: Debora Sherman

Production Associates: Frank Metz (art), Helen Barrow (design),
Suzanne Frisbie, Susan Edwards, Tom Kieran, Ruth Randall

Cover design by Peter Schaumann

A Touchstone Book
Published by Simon and Schuster
Rockefeller Center, 630 Fifth Avenue
New York, New York 10020

FIRST PRINTING

SBN 671–21220–6 Touchstone paperback edition
Library of Congress Catalog Card Number: 67–27377
Manufactured in the United States of America

The editors invite submissions. Manuscripts will
not be returned unless accompanied
by stamped self-addressed envelope.

Contents

Editors' Notes

ONE OF THE virtues of Randall Reid's story "Detritus" is that it places a cool, astringent intelligence upon the inflamed interests we bring these days to any fiction that deals with sex, which is to say almost any fiction. The virtual elimination of censorship and taboos in literature, as in other of the arts and trades, has had the peculiar effect of making the formerly forbidden details common-place without particularly reducing the desire for them. Or so one would gather from reading and going to films or stopping in the porno shops, which appear to be the most rapidly expanding industry in America. Recently a shop opened in New York which had a number of booths arranged in a circle around a small stage. One dropped in his quarter, a panel opened in the booth, and there before one's eyes was a naked woman doing her poses. For some reason this shop was quickly closed by the police, but it lingers in the mind as a reverberating image of how things are with us sexual-culturally. One enters the novel or film or play and waits for the panel to open, and when it does, our interest picks up and the cameras of fantasy begin to roll.

But not for very long, I would guess. One's interest tends to run out like the time bought by a quarter. For it is not imagination that is being engaged so much as that avid and compulsive peeker, quickly bored but never satisfied, known as curiosity. "I Am Curious" is not only the title of two recent "panel" films but rather a kind of proclamation of public taste: it seems more than a sign of effective law enforcement that on those blocks in midtown Manhattan where the stylish hookers once cruised, there are now the storefront movie houses and bookstores and the men making change.

The wave of porn, however teasing and unseemly, may have certain benefits in relaxing repressions and providing information. There is a lot of polemic about its side effects, but nobody really knows, except each of us personally. Still, all of these images and scenes of bodies and positions taken out of context do tend to stimulate the nerves while impoverishing understanding. The problem and opportunity of earlier authors in portraying sex is that they had to make the context everything in the hope that the development and ramifications of a passion such as Kate Croy's or Count Vronsky's might charge the book with a sensuality that glowed and hummed between the lines. Just as Anna's magnificent shoulders had to suggest the whole panoply of charms that she would deliver up to her lover, so too the erotic power of the relationship had to be indicated by the web of circumstances that fostered and resisted it: physical, mental, marital, social, moral, religious, etc. This need to imply and externalize the erotic was not always an unmitigated boon. While it benefited a Tolstoy, and for certain additional reasons, a James or a Charlotte Brontë (I am drawing here on a recent conversation with another contributor to this issue, Reynolds Price), it seems finally to be a handicap to writers like Stendhal and Flaubert, and again, for additional reasons, Dostoevsky. Be that as it may, there was an across-the-board benefit to suggestiveness and intelligence by having to make sexual interest reside in the before and the after, by locating it in the world and in the mind rather than in the bedroom and genitals. As Dr. Johnson put it, with a cool sanity that isn't so prevalent these days, "Were it not for imagination, Sir, a man would be as happy in the arms of a chambermaid as of a duchess."

The sensualist who speaks in Randall Reid's story "Detritus" calls himself by that old-fashioned term "roué" rather than by our symptomatic term "stud." And there is an old-fashioned deliberateness and circumspection about his memories of women which, joined to his up-to-date candor, produces a most astonishing range of consciousness.

(continued on page 248)

Detritus

Randall Reid

I suppose I'm bored. That is an affectation, of course. And as a way to begin it is as banal as *Once upon a time*. But it doesn't matter, I don't aspire to novelty. Just memory and malice. And vanity. Portrait of a man alone with a mirror, making faces in the glass.

What next?

Wives are the best. Their purity has already gone to market, and they need not guard it anymore.

"But my husband, my children, my responsibilities—"

"You are too good for all that."

Secretly, at least, she will of course agree. And security palls. You appeal to her sense of freedom, her desire to be rid of it all. A little flattery, a little wicked titillation, and then the unanswerable question: "Why not?"

Well, why not?

•

Stopped for cigarettes at a newsstand and found myself staring at a magazine nude tacked to the wall. Another commodity. They have rouged and retouched her skin until it looks made of orange fudge. Enticing, of course— and her breasts are magnificent, or at least huge. But her groin is just another armpit, shaven and scented and sex- less. Our modern mermaid, the girl with no way in. All her cleavage is above the belt.

I gathered my change. Her nipples watched me like fleshy pink eyes, her eyes saw nothing but the camera.

•

P.M.: Philip was here, talking of betrayal and heedless- ness in his tormented voice. I tried to calm him. Useless. He is right, of course, but it doesn't matter.

•

I fell in love with Laura because her shoes did not fit. They made her totter when she walked, and her huge round eyes had a terror in them, as if she were always about to fall. It was comic in its way. There she was, with arms like thighs and breasts the size of cabbages. She could have given birth to an army and scarcely felt the pain. Yet she reminded me of a child. I pitied her, I wanted to touch her and tell her not to be afraid of the dark.

My sympathy made her cry. And tears made her helpless. She thought it very good of me to console her, in my way.

Treat a big woman as if she were very frail. Usually she is.

•

When Harriet left, I lived with two girls named Anne and Suzanne whom I fucked endlessly, separately and together, until they became for me a composite body with mouths everywhere, and too many nipples, and soft, superfluous thighs. They proposed a "real" orgy. I should do everything possible to each of them, and they would do everything to each other, and we would all watch. We did. And it excited me, even profoundly excited me. All those tongues and thighs and breasts, endlessly duplicated by the mirrors and our eyes. But at last something seemed to get stuck. Images repeated themselves: mouths sucking, hands grasping, orifices being plugged. It went on and on, like some dreadful labor we were condemned eternally to perform.

The next day I received a letter with an invitation— an old friend had purchased a house with forty acres of woods and meadow. I went into the country for the sake of my health and the good of my soul.

Curiously enough, it worked. My senses blossomed, I discovered smells that were not recognizably female—oak leaves, hot dust at the edge of the road, the sweet, boggy smell of horses and meadow grass. Very trite, of course, but very pleasant. And my friend turned out better than I expected. The years had worn away his illusions without damaging his heart; he was that rare creature, a nice man who was not a fool. It pleased me to pat his dogs, admire his view, compliment his wife. I even acquired a remote and sentimental love for his daughter, home from her first year at college. She was such a little thing. Her clear gray eyes grew wide whenever you spoke to her, and she smelled as clean and pink as a new eraser. I felt strangely protective; it was a pleasure not to touch her, to leave her fragile and intact beside me.

We rode together sometimes, or drove into town for the papers and stopped for a picnic on the way home. Once we found a quiet place near the river, a grove of trees where a path led down to a pasture and a little spring. The day was still, hot. We ate our sandwiches in the shade and shared our silence. I had a pleasant regret to nurse, born of my approaching departure. Later, she wandered down to the spring and I went back to the car for cigarettes. I returned to find her stretched naked on a beach towel, asleep. There was no breeze, only the pure and soundless heat; her firm young buttocks glowed in the sun. I touched her, and her lips came apart. She whispered something I could not hear. But her arms reached for me, and we rolled together on the grass. Again and again, until the sweat stung my eyes. At last she slept, while I sat dazed and trembling in the sun.

That was ecstasy, if you like. Of course the sequel was not so pretty—tears, confessions, my friend compelled to act the outraged father, but too aware of his comic position and too confused in his outrage to be impressive. Instead of indignation, it produced only confused shame, as if we had all dirtied ourselves publicly. I left amid mutually averted eyes.

•

I saw Shriver today. He looked dried up, made of dandruff and parchment. Still very dapper, of course, but his eyes are fever-ridden. Those spiderish lusts of his. He loves delirium, fantasy, orgy—in his dreams, convent girls squirm in perpetual coition with monks and Great Danes.

I despise all voyeurs of the forbidden.

And the gourmet of handsome flesh, too. You know the type; he is found wherever luxury can be purchased—a fat, balding man with the mouth of a carp. To him, the flesh of young girls is a sensuous pleasure, like cigars and vintage wines, and a material solace, like money.

I am a seducer, not a satanist. A semiretired roué.

•

Dreams again, that drastic vaporous light. The sea is made of glass and the beach is patrolled by aging fairies with orange hair and purplish tans.

•

I seem to have settled at last. Here, on my unfashionable hill, with a view of freeway loops and a glimpse of the bridge, I sit like some bit of debris beached by the tide.

I do no work, but I have an income—now, like other things, rather drastically reduced. My career? Thirty years a lover—until one night I humped MacGregor's wife on a borrowed bed, and caught a chill.

Blue veins and congealed fat. Pubic hair like dead moss. And an awful, sourceless cold like an emanation. The sheets smelled of it—snot-cold, fog-cold. She tried so hard to feel some pleasure. And I pumped and stared at that flat face, stupid with effort, until the spasm came. Then nothing. A seeping cold that made me shiver in her arms. She cried a little. When I withdrew, I saw it hanging there, weak and cold and small, like a shriveled teat. And the cold has proved ineradicable.

But I see a question quivering on your tongue.

"Are you still . . . I mean, can you?"

The answer, madam, is yes—yes to the question as you meant it, though perhaps I should say no. When the moment of revelation came, I was not visited by a penitential impotence. No, the machinery still works, obeying some law of its own. It works in spite of me. My orgasm is like a gun going off in another room; I scarcely hear the report.

•

Banal idea: Every desire breeds its opposite. To love is to hate, to hate is to love, ambivalence is the law of life, et cetera. And it doesn't stop there. Pleasure calls for pain. To desire success is to lust after failure. If freedom lures us, so does slavery—not just also, but *because:* desiring freedom makes us desire slavery. Hence vacillation, frustration, despair. A man cannot act without betraying a part of himself.

Antitheses are like sexes that blindly seek to couple and complete themselves—the secret love of vice for virtue and of virtue for vice.

•

Mara was not pretty, but she had a certain sluttish elegance. Her shoulders were always bare and round and buttery soft, cut by two little straps. When she bent down, her breasts would spill like water over the top of her dress.

Those were the days when every girl had a mouth like a whore's. Lipstick so red and thick you could see it shine. She had a whore's laugh, too. I hated her laugh.

It excited me.

•

I was a pale and delicate child. My school pictures would amuse you—I sit like a little seraph amidst the grosser substance of my classmates. Beware the delicate child. Beware anyone who wears his sensitivity like a suit of clothes.

•

Women should always dress so that they can be gracefully undressed. The process, not the mere result of nakedness, is what matters; it is an art to be performed and prolonged.

And suspense is its soul. To be almost seduced, with the final act imminent but still unperformed, is to be deliciously helpless with anticipation. So I always let the final garment stay for a moment. I kiss her throat and breasts, brush my lips against the muscles of her spine, until at last my hands slide beneath the elastic and begin to draw her panties down. But slowly, slowly, so that she feels herself being exposed. Voluptuous sensation! The gliding silk against her skin, my eyes and hands caressing her—even the air whispers her nakedness. A little hesitation to savor it. Then down, all the way down, and that lovely mound is revealed, so warm and swollen, so exquisitely wet with her surrender.

And so it goes. Memories, little pictures from the past. Sometimes only the nerves remember. Whoever she was, she remains nameless. I am aware only of her freckled shoulders, the special flavor of her mouth.

They seem to be increasing, these phantoms of the

senses. And all mixed up with the women are smells of forgotten rooms, the taste of some breakfast food I had as a child. Symptomatic, I suppose, the efflorescence of decay.

•

Things wear out, but not quite. Something is left, something meaningless but sufficient. I am quite safe.

•

Philip accused me of his mother's death. She is dead, I said, what does it matter? Take the guilt if you want it, mine or hers. And of course he has. You can see death in him. He has that terrible bodiless rage—white face, pinched nostrils, a screaming horror in the voice. It is a convulsion of the nerves, with no flesh or bone to sustain it.

•

In one of those treacherously serene states which follows a debauch, I found myself paired at a dinner party with a girl who said she knew of me through friends. She was small, very plain, past thirty—one of those colorless little virgins who can be found aging in every library, every school. She bored me, but I didn't mind. In such a mood, to be bored seems virtuous, both charitable and ascetic. Some whim of gallantry even made me offer to see her home.

Whatever we talked about, it must have charmed her. She invited me in for coffee. I was inattentive; caresses were a reflex, and so were words.

But not for her. Soon she was half-undressed and quivering beneath me on the couch.

Her eyes were so helpless. I felt a qualm, or something, and I did a strange thing—I stopped. A pretty scene. There she was, with her skirt up and her dignity down, and I began to talk. I moralized, apologized, stalled. And every moment her bare loins grew more ugly in my eyes and in hers. The moment prolonged itself unbearably. She could not move, could not even cover herself. She just shriveled up until there was not enough left of her to cry.

There was destruction for you, admirably thorough. I leave it to those who have a taste for it.

•

I am troubled by dreams. Amuse yourselves with this

one. A woman with no mouth and huge breasts—mottled, sausage-colored breasts. When I squeeze them, they pop like boils.

•

Conventional bric-a-brac. Roués exude triteness, even in their dreams.

•

"But don't you really believe a married woman should be chaste?"

"No." My denial was as abrupt and titillating as a slap in the face. She found it irresistible.

Radical ideas induce tumescence of the brain.

•

I write by fits and starts, flirting with subjects as promiscuously as if they were women.

Scriptus interruptus.

•

Women are attractive only when they are frightened or aroused. Left to themselves, they run to teacups and little hats and fat—not woman fat, but steer fat: sluggish, neutered flesh. One torments them out of love and pity; one cannot bear to see them be so dull.

•

Carolyn was rich. And cultured and passionate and sensitive—one of those women whose appetites are insatiable but exquisitely refined. We had to make love to Mozart, or watch the evening darken while a flute sang in another room. Very pure it was, and very pretty, and it made me ill.

I despise serious music; it is ashamed to let its vulgarity show. Give me drums that pound and saxophones that wallow in their own ooze. Or moonlight and sweet dreams —lies too old and artless to conceal the truth.

•

The truth, indeed, as if I could tell it.

I try to speak, but my tongue misquotes me, my hands gesture blandly of themselves. I have the mannerisms of a veteran salesman or a veteran whore.

•

Rain today, cold and damp. I sit and watch the blue

flames of my stove, huddled close, with memories wrapped like a shawl around me.

And I have been rereading what I have written. I do not like it; it smells as withered and faintly rotten as an old apple. It is false, too; memories are only retrospective fantasies, not to be trusted. And why tell them? To write one's memoirs is only a complicated form of self-abuse.

I have begun to leak aphorisms. Onanism and morality. In his old age, Don Juan becomes just another sententiously nasty old man.

My dotage: I shall acquire kidney stones and prostate trouble, affect a cane and wear a flower in my lapel. Perhaps I shall even find a wife—a middle-aged practical nurse who believes in laxatives and the power of prayer, or one of those dowagers whose bosoms emit little geysers of lavender scent at every breath.

No, those dowagers no longer exist. Grandma wears stretch pants and rubber breasts and an orange wig.

•

An aphorism on aphorisms: they are the mark of a promiscuous mind. An aphorist avoids philosophy as a roué avoids marriage; he is afraid to commit himself.

•

Certain lies speak to us more powerfully than any truth. Therefore they are the truth. About us.

•

I became a seducer because I could not bear to lie. So flattery, betrayal, the violation of all my anguished candor. On principle. Like the gratuitous cruelty of the tenderhearted, with the vicious little pleasure such a violation always brings.

. . . Another lie.

•

Now every magazine has its flawless nudes. They are worse than travel posters, those assertions of ideal flesh. Like visions of Rhine valleys and castles and happy picturesque folk. Somewhere that never was.

It isn't just the magazines. Ideals are nasty things no matter where they come from. All that dirty Greek marble —petrified daydreams, the destroyers of life.

•

That little white-haired man was in the papers again, still cackling out pronouncements at ninety. He is a living reproach, I suppose. Rationality, the strenuous pleasures of the mind, *mens sana in corpore sano,* the public self—one of those who strut around in the light of reason like sun-worshipers at a beach.

Well, reason *is* a light. And like any light it blinds while it illuminates. Stay in the sun too long and you can't see in the dark at all.

•

You cannot make love with your eyes; close them. Our loves should be as private as our dreams.

•

I could feel her presence beside me in the bus. A curious intimacy: the night heavy with sleep and motion, two strangers traveling together in the dark. I knew nothing about her except the smell of her hair and skin, the texture of her dress, the whisper of her stockings as she crossed her legs. And I wanted her. The aura which enclosed us was as palpable as any touch.

We romanticize our urgency and make it the measure of our desire, and that is nonsense. I have never been less urgent, and I have never desired anyone more. The soft pressure of her thigh stirred me. I wanted to touch it—not possess it or violate it, just touch it—the way one touches animals or smooth stones.

She accepted a cigarette. Her hand touched mine, and in the flaring match I saw her eyes and knew. So we spoke, kissed. Whispering a little, we made what love we could.

As we neared San Francisco, the lights came on and we were confronted by the absurdity of other people. She withdrew, straightening her skirt. I put my lips against her ear. "Get off with me," I said. "Here."

She nodded at last, not looking at me. "I must make a call."

The depot was full of that peculiar smell that public places have—rest rooms, buses, lunch counters—a smell composed of too many strangenesses mingled and cancelled.

She made her call and we found a room two blocks from Market. The fading prints of elastic at her waist and thighs were like the marks left by fetters. I smoothed them with my lips.

And then for once I forgot myself and her, and made nothing but love. The dark was full of it.

I woke at noon and found her curled in sleep against me. Against my chest, the faint suspiration of her breath —a rhythm I could enter. My thrust was as deep and slow and effortless as her sleep.

In that long tranquillity of desire, there is ease, not frenzy—a perfect closeness in which sensations flow back and forth like tides.

Then sleep again. At last I dressed, went down to the cafeteria on the corner, and brought back coffee in lidded paper cups.

She had put on my discarded shirt and was sitting up in bed. The shirt queerly accented her femininity. In that mannish collar, her neck looked frail and bare, and the dark circles of her nipples showed against the cloth. We sipped the coffee and did not talk. Outside: streetcar bells, traffic, the vague noises of the street. They were better than bird songs.

Soon it was time. I watched her resume the constrictions of bra and girdle, bend to the mirror and redraw her mask. When she had gathered her self about her, she touched my lips and eyes and disappeared. Where? To the depot, I suppose, and another bus, something which would carry her back to whatever she had left.

The ring she wore proclaimed that she was married. And there were signs of children—faint stretch marks on the abdomen, nipples that looked as if they had given suck. But I did not ask. We shared an intimacy that only the anonymous can ever know. Without identities, we could be ourselves.

●

I have spoiled it. It smells of my aphoristic smut. Yet I remember that time with pleasure, and there are not many such times.

Real abandonment is rare. Our selves, our moralities, our constraints seldom slip away. Instead, we nerve ourselves to violate them, and the result is hysteria, not release.

It is like sleep, the ability to slip quietly into another self and be restored. But few can do it. Most are like insomniacs, our waking dead. I have heard them cry out in their pleasure as they cry out in their sleep.

•

Never mind all that. What about the smut?

Excuse me, I have neglected a duty. Certain things are expected when a roué tells all.

Anatomical secrets: Chinese girls are crosswise. If niggers don't get it twice a day, their glands swell up and they go crazy. I knew a girl in New Jersey who could pick up pennies with her pussy.

Novelty: French ticklers. The sixty-nine secret positions of a Tibetan goatherd. Do it under water if you really want a thrill.

Satisfied?

No, tell me more.

They are all lies. All the novelty there is lurks hidden in the familiar gesture, the customary act.

Novelty is a pimp's invention, a fraud.

Forbidden glimpses. Dreams. They are made for the solitary one, the little masturbator in his soiled sheets. Alone, with flushed cheeks and furtive hand, he pursues his phantoms: black stockings, the pale gleam of flesh swollen around a garter; a nighttime world where nipples glow and wink like neon lights. His pleasure ends in the smell of his own semen, cold as snot against the skin.

And what about you, buddy? You and the wife read any good dirty books lately? The bedside shelf, Marriage Manuals and Erotic Classics. How-to-do-it books. Before long, someone will be selling blueprints for orgies, and the guests can fit themselves together like prefabricated pieces in the latest erector set.

•

Philip again, looking worse. A hemophiliac, he is forced quite literally to live on the blood of others, and he would rather die. So he wears that look of ghastly suffering, like a vampire Christ.

•

Pills seem to stick in the throat even after swallowing. They have a taste, too, no matter what they're made of.

Bitter, chalky things. They made me take them every morning as a child.

Enemas, syringes, syrups, pills. The smell of rubber sheets and vaseline. All those implements they use. Cold, passionless fingers that probe into you, proud of their indifference. There is no violation worse than that impersonal touch.

•

They told me witches were not real, but I knew they were; I had seen them. I had seen Hansel, too, and Gretel, and that sweet hideous house. It tasted like the candy flowers on birthday cakes. . . .

Hand in hand the lost boy and girl stand together in the darkness. The house lures them, frightens them. It is forbidden, they know, all sweetness is. They taste, and the vision of sweetness turns to stale confectionary sugar on the tongue. And then the witch's voice, with its unspeakable invitation.

•

On the day before my seventh birthday, I found a mouse fresh caught in a trap. It was squeezed flat in the middle, like a pinched sack full of something soft, but it was still alive. And it would not die. The mouth gaped and closed, gaped and closed, until I screamed and old Maria came and smashed its head with a bookend.

Then she dried my tears. "You are a very tender-hearted boy," she said. "But why don't you ever cry for yourself?"

•

My first love was the sun-warmed trunk of a dead eucalyptus tree. It lay in a tangle of morning glories and mallow weeds behind the garage—a narrow, forgotten place where no one ever went. I used to crawl in there and lie hidden in the sun. Hidden and naked. I liked to stretch on my belly, feeling the sun on my back and the warm smooth wood against my loins. And I would begin to rock, gently. I thought of nothing—only the warmth and the smell of weeds and hot tar paper roofs, and the pleasure of my secret flesh.

I never told anyone and no one ever found me, so I felt no shame.

When I was nine, she came to live in the duplex on the corner. Her name was Lucille, though I never called her that. I never spoke her name, except to myself. She was young, married but still childless, a thin girl with pale cheeks and long white hands. She let me sit in her kitchen and talk to her while she worked. Her white hands looked cool and soft, and when she bent over me, I could see the little shadow between her breasts. I wanted to put my lips there.

I was teased, of course—by parents and playmates. But it did not matter. Each evening I watched her come out on the step to greet her husband, lifting her lips and her pale hands to his face. A beautiful gesture. If I was jealous, I do not remember it. I simply wanted her; it did not occur to me to want her all to myself.

She kissed me once, laughing, while I stood like a stricken fool beneath the Christmas mistletoe. I could only look at her until she saw my eyes and something in them made her laughter stop.

And then she was gone. They moved away and had a baby and I did not see her again.

•

Childhood memories are all lies. We condescend to them, we posture, we affect to be amused, we formulate official autobiographies which we tell ourselves and others —and all to forget the wounds that never heal. We cannot forgive ourselves for having suffered; it is a weakness and we despise it. We like to pretend that the child grew up.

•

Recess. A numbed girl with pimples and breasts sleepwalks through the corridors. Her eyes, behind the rimless glasses, are watery and pale, and her flesh tries to shrink up and conceal itself within her clothes. Whispers buzz like flies around her. Jackal laughter—all the bastards snicker and rub themselves through their pants.

•

It was her husband's idea, the portrait. He was young and rather stupid, therefore impressed by me. I knew books, could sketch a little—a man of many talents, all of them small.

But my pencil lied as easily as my tongue, so the portrait pleased her. I suggested a nude. She blushed, looked vaguely frightened. No, she couldn't do that.

"But you have a lovely body."

We settled on another portrait, this time in oils. She would sit for it in my apartment where the light was right.

And all the time she sat I talked quite shamelessly about myself and women, sometimes adding praises of her eyes and the voluptuous curve of her neck. She was fascinated, of course. To a virtuous woman, nothing is more exciting than the attentions of a roué.

I asked her to sleep with me, and she refused. A day or two later, I asked again. No. When I took her in my arms and kissed her hair and eyes, she trembled, went rigid, then broke away. Her speech was what you might expect. She said I had made her trust me and tried to take advantage of it. She said she loved her husband. She was not the sort. I had no right.

I agreed, apologized, and promised not to bother her again. Her disappointment was visible. Within a few days she called me and virtually begged me to resume my siege. And I did, with predictable results—despite her tears, fears, and equivocations.

But why laugh? She wanted intensely to remain chaste and she wanted intensely to succumb. What was she to do? The little drama I had launched was very exciting—it aroused both of her desires—but dramas, like syllogisms, require conclusions. There must be a final act.

And then what? The drama is over, but life isn't. One must somehow fabricate another play, one in which there is something precious to be lost, something alluring to be gained. . . .

•

A curious point. Have you ever noticed that a seducer always ends his triumph by intimating that it wasn't a triumph at all? All he did was offer a pretext; his victim, he suggests, was really dying to fall.

The rapist: I made her do what I wanted her to.

The seducer: I made her do what *she* wanted to.

A true gentleman, the rapist exonerates the lady and takes full responsibility for his act. Not exactly. There is sovereign contempt in him, but no courtesy. He would no more grant her the right to say yes than to say no. He is the conqueror, the violator, the bloody lord.

The seducer, however, persuades the lady to violate herself.

The bully versus the cad, eternal opposites. They were all together in the Garden: the lordly rapist, the seductive serpent, the woman—and Adam, your eternal husband, placid, steady, dull, cheated.

It was Paradise, ruled by the inventor and sole proprietor, Old Omnipotence himself. Adam and Eve were his prize serfs. They didn't know they were naked, but God did. His little joke. Made for his pleasure, they were as innocent as animals, and as easily used.

But Paradise can never last, even for God. The serpent coils and waits. He has already had his encounter with Omnipotence—and is its victim, doomed and knowing it, a weakling who cannot fight but will not fawn. God, the lordly bully, strides the Garden as if it were a manor or a playground. Adam tugs his forelock, Eve spreads her thighs obediently at God's approach.

The serpent feels the tremor of those heavy boots. Sounds reach him: Eve's little shudder, the smack of flesh on flesh, that dreadful thrust. At last the lordly one is done. Sated, he rises and buttons his pants, while she lies disregarded in the dust.

The footsteps fade. In the streaming sun, she lies dazed and helpless, soiled. The serpent glides nearer. Her eyes wound him. He too has known what it means to squirm for God.

Goddess, he calls her, immortal beauty, adored by all creation. He positively seethes with desire—and with love, that unclean thing, born of his wounds. Caressing her, he takes pity upon himself.

Eve feels his words like a touch. His eyes, too, and the radiance of that supple insinuating form, so perilously erect.

In all those glittering scales, the same image is reflected, clothed in opalescent shimmers and nothing else. She has always been beautiful, but now she knows it. She is inflamed with visions: her mouth, her pomegranate breasts, her soft, dissolving thighs. Surrender is triumph, the consummation of herself.

So in exquisite apprehension she reaches for the apple.

The usual ecstasy. But as usual it subsides. Forbidden fruit, once eaten, tastes like everything else.

Yet something is ominously different. Though the visions fade, sight doesn't. She is still aware of herself. And the self she sees is not a goddess but a woman, a woman exposed, vulgar and vulgarly betrayed. By what? That limp little thing in the dust, the worm in the apple. It lies there, too spent even to wriggle, with nothing but malice left in its eyes.

And everybody knows. The serpent sees to that. It is his revenge for having betrayed himself to Eve. The final humiliation is his—the moment when she understands his impotence, that having seduced her he doesn't know what to do with her now.

Now she must endure Adam's stupid tears. And God isn't even jealous. He simply discards her—a trivial plaything that someone else has soiled.

She is no longer pretty. Her face is dull and her body feels heavy and unclean. She spends her days in hating—herself, the serpent for what he has done to her, Adam for what she has done to him. It is of course the rapist she really desires. If only God cared a little, or if only Adam would stand up to God.

But God doesn't want her. And Adam will submit to anything—his God, his fate, his wife. Numb shock followed by helpless self-pity—that is his only response. Then stupid submission, acceptance. Even of her beauty. He does not understand it, just as he does not understand the motive for her shame. To live with him, she must become as dull as he is, breeding and suffering with stupid equanimity. That is her final lot. After violation and betrayal, she must mutilate herself. She performs it. She lets everything go —her looks, her desires, her dreams. She becomes at last Adam's wife.

A happy ending, as stories go.

Ladies, I give you your choice: the rapist, the seducer,

or the eternal husband? That's all there is, in or out of Eden.

•

And where did he come from, that poor fool on the cross? He was the serpent's brother, a younger son.

•

Philip on crutches, flanked by his fiancée, her eyes aglow with the trivial fanaticism of sacrifice. A lovely pair.

But it didn't work. I could see hatred growing in him, and she, sweet stupid girl, she didn't understand. She tried to be even more devoted. He called her a smothering bitch and left her crying in my rooms.

"But I love him. What can I do?"

"Get sick," I said. "Go blind or lose a leg. Let him immolate himself for you."

She didn't, of course. And so it ended, as it should. We want no heirs.

•

At Bilstein's house, I turned from the bar and saw Harriett looking at me. Her eyes glazed quickly, but it was too late, I had seen. I crossed the room like a man walking toward a cliff. And I asked her to dance. While our bodies touched, we did not have to look at each other.

I have always been afraid of eyes. They ask too much, betray too much. They embarrass me like the nakedness of a woman I do not desire. But there are moments, of course. Eyes look at us, and we glimpse something incurable in them, something which is also incurable in us.

•

If I could have met her in the night, always in the night, with no face to look at, no face of my own to be seen.

This arranging of faces, this smoothing of hair, this conversation at breakfast when every word makes it more impossible to talk. We soon despise each other.

•

In the twilight of that summer, Harriet sits in the porch swing, watching the sky fade and darken. Her bare legs glow in a patch of light. They are classic legs: full thighs, long slender calves, thin ankles with the bone white against the skin. But now they are marred with dark sores, mosquito bites which she scratches until the blood comes, then scratches again, tearing at the scabs that form.

•

Harriet betrayed me and lied about it. And I understood why she betrayed me and why she lied.

Definition of a pervert: the rabbit who empathized with the dog who ate him.

Destroy sympathy. It is a disease. Cruelty and indifference are better.

•

With that tremor of the eyelids, that faint crouch of the body, Harriet seemed always to be trying to shrink, as if every touch were painful. Yet her most disquieting tendency was a total absence of reserve. She would tell anything: her morbidities, fears, humiliations—the time a teacher yelled at her and she wet herself in front of the class. And these same things would make her writhe in anguish. So she fascinated the vulgar souls, those who were flattered or titillated by so much intimacy. But it was not trust and it was not perverse self-advertisement. For her, confession was a desperate strategy. She reminded me of those sea creatures who eviscerate themselves when threatened, leaving their guts to fascinate the pursuer while they escape and grow new ones.

•

We had beer and cold crab and tacos, and we danced all that afternoon. Something came alive in her eyes, something I had not seen before. She arched her back and stuck her butt out in a proud little strut; her skirt whipped and swirled about her thighs. While the song sustained her, she was not afraid of anything, even herself.

•

Stillbirth: ominously appropriate. The next day I found her dressed and sitting in the corridor, making perfectly audible comments on the nurses as they passed. Then it stopped; her face went dead as suddenly as if someone had blown out the light. I led her in silence back to her room. No tears—she just sat there, her breasts swollen, the useless milk staining her blouse.

A year later there was Philip.

•

Real love is terrifying, unflattering, ugly. It is a violation.
To be loved is to have your nakedness exposed, to the
lover's eyes and to your own. Unbearable. To be seduced
is to be given a flattering version of yourself, cosmetically
clothed and unreal, incapable of being hurt.

•

And now a document:

Dear Joe,
I tried not to write because I knew you'd despise me
for begging, and you're right, but here I am.
I want you to come back, Joe. I always knew I'd lose
you and now I have, only come back to me please. I did
that thing so you'd hate me, because I hated me and you
should too. That makes no sense but that's why I did it.
When you first came to me, I didn't believe it, it was too
good, you made me so happy, and I wouldn't show how
I felt because I didn't dare, because if they know how
you're happy they know how to hurt you.
So I wrecked it, but please. It's not your fault, but
I'm no good alone, I don't know what to do or think and
I get frightened. Joe, Joe, I'm so mixed up. This baby,
too, it cries and I can't help it. I'm no good at loving, I
never was.
Oh God, Joe. I'll be whatever you want if you want
me. Please come.

Harriett

•

Perhaps betrayal is the most intimate of all acts, the one
in which complicity is most secret and most shared.

•

She stands brushing her hair while I lie in bed beside
her. Her face is averted, her bare thighs an inch or two
from my lips. And all the curving lines of belly and thigh
converge on that little mound, there where her flesh opens
in folds as smooth and intricate as the involutions of a
shell.

I am married to that, even now.

I do not believe in divorce. I do not believe it is possible.

•

The fire began in her apartment they said. A careless cigarette, probably—something which smouldered in the couch and then burst and ran up the walls. It happened in the middle of the day and she was home, but she gave no alarm. When someone above noticed the smoke, the stairway was already in flames.

They said she must have been drunk or doped, but I know she wasn't. She was just afraid—afraid to sound the alarm because they would know the fire was her fault and blame her. It was easier to die.

So she burned. And so did the others who lived in that house—a widow, a retired couple, three children who were home alone because their mother worked.

She lived alone, said the newspapers. Her one child, Philip, had resided with his grandmother in San Jose since the separation of his parents.

•

My son who looks like a ghoul, who bleeds if you touch him.

•

And so it happens. A new love—as sudden as an apparition. My neighbor, she says, she had "noticed" me before. Perhaps "recognized" says it better. And whatever the signs were, they must have been unmistakable. They brought her to my door, with perfect confidence, at two in the afternoon.

She has all the equipment of youth—firm breasts, firm thighs, a blue-white milky skin. But her eyes are the color of a bruise, her mouth limp and stretched like old elastic.

Please God, her name is Sharon.

•

I don't want her. I didn't want any of them. I wanted to be alone and quiet, and I never was.

•

Love affairs: a dismally expressive phrase, self-cancelling. Words soon couple and exhaust themselves. Caresses turn into gestures. Whatever it was becomes a charade, a game, a dance.

And the alternatives? Hysteria or habit. Blow your mind, as they say—and a lovely saying it is: cerebral self-fellatio, the beatific transport of the young. Or take the sanative fucking of the decently married, who void their lusts as they void their stools. Or take nothing at all.

I am tired of it. The flavor of lies and cleverness, epigrams.

•

My little Sharon again, as regular as any fate. But why? She does not talk. If irritation makes me speak, she smiles and murmurs something. When I mention my age, she says she prefers an older man.

She has a peculiar voice. It is echoless, unresonantly empty.

•

Now Sharon comes every day and fixes lunch. Her own idea. She is very efficient, too, even garnishing the plates with little sprays of carrot curl and parsley.

When the meal is done, she sits beside me. The afternoon wanes. There being nothing else to do, I pull down the blinds and we lie together on my couch. Her thighs part with the ease of many accommodations, her mouth releases little pleasure sounds. Yet even then that mild, dead voice never quickens. It is vibrationless, spent.

And that is our love. Perhaps we shall marry. She could accommodate herself to that.

•

Sat in the park among the pigeon-feeders. As usual, I watched the women—mothers, mostly, out with the tots for an airing. In front of me, a dark-haired girl with a blurred mouth lay dozing on the grass. She had that slack, stupid look. But her skirt twisted as she rolled over, and I saw plump white thighs, a curve of buttocks swelling out of her panties. It made me hot and faint. Walking home, I was actually trembling with desire, but when Sharon came, it vanished, and I was cold again.

•

A.M.: Dreamed about the woman in the park.

•

Went to see Philip at the County Hospital. He has been

there a week, it seems, but I was not informed until today. Acute internal hemorrhages, prognosis reserved.

I have my own prognosis. His face has begun to collapse, and his arms have great yellow-green bruises from intravenous feeding. There was nothing to say. He lay in that ward and stared at me as if I were part of the wall.

I decided to walk back. The morning was appropriately gray, cold, and oppressive. Coming up the hill, I crossed the street to avoid a little tableau—a man and woman in sullen confrontation against the wall. He held her wrist in one hand and had the other raised as if to strike her, but he never did. Perhaps he enjoyed the suspense of that threatening hand. He cursed her, too, methodically. She stood with her head down, limp, as if she did not care enough even to cringe. A trivial scene. But as I passed, I felt a novel chill. It looked like Sharon.

Was it? I don't know. If it was, she did not see me, and I did not look back. Let secrets remain secrets. I don't want to know them.

●

Can one graph a recurring point in all the spiral wanderings of the self? Perhaps. And that recurring point, of course, would be the stake to which one is tethered, and one's spiritual voyages then would be the futile dashes and retreats of a dog on a chain.

I do not know what a recurring zero is, but I like the taste of the phrase. It is descriptive.

●

Sharon was here. She was as willing as ever, but afterwards, as she stooped and washed herself, she looked at me with her clotted eyes. "It's not much fun," she said. "Is it?"

●

At Grencher's party, we all stood around in the den, surveying our host's collection of trivial pornography. Someone gave me a little peep show telescope and told me to look into it. They said I would see something very special, and I did. I saw my own eye, hideously distorted and magnified by the mirror in the tube. It stared back at me, fat, with a fried-egg look, obscene. My face betrayed something, I suppose—enough to detonate their laughter. I excused myself and went outside to be sick on my host's lawn.

•

There is a child in the yard next door—a pale child with pale hair and bloated flesh. His eyes look like bits of celluloid left too long in the sun.

•

Philip falling on the steps, cutting his chin. He bled like some dreadful fountain.

•

Every animal suffers, we are told, the post-coital blues. But what about that peculiar desolation and resentment, that sense of irrelevance? We don't like to admit it. Instead, we claim the weariness of too much bliss. And we graceful lovers cover our retreat with kisses and endearments, withdrawal poetry. We lie our way out as we lie our way in.

I know all about exhaustion, the sag of spirits with the flesh, and I say it doesn't matter. The point is: something is not exhausted, something has been tricked.

Ladies, after all our ecstasies, I have but one honest thing to say: "I'm sorry. That isn't what I meant."

•

A.M.: Services for Philip.

•

Fog now, many days of fog. You can smell it in the curtains and the rug. I have not seen Sharon for more than a week. I should inquire, I suppose, but I prefer not to know where she has gone. I am alone again, and that is enough—an old man, a liar still, with no self but my own to betray.

Days of 1971

James Merrill

FALLEN from the clouds, well-met.
This way to the limousine.
How are things? Don't tell me yet!
Have a Gauloise first, I mean.

Matches now, did I forget—
With a flourish and no word
Out came the sentry-silhouette
Black against a big, flame-feathered bird,

Emblem of your "new" regime
Held, for its repressive ways,
In pretty general disesteem

Which to share just then was hard,
Borne up so far on a strategic blaze
Struck by you, and quite off guard.

In Paris you remark each small
Caged creature, marmoset, bat, newt, for sale;
Also the sparkling gutters, and the smelly
Seine this afternoon when we embark.

And the Bateau Mouche is spoiled by a party of cripples.
Look at what's left of that young fellow strapped
Into his wheelchair. How you pity him!
The city ripples, your eyes sicken and swim.

The boy includes you in his sightseeing,
Nodding sociably as if who of us
Here below were more than half a man.

There goes the Louvre, its Egyptian wing
Dense with basalt limbs and heads to use
Only as one's imagination can.

Can-can from last night's *Orphée aux Enfers*

Since daybreak you've been whistling till I wince.
Well, you were a handsome devil once.
Take the wheel. You're still a fair chauffeur.

Our trip. I'd pictured it another way—
Asthmatic pilgrim and his "nun of speed,"
In either mind a music spun of need . . .
That last turnoff went to Illiers.

Proust's Law (are you listening?) is twofold:
a) What least thing our self-love longs for most
Others instinctively withhold;

b) Only when time has slain desire
Is his wish granted to a smiling ghost
Neither harmed nor warmed, now, by the fire.

Stephen in the Pyrenees—our first
Real stop. You promptly got a stomachache.
Days of groans and grimaces interspersed
With marathon slumbers. Evenings, you'd wake

And stagger forth to find us talking. Not
Still about poetry! Alas . . .
So bottles were produced, and something hot.
The jokes you told translated, more or less.

Predictably departure cured you. Stephen
Investing me with a Basque walking-stick,
"How much further, James, will you be driven?"

He didn't ask. He stood there, thin, pale, kind
As candlelight. Ah, what if *I* took sick?
You raced the motor, having read my mind.

Sucked by haste into the car,
Pressing his frantic buzzer, Bee!
Suppose he stings—why such hilarity?
These things occur.

Get rid of him at once
While we can! His wrath
Is almost human, the windshield's warpath
Dins with a song and dance

In one respect unlike our own:
Readily let out into the open.

There. Good creature, also he had known
The cost of self-as-weapon;

Venom unspent, barb idle, knows
Where they lead now—thyme, lavender, musk-rose,

Toulouse, Toulon, the border. Driven?
At ease, rather, among fleeting scenes.
The O L I V E T T I signs
Whizz by, and azure Lombardy is given

Back, as the Virgin of Officialdom
Severely draped twists on her throne to peek
At the forbidden crags of kingdom come
Before resuming her deft hunt and peck.

One V sticks. Venice. Its vertiginous pastry
Maze we scurry through like mice, and will
Never see the likes of in our lives.

It is too pink, white, stale to taste,
Crumbling in the gleam of slimy knives.
Have your cake and eat it? Take the wheel.

Wait—now where are we? Who is everyone?
Well, that's a Princess, that's the butler . . . no,
Probably by now the butler's son.
We were stopping till tomorrow with Umberto

Among trompe-l'oeil, old volumes, photographs
Of faded people wearing crowns and stars.
Welcome to the Time Machine, he laughed
Leaning on us both up its cold stairs.

At table the others recalled phrases from
Homer and Sappho, and you seemed to brighten.
Your sheets would entertain the "priest" that night
(Dish of embers in a wooden frame)

And eyes glaze on the bedside book, remote
But near, pristine but mildewed, which I wrote.

Take the wheel. San Zeno will survive
Whether or not visited.
Power is knowledge in your head.
(Sorry, I must have been thinking aloud. Drive, drive.)

Time and again the novel I began
Took aim at that unwritten part
In which the hero, named Sebastian,
Came to his senses through a work of art.

O book of hours, those last
Illuminated castles built
In air, O chariot-motif

Bearing down a margin good as gilt
Past fields of ever purer leaf
Its burning rubric, to get nowhere fast. . . .

The road stopped where a Greek mountain fell
Early that week. Backed-up cars glared in the dusk.
Night fell next, and still five stupid slack-
Jawed ferries hadn't got their fill of us.

Tempers shortened. One self-righteous truck
Knocked the shit out of a eucalyptus
Whose whitewashed trunk lay twitching brokenly—
Nijinsky in *Petrouchka*—on the quai.

Later, past caring, packed like sheep,
Some may have felt the breathless lounge redeemed
By a transistor singing to the doomed

At last in their own tongue. You fell asleep
Life-sentenced to the honey-cell of song,
Harsh melisma, torturous diphthong.

Strato, each year's poem
Says goodbye to you.
Again, though, we've come through
Without losing temper or face.

If care rumpled your face
The other day in Rome,
Tonight just dump my suitcase
Inside the door and make a dash for home

While I unpack what we saw made
At Murano, and you gave to me—
Two ounces of white heat
Twirled and tweezered into shape,

Ecco! another fanciful
Little horse, still blushing, set to cool.

For Ernest Hemingway

Reynolds Price

I F I HAD BEEN conscious of caring enough, as late as the spring of 1970, to check the state of my own feelings about the work of Hemingway (nine years after his death and at least five since I'd read more of him than an occasional story for teaching purposes), I'd probably have come up with a reading close to the postmortem consensus—that once one has abandoned illusions of his being a novelist and has set aside, as thoroughly as any spectator can, the decades of increasingly public descent into artistic senility (dosing those memories with the sad and sterile revelations of Carlos Baker's biography), then one can honor him, in Patrick Cruttwell's words, as "a minor Romantic poet" who wrote a lovely early novel, *The Sun Also Rises,* and a handful of early stories of the north woods, the first war, postwar Americans in Europe which are likely to remain readable and, despite their truculent preciosity, leanly but steadily rewarding. But I don't remember caring enough to come up with even that grudging an estimate.

Why?—partly a participation in the understandable, if unlikable, international sigh of relief at the flattening of one more Sitting Bull, especially one who had made strenuous attempts to publicize his own worst nature; partly an attenuation of my lines to the work itself; partly a response to the discovery that, in my first three years of teaching, *A Farewell to Arms* had dissolved with alarming ease, under the corrosive of prolonged scrutiny, into its soft components (narcissism and blindness) when a superficially softer-looking book like *The Great Gatsby* proved diamond; but mostly the two common responses to any family death: forgetfulness and ingratitude.

Then two reminding signals. In the summer of '70, I visited Key West and wandered with a friend one morning down Whitehead to the Hemingway house, tall, square, and iron-galleried, with high airy rooms on ample grounds thick with tropic green, still privately owned (though not by his heirs) and casually open, once you've paid your dollar, for the sort of slow unattended poking-around all but universally forbidden in other American Shrines. His bed, his tile bath, his war souvenirs (all distinctly small-town Southern, human-sized; middle-class careless well-to-do—the surroundings of, say, a taciturn literate doctor and his tanned leggy wife, just gone for two weeks with their kin in Charleston or to Asheville, cool and golfy; and you inexplicably permitted to hang spectral in their momentarily cast shell). But more—the large room over the yard-house in which Hemingway wrote a good part of his work between 1931 and 1939 (six books) at a small round table, dark brown and unsteady; the small swimming pool beneath, prowled by the dozens of deformed multi-toed cats descended from a Hemingway pair of the thirties. Green shade, hustling surly old Key West silent behind walls, a rising scent of sadness—that Eden survived, not destroyed at all but here and reachable, though not by its intended inhabitants who are barred by the simple choices of their lives and, now, by death (Hemingway lost the house in 1939 at his second divorce). The rising sense that I am surrounded, accompanied by more than my friend—

> I am moved by fancies that are curled
> Around these images, and cling:
> The notion of some infinitely gentle
> Infinitely suffering thing.

The center of my strong and unexpected response began to clarify when I discovered, at home, that I had recalled Eliot's first adjective as *delicate*—"some infinitely delicate, Infinitely suffering thing." What thing?

In October, the second signal. *Islands in the Stream* was published, and received with one or two enthusiastic notices, a few sane ones (Irving Howe, John Aldridge), and a number of tantrums of the beat-it-to-death, scatter-the-ashes sort. In fact, the kinds of notices calculated to rush serious readers to a bookstore (such response being a fairly sure sign that a book is alive and scary, capable of harm); and no doubt I'd have read the book eventually, but a combination of my fresh memories of Key West and a natural surge of sympathy after such a press sent me out to buy it, a ten-dollar vote of—what? *Thanks,* I suddenly knew, to Hemingway.

For what? For being a strong force in both my own early awareness of a need to write and my early sense of how to write. Maybe the strongest. A fact I'd handily forgot but was firmly returned to now, by *Islands in the Stream.*

A long novel—466 pages—it threatens for nearly half its length to be his best. And the first of its three parts— "Bimini," 200 pages—is his finest sustained fiction, itself an independent novella. Finest, I think, for a number of reasons that will be self-evident to anyone who can bury his conditioned responses to the Hemingway of post-1940, but chiefly because in it Hemingway deals for the first time substantially, masterfully, and to crushing effect with the only one of the four possible human relations which he had previously avoided—parental devotion, filial return. (The other three relations—with God, with the earth, with a female or male lover or friend—he had worked from the start, failing almost always with the first, puzzlingly often with the third, succeeding as richly as anyone with the second.)

It would violate the apparent loose-handedness of those 200 pages to pick in them for exhibits. Hemingway, unlike Faulkner, is always badly served by spot-quotation, as anyone will know who turns from critical discussions of him (with their repertoire of a dozen Great Paragraphs) back to the works themselves. Faulkner, so often short-winded, can be flattered by brief citation, shown at the stunning moment of triumph. But Hemingway's power, despite his continued fame for "style," is always built upon *breath,* long breath, even in the shortest piece—upon a sustained legato of quiet pleading which acts on a willing reader in almost exactly the same way as the opening phrase of Handel's *Care selve* or *Ombra mai fù.* What the words are ostensibly saying in both Hemingway and Handel is less true, less complete, than the slow arc of their total movement throughout their length. Therefore any excerpt is likely to emphasize momentary weakness—artificiality of pose, frailty of emotion—which may well dissolve in the context of their intended whole. The words of *Ombra mai fù* translate literally as "Never was the shade of my dear and lovable vegetable so soothing"; and any three lines from, say, the beautifully built trout-fishing pages of *The Sun Also Rises* are likely to read as equally simple-minded, dangerously vapid—

He was a good trout, and I banged his head against the timber so that he quivered out straight, and then slipped him into my bag.

So may this from Part I of *Islands in the Stream*—

The boys slept on cots on the screened porch and it is much less lonely sleeping when you can hear children breathing when you wake in the night.

But in the last novel, the love among Thomas Hudson, a good marine painter, and his three sons is created—compelled in the reader—by a slow lateral and spiral movement of episodes (lateral and spiral because no episode reaches a clear climax or peaks the others in revelation). All the episodes are built not on "style" or charged moments, though there are lovely moments, or on the ground-bass hum of a cerebral dynamo like Conrad's or Mann's, but on simple *threat*—potentially serious physical or psychic damage avoided: the middle son's encounter with a shark while spear-fishing, the same boy's six-hour battle to bloody near-collapse with a giant marlin who escapes at the last moment (the only passage outside *The Old Man and the Sea* where I'm seduced into brief comprehension of his love of hunting), the boys' joint participation in a funny but sinister practical joke at a local bar (they convincingly pretend to be juvenile alcoholics, to the alarm of tourists). Threats which delay their action for the short interim of the visit with their father but prove at the end of the section to have been dire warnings or prophecies (warnings imply a chance of escape)—the two younger boys are killed with their mother in a car wreck, shortly after their return to France. Only when we—and Thomas Hudson—are possessed of that news can the helix of episodes deliver, decode, its appalling message to us and to him. The lovely-seeming lazy days were white with the effort to speak their knowledge. *Avoid dependence, contingency.* The rest of the novel (a little more than half) tries to face those injunctions (restated in further calamities) and seems to me to fail, for reasons I'll guess at later; but the first part stands, firm and independent, simultaneously a populated accurate picture and an elaborate unanswerable statement about that picture. Or scenes with music.

For in that first 200 pages, the junction of love and threat, encountered for the first time in Hemingway within a family of blood-kin, exacts from him a prose which, despite my claims of its unexcerptibility, is as patient and attentive to the forms of life which pass before it and as richly elliptical as any he wrote, requiring our rendezvous with him in the job—and all that as late as the early 1950's, just after the debacle of *Across the River and Into the Trees.* Take this exchange between Hudson and young Tom, his eldest—

"Can you remember Christmas there?"
"No. Just you and snow and our dog Schnautz and my nurse. She was beautiful. And I remember mother on skis and how beautiful she was. I can remember seeing you and mother coming down skiing through an orchard. I don't know where it was. But I can remember the Jardin du Luxembourg well. I can remember afternoons with the boats on the lake by the fountain in the big garden with the trees . . ."

(That last sentence, incidentally, reestablishes Hemingway's mastery of one of the most treacherous but potentially revealing components of narrative—the preposition, a genuine cadenza of prepositions set naturally in the mouth of a boy, not for exhibit but as a function of a vision based as profoundly as Cézanne's on the *stance* of objects in relation to one another: a child, late light, boats on water near shore, flowers, shade.)

Such prose, recognizable and yet renewed within the old forms by the fertility of its new impetus—family love—is only the first indication, coming as late as it does, of how terribly Hemingway maimed himself as an artist by generally banishing such passionate tenderness and emotional reciprocity from the previous thirty years of his work (it is clear enough from *A Moveable Feast*, the Baker biography, and private anecdotes from some of his more credible friends that such responses and returns were an important component of his daily life). The remaining 260 pages suggest—in their attempt to chart Hudson's strategies for dealing with external and internal calamity, his final almost glad acceptance of solitude and bareness —an even more melancholy possibility: that the years of avoiding permanent emotional relations in his work left him at the end unable to define his profoundest subject, prevented his even seeing that after the initial energy of his north-woods-and-war youth had spent itself (by 1933), he began to fail as artist and man not because of exhaustion of limited resource but because he could not or would not proceed from that first worked vein on into a richer, maybe endless vein, darker, heavier, more inaccessible but of proportionately greater value to him and his readers; a vein that might have fueled him through a long yielding life with his truest subject (because his truest need).

Wasn't his lifelong subject *saintliness*? Wasn't it generally as secret from him (a lapsing but never quite lost Christian) as from his readers? And doesn't that refusal, or inability, to identify and then attempt understanding of his central concern constitute the forced end of his work— and our failure as his readers, collusive in blindness? Hasn't the enormous and repetitive critical literature devoted to dissecting his obsession with codes and rituals, which may permit brief happiness in a meaningless world, discovered only a small (and unrealistic, intellectually jejune) portion of his long search? But doesn't he discover at last—and tell us in *Islands in the Stream*—that his search was not for survival and the techniques of survival but for goodness, thus victory?

What kind of goodness? Granted that a depressing amount of the work till 1940 (till *For Whom the Bell*

Tolls) is so obsessed with codes of behavior as to come perilously close to comprising another of those deadest of all ducks—etiquettes: Castiglione, Elyot, Post (and anyone reared in middle-class America in the past forty years has known at least one Youth, generally aging, who was using Hemingway thus—a use which his own public person and need for disciples persistently encouraged). Yet beneath the thirty years of posturing, his serious readers detected, and honored, great pain and the groping for unspecific, often brutal anodynes—pain whose precise nature and origin he did not begin to face until the last pages of *For Whom the Bell Tolls* and which, though he can diagnose in *Islands in the Stream,* he could not adequately dramatize: the polar agonies of love, need, contingency and of solitude, hate, freedom. What seems to me strange and sad now is that few of his admirers and none of his abusers appear to have sighted what surfaces so often in his last three novels and in *A Moveable Feast*—the signs that the old quest for manly skills (of necessity, temporary skills) became a quest for virtue. The quest for skills was clearly related to *danger*—danger of damage to the self by Nada, Chance, or Frederic Henry's "They": "They threw you in and told you the rules and the first time they caught you off base they killed you." But the quest of Colonel Cantwell in *Across the River* (which metamorphoses from obsession with narcotic rituals for living well to the study of how to die), the unconscious quest of Santiago in *The Old Man and the Sea* (too heavily and obscurely underscored by crucifixion imagery), the clear fact that the subject of *A Moveable Feast* is Hemingway's own early failure as a man (husband, father, friend), and the fully altered quest of Thomas Hudson in *Islands in the Stream* (from good father and comrade in life to good solitary animal in death)—all are related not so much to danger as to mystery. No longer the easy late-Victorian "They" or the sophomore's Nada (both no more adequate responses to human experience than the tub-thumping of Henley's "Invictus") but something that might approximately be described as God, Order, the Source of Vaguely Discernible Law. The attempt not so much to "understand" apparent Order and Law as to detect its outlines (as by Braille in darkness), to strain to hear and obey some of its demands.

What demands did he hear?—most clearly, I think, the demand to survive the end of pleasure (and to end bad, useless pleasures). That is obviously a demand most often heard by the aged or middle-aged, droning through the deaths of friends, lovers, family, their own fading faculties. But Hemingway's characters from the first have heard it, and early in their lives—Nick Adams faced on all sides with disintegrated hopes, Jake Barnes deprived of genitals, Frederic Henry of Catherine and their son, the Italian major of his family in "In Another Country," Marie Morgan of her Harry, and on and on. Those early characters generally face deprivation with a common answer—activity. And it is surprising how often the activity is artistic. Nick Adams becomes a writer after the war (the author of his own stories); Jake Barnes is a journalist with ambitions (and, not at all incidentally, a good Catholic); Frederic Henry, without love, becomes the man who dictates to us *A Farewell to Arms;* Robert Jordan hopes to return, once the Spanish Civil War is over, to his university teaching in Missoula, Montana, and to write a good book. But, whatever its nature, activity remains their aim and their only hope of survival intact—activity as waiting tactic (waiting for the end, total death), as gyrostabilizer, narcotic. In the last novels, however—most explicitly in *Islands in the Stream*—deprivation is met by *duty*, what the last heroes see as the performance of duty (there are earlier heroes with notions of duty—Nick, Jake—but their duty is more nearly chivalry, a self-consciously graceful *noblesse oblige*).

The duty is not to survive or to grace the lives of their waiting-companions but to do their work—lonely fishing, lonely soldiering, lonely painting and submarine-hunting. For whom? Not for family (wives, sons) or lovers (there are none; Cantwell knows his teen-age contessa is a moment's dream). Well, for one's human witnesses then. Why? Cantwell goes on apparently, and a little incredibly, because any form of stop would diminish the vitality of his men, his friend the headwaiter, his girl—their grip upon the rims of their own abysses. Santiago endures his ordeal largely for the boy Manolin, that he not be ashamed of his aging friend and withdraw love and care. Thomas Hudson asks himself in a crucial passage in Part III (when he has, disastrously for his soul, stopped painting after the deaths of his three sons and gone to chasing Nazi subs off Cuba)—

> Well, it keeps your mind off things. What things? There aren't any things any more. Oh yes, there are. There is this ship and the people on her and the sea and the bastards you are hunting. Afterwards you will see your animals and go into town and get drunk as you can and your ashes dragged and then get ready to go out and do it again.

Hudson deals a few lines later with the fact that his present work is literally murder, that he does it "Because we are all murderers"; and he never really faces up to the tragedy of having permitted family sorrow to derail his true work —his rudder, his *use* to God and men as maker of ordered reflection—but those few lines, which out of context sound like a dozen Stoic monologues in the earlier work, actually bring Hudson nearer than any other Hemingway hero toward an explicit statement of that yearning for goodness which I suspect in all the work, from the very start—the generally suppressed intimation that *happiness* for all the young sufferers, or at least *rest*, would lie at the pole opposite their present position, the pole of pure solitude, detachment from the love of other created beings (in the words of John of the Cross), and only then in work for the two remaining witnesses: one's self and the inhuman universe. "There is this ship and the people on her and the sea and the bastards you are hunting"—brothers, the Mother, enemies: all the categories of created things. Hudson, and Hemingway, halt one step short of defining the traditional goal of virtue—the heart of God. And two pages before the end, when Hudson has taken fatal wounds from a wrecked sub crew, he struggles to stay alive by thinking—

> Think about the war and when you will paint again . . . You can paint the sea better than anyone now if you will do it and not get mixed up in other things. Hang on good now to how you truly want to do it.

You must hold hard to life to do it. But life is a cheap thing beside a man's work. The only thing is that you need it. Hold it tight. Now is the true time you make your play. Make it now without hope of anything. You always coagulated well and you can make one more real play. We are not the lumpenproletariat. We are the best and we do it for free.

But again, do it for whom? Most of Hudson's prewar pictures have been described as intended for this or that person—he paints for his middle son the lost giant marlin, Caribbean waterspouts for his bartender, a portrait of his loved-and-lost first wife (which he later gives her). Intended then as gifts, *from* love and *for* love, like most gifts. But now, in death, the reverberations threaten to deepen —Thomas Hudson's paintings (and by intimation, the clenched dignity of Nick Adams and Jake Barnes, Robert Jordan's inconsistent but passionate hunger for justice, Cantwell's tidy death, Santiago's mad endurance—most of Hemingway's work) seem intended to enhance, even to create if necessary the love of creation in its witnesses and thereby to confirm an approach by the worker toward goodness, literal virtue, the manly performance of the will of God. *Saintliness,* I've called it (*goodness* if you'd rather, though *saintliness* suggests at least the fierce need, its desperation)—a saint being, by one definition, a life which shows God lovable.

Any God is seldom mentioned (never seriously by Hudson, though Jake Barnes is a quiet Catholic, Santiago a rainy-day one—and though Hemingway himself nursed an intense if sporadic relation with the Church, from his mid-twenties on, saying in 1955, "I like to think I am [a Catholic] insofar as I can be" and in 1958 that he "believed in belief"). Isn't that the most damaging lack of all, in the life and the work?—from the beginning but most desperate toward the end, as the body and its satellites dissolved in age and the abuse of decades? I mean the simple fact that neither Hemingway nor any of his heroes (except maybe Santiago and, long before, the young priest from the Abruzzi who lingers in the mind, with Count Greffi, as one of the two polar heroes of *A Farewell to Arms*) could make the leap from an enduring love of creatures to a usable love of a Creator, a leap which (barring prevenient grace, some personal experience of the supernal) would have been the wildest, most dangerous act of all. Maybe, though, the *saving* one—leap into a still, or stiller, harbor from which (with the strengths of his life's vision about him, none cancelled or denied but their natural arcs now permitted completion) he could have made further and final works, good for him and us. That he didn't (not necessarily *couldn't,* though of modern novelists maybe only Tolstoy, Dostoevsky, and Bernanos have given us sustained great work from such a choice) has become the single most famous fact of his life—its end: blind, baffled.

But he wrote a good deal, not one of the Monster Oeuvres yet much more than one might guess who followed the news reports of his leisure; and there remain apparently hundreds of pages of unpublished manuscript. What does it come to?—what does it tell us, do to us, for us, against us?

I've mentioned the present low standing of his stock, among critics and reviewers and older readers. Young people don't seem to read him. My university students— the youngest of whom were nine when he died—seem to have no special relations with him. What seemed to us cool grace seems to many of them huffery-puffery. But then, as is famous, a depressing majority of students have special relations with only the feyest available books. (Will Hemingway prove to be the last Classic Author upon whom a generation modeled its lives?—for *classic* read *good.*) Even his two earliest, most enthusiastic and most careful academic critics have lately beat sad retreat. Carlos Baker's long love visibly disintegrates as he tallies each breath of the sixty-two years; and Philip Young nears the end of the revised edition of his influential "trauma" study (which caused Hemingway such pain) with this—

> Hemingway wrote two very good early novels, several very good stories and a few great ones . . . and an excellent if quite small book of reminiscence. That's all it takes. This is such stuff as immortalities are made on.

The hope is that the good books will survive a depression inevitable after so many years of inflation (Eliot is presently suffering as badly; Faulkner, after decades of neglect, has swollen and will probably assuage until we see him again as a very deep but narrow trench, not the Great Meteor Crater he now seems to many)—and that we may even, as Young wagers gingerly, come to see some of the repugnant late work in the light of Hemingway's own puzzling claim that in it he had gone beyond mathematics into the calculus (differential calculus is defined, for instance, as "the branch of higher mathematics that deals with the relations of differentials to the constant on which they depend"—isn't his constant clarifying now, whatever his reluctance to search it out, his failures to dramatize its demands?).

BUT SINCE no reader can wait for the verdict of years, what can one feel now? What do I feel?—an American novelist, age thirty-eight (the age at which Hemingway published his eighth book, *To Have and Have Not;* his collected stories appeared a year later), whose work would appear to have slim relations, in matter or manner, with the work of Hemingway and whose life might well have had his scorn? (he was healthily inconsistent with his scorn).

I have to return to my intense responses of a year ago— to the powerful presence of a profoundly attractive and needy man still residing in the Key West house and to the reception of his final novel. I've hinted that these responses were in the nature of neglected long-due debts, payment offered too late to be of any likely use to the lender. All the same—what debts?

To go back some years short of the start—in the summer of 1961, I was twenty-eight years old and had been writing seriously for six years. I had completed a novel but had only published stories, and those in England. Still, the novel was in proof at Atheneum—*A Long and Happy Life*—and was scheduled for publication in the fall. I had taken a year's leave from teaching and was heading to England for steady writing—and to be out of reach on publication day. On my way in mid-July I stopped in New

York and met my publishers. They had asked me to list
the names of literary people who might be interested
enough in my book to help it; and I had listed the writers
who had previously been helpful. But as we speculated
that July (no one on the list had then replied)—and as
we brushed over the death of Hemingway ten days before
—Michael Bessie startled me by saying that he had seen
Hemingway in April, had given him a copy of the proofs
of *A Long and Happy Life* and had (on the basis of past
kindnesses Hemingway had done for young writers) half-
hoped for a comment. None had come. But I boarded my
ship with three feelings. One was a response to Bessie's
reply to my asking, "How did you feel about Hemingway
when you saw him?"—"That he was a wounded animal who
should be allowed to go off and die as he chose." The
second was my own obvious curiosity—had Hemingway
read my novel? what had he thought? was there a sentence about it, somewhere, in his hand or had he, as
seemed likely, been far beyond reading and responding?
The third was more than a little self-protective and was
an index to the degree to which I'd suppressed my debts
to Hemingway—what had possessed Bessie in thinking that
Hemingway might conceivably have liked my novel, the
story of a twenty-year-old North Carolina farm girl with
elaborate emotional hesitations and scruples?

My feelings, about a dead man, were so near to baffled
revulsion that I can only attribute them to two sources.
First, the success of Hemingway's public relations in the
forties and fifties. He had managed to displace the un-
assailable core of the work itself from my memory and
replace it with the coarse, useless icon of Self which he
planted, or permitted, in dozens of issues of *Life* and
Look, gossip columns, *Photoplay*—an icon which the apparent sclerosis of the later work had till then, for me at least,
not made human. Second, emotions of which I was unconscious—filial envy, the need of most young writers to believe in their own utter newness, the suppression of my
own early bonds with Hemingway. In short, and awfully,
I had come close to accepting his last verdict on himself—
forgetting that he laid the death sentence on his life, not
on the work.

Yet, a month later, I received a statement which Stephen Spender had written, knowing nothing of the recent distant pass with Hemingway. It said, in part, that I was a " 'kinetic' writer of a kind that recalls certain pages of Hemingway, and Joyce . . ." I was pleased, of course, especially by Joyce's name ("The Dead" having long seemed to me about as great as narrative prose gets—certain pages of the Bible excepted); but again I was surprised by the presence of Hemingway. Spender had known my work since 1957. He was the first editor to publish a story of mine, in *Encounter;* and in his own *World Within World*, he had written briefly but with great freshness of his own acquaintance with Hemingway in Spain during the Civil War (one of the first memoirs to counter the received image of Loud Fist). So I might well have paused in my elation to think out whatever resemblance Spender saw. But I was deep in a second book—and in the heady impetus toward publication of the first—and a sober rereading of Hemingway (or a reading; I'd read by no means half his work) was low on my list of priorities.

It should have been high; for if I had attempted to trace and understand Hemingway's help in my own work, I'd have been much better equipped for dealing with (in my own head at least) a comment that greeted *A Long and Happy Life* from almost all quarters, even the most sympathetic—that it sprang from the side of Faulkner. It didn't; but in my resentment at being looped into the long and crowded cow-chain that stretched behind a writer for whom I felt admiration but no attraction, I expended a fair amount of energy in denials and in the offering of alternate masters—the Bible, Milton, Tolstoy, Eudora Welty. If I had been able to follow the lead offered by Bessie and Spender, I could have offered a still more accurate, more revealing name.

So IT WAS TEN YEARS before my morning in the house in Key West and my admiration for *Islands in the Stream* reminded me that, for me as a high-school student in Raleigh in the early fifties and as an undergraduate at Duke, the most visible model of Novelist was Hemingway (*artist* of any sort, except maybe Picasso, with whom

Hemingway shared many external attributes but whose central faculty—continuous intellectual imagination, a mind like a frightening infallible engine endowed with the power of growth—he lacked). For how many writers born in the twenties and thirties can Hemingway not have been a breathing Mount Rushmore? though his presence and pressure seem to have taken a far heavier toll on the older generation, who not only read Hemingway but took him to war as well. Not only most visible but, oddly, most universally *certified.* Even our public-school teachers admired him, when they had been so clearly pained by Faulkner's Nobel—the author of *Sanctuary* and other sex books. In fact, when I reconstruct the chronology of my introduction to Hemingway, I discover that I must have encountered the work first, at a distant remove, in movies of the forties—*The Short Happy Life of Francis Macomber, For Whom the Bell Tolls.* It was apparently not until the tenth or eleventh grade—age fifteen or sixteen—that I read any of him. As the first thing, I remember "Old Man at the Bridge" in a textbook. And then, for an "oral book-report" in the eleventh grade, *A Farewell to Arms.* (I remember standing on my feet before forty healthy adolescents—it was only 1949—and saying that Hemingway had shown me that illicit love could be pure and worth having. I don't remember remarking that, like water, it could also kill you —or your Juliet—but I must have acquired, subliminally at least, the welcome news that it made Frederic Henry, a would-be-architect, into a highly skilled novelist.)

It was not till my freshman year in college, however, that the effect began to show (in high school, like everyone else, I'd been a poet). My first serious pieces of prose narrative have a kind of grave faith in the eyes, the gaze of the narrator at the moving objects who are his study —a narrowed gaze, through lashes that screen eighty percent of "detail" from the language and the helpless reader, which seems now surely helped onward, if not grounded in, early Hemingway. Here, for example, is the end of the first "theme" I remember writing in freshman English, a five-hundred-word memory of the death of my aunt's dog Mick:

It was still hot for late afternoon, but I kept walking. Mick must have been getting tired; but she bounced along, doing her best to look about as pert as a race-horse. My head was down, and I was thinking that I would turn around and head home as soon as I could tear that auction sale sign off the telephone pole down the road. A car passed. It sounded as if it threw a rock up under the fender. I looked up at the highway. Mick was lying there. The car did not stop. I went over and picked her up. I carried her to the shoulder of the road and laid her down in the dry, gray dust. She was hardly bleeding, but her side was split open like a ripe grape, and the skin underneath was as white and waxy as soap. I was really sorry that it had happened to Mick. I really was. I sat down in the dust, and Mick was in front of me. I just sat there for a long time thinking, and then I got up and went home. It was almost supper time.

The fact that I'd read *The Catcher in the Rye* a couple of months earlier may account for the *about* in the second sentence and the *I really was*, though they are normal in the context; but it would be hard to maintain now, in the face of the elaborate syntax required by my later work, that this early sketch wasn't actually a piece of ventriloquism—the lips of my memory worked by Hemingway, or by my notion of Hemingway. This was remarked on, and mildly lamented, by my instructor, an otherwise helpful man who would probably have been better advised to wonder "Why is this boy, visibly so polar to Hemingway or Hemingway's apparent heroes, nonetheless needful of lessons from him, and lessons in vision not behavior?" (strangely, the man shot himself three years later). Maybe it's as well that he didn't. I suspect now that I was responding, at the butt end of an adolescence perceived as monstrously lonely and rejected, to the siren song in the little Hemingway I'd read and that I heard it this way —"If you can tell what you know about pain and loss (physical and spiritual damage, incomprehension, bad love) and tell it in language so magically bare in its bones, so lean and irresistible in its threnody as to be instantly audible to any passerby, then by your clarity and skill, the depth and validity of your own precarious experience, you will compel large amounts of good love from those same passers, who'll restore your losses or repair them." And if I'd been conscious of the degree of self-pity involved in that first exchange, I might have been revolted and turned from narrative (as I'd turned, two years before, from drawing and painting). But I was only warned that I "sounded like Hemingway"; and since I knew perfectly well that everyone in America sounded like Hemingway, that was no obstacle. So I had written several sketches and my first real story, "Michael Egerton"—all under the tutelage of Hemingway's voice and stance—before I had read more than one or two of his stories and *A Farewell to Arms*. An "influence" can be exerted by the blinking of an eye, the literal movement of a hand from here to there, five words spoken in a memorable voice; and the almost universal sterility of academic-journalistic influence-hunting has followed from a refusal to go beyond merely symptomatic surface likenesses toward causes and the necessary question "Why was this writer hungry for this; what lack or taste was nourished by this?"

I did go on. One of the exciting nights of my life was spent in early September, 1952, reading *The Old Man and the Sea* in *Life* magazine, straight through by a naked light bulb, in the bed in which I was born (reread now, after years of accepting secondhand opinions on its weakness, it again seems fresh and dangerous, and though a little rigid, one of the great long stories). I remember reading, admiring, and—better—feeling affection for *The Sun Also Rises* during a course at Harvard in the summer of 1954; and I still have my old Modern Library edition of the first forty-nine stories, with neat stern notes to less than half the stories in my college-senior's hand—the notes of a technician, and as knowing and disapproving as only a young technician can be, but so unnaturally attentive as to signal clearly that some sort of unspoken love was involved, exchanged in fact—the exchange I began to define above, and to which I'll return. But, oddly, that was it—after 1955, I don't recall reading any more Hemingway till 1963, *A Moveable Feast,* well after I'd written two books of my own—and then not again till 1971 when I reread all I'd covered and the two-thirds I hadn't.

WHY? Not *why was I rereading?* but why had I read him in the first place, more than twenty years ago; and why had he helped so powerfully that I felt last summer —and still—this strong rush of gratitude? And why did I put him down so soon? Maybe another piece of Spender's comment will crack the door. He suggested that *A Long and Happy Life* advanced the chief discovery of Joyce and Hemingway, "which was to involve the reader, as with his blood and muscles, in the texture of the intensely observed and vividly imagistic writing." Assuming what I hope is true—that I needn't drown in self-contemplation if I think that out a little, and that I'm not pressing to death a comment made in kindness—what can Spender have meant? I remember, at the time, being especially pleased by his calling the prose "kinetic," which I took to mean concerned with and productive of movement. I don't recall telling Spender, but it had been my premise or faith before beginning *A Long and Happy Life* that by describing fully and accurately every physical gesture of three widely separated days in the lives of two people, I could convey the people—literally deliver them—to you, your room, your senses (I considered *thought* a physical gesture, which it is, though often invisible to the ordinary spectator). That faith, consciously held, guided the book through two years of writing and seems to me still the motive force of its claim on readers.

Isn't it also Hemingway's faith, in every line he wrote? Isn't it Tolstoy's, Flaubert's? Doesn't it provide the terrible force of the greatest narratives of the Bible?—*Genesis 22, John* 21. I'd read those as well, long before my discovery of Hemingway; and from the ninth grade, after *Anna Karenina,* I'd had my answer to the question "Who's best?" But as a tyro, I clearly took light from Hemingway. He was there, alive in Cuba, nine hundred miles from the desk in my bedroom, still writing—ergo, *writing was possible.* The texture of his work, his method, was apparently more lucid than Tolstoy's, unquestionably more human than Flaubert's (at least as I knew them in translation); and everything was briefer and thus more readily usable. But far more important—again I don't remember thinking about it—was what lay beneath that apparent lucidity. He said more than once that a good writer could omit anything from a story—knowingly, purposely—and the reader would respond to its presence with an intensity beyond mere understanding. There are striking examples —the famous one of "Big Two-Hearted River" which is utterly silent about its subject, and now *Islands in the Stream* which has a huge secret embedded in its heart, its claim against love, against life (as terrible as Tolstoy's in *The Kreutzer Sonata* or Céline's, though entirely personal and, like theirs, not dramatized). But what I discovered, detected with the sensing devices no one possesses after, say, sixteen, was both more general and more nourishingly specific—the knowledge that Hemingway had begun to write, and continued, for the reasons that were rapidly gathering behind me as my nearly terminal case of adolescence was beginning to relent: write or choke in self-loathing; write to comprehend and control fear. Loathing and fear of what? Anyone who has read my early fiction will probably know (they are not rare fears), and in the only way that might conceivably matter to anyone but me; nor is it wise-guy reductive to say that any sympathetic reader of Hemingway has possessed that knowledge of him since *In Our Time*—and that such knowledge is precisely what Hemingway intended, knowledge acquired from the work, not directly from the life. But the magnetic fields of fear in both cases—or so I felt, and feel—are located in simultaneous desperate love and dread of parents, imagined and actual abandonment by one's earliest peers, the early discovery that the certified emotions (affection, love, loyalty) are as likely to produce waste, pain, and damage to the animal self as are hate, solitude, freedom—perhaps more likely.

But Hemingway's work, at least, is complete and no damage can be done him or it by one more consideration of his technical procedures and their engines, their impetus (harm to a dead writer could only be the destruction of all copies of his work). And, oddly, in all that I know of the vast body of Hemingway criticism, there is almost no close attention to the bones of language, of the illuminating sort which Proust, for instance, gave to Flaubert. This despite the fact that most of his readers have always acknowledged that he gave as passionate a care to word and rhythm as Mallarmé. The most interesting discussion of his method is in fact by a writer—Frank O'Connor in his study of the short story, *The Lonely Voice*— and though it is finally destructive in its wrongheadedness and envy, it is near enough to insight to be worth a look. O'Connor feels that Hemingway studied and understood Joyce's early method and then proceeded to set up shop with Joyce's tools—"and a handsome little business he made of it." And regardless of the justice of that (it's at least a refreshing alternate to the usual references to Gertrude Stein and Sherwood Anderson), it is in O'Connor's description of the Joyce of *Dubliners* that he casts indirect light on Hemingway—

> It is a style that originated with Walter Pater but was then modeled very closely on that of Flaubert. It is a highly pictorial style; one intended to exclude the reader from the action and instead to present him with a series of images of the events described, which he may accept or reject but cannot modify to suit his own mood or environment.

The following, however, is as far as he goes toward an attempt at understanding the motive for such procedure, in either Joyce or Hemingway—

> By the repetition of key words and key phrases . . . it slows down the whole conversational movement of prose, the casual, sinuous, evocative quality that distinguishes it from poetry and is intended to link author and reader in a common perception of the object, and replaces it by a series of verbal rituals which are intended to evoke the object as it may be supposed to be. At an extreme point it attempts to substitute the image for the reality. It is a rhetorician's dream.

And finally—

> . . . in neither of these passages [from Joyce and Hemingway] is there what you could call a human voice

speaking, nobody resembling yourself who is trying to persuade you to share in an experience of his own, and whom you can imagine yourself questioning about its nature—nothing but an old magician sitting over his crystal ball, or a hypnotist waving his hands gently before your eyes and muttering, "You are falling asleep; you are falling asleep; slowly, slowly your eyes are beginning to close; your eyelids are growing heavy; you are—falling—asleep."

Despite the fact that *I* feel strong bonds with the voice in early Hemingway at least, the core of that seems roughly true of both writers—Joyce in the cold dexterity of *A Portrait of the Artist* and Hemingway all his life, though in an entirely different way. Why true? Surely the motives are different and infinitely complex in each case (though one might suspect, especially after Ellmann's biography, that Joyce's production of such a distancing method was only one more cast skin of an essentially reptilian nature). If I attempt my own description of Hemingway's procedure (a description largely coincident with what I *felt* as a student and what drew me to him as I began to write), then I can guess more legitimately at motives.

Hemingway's attempt, in all his fiction, is *not* to work magic spells on a reader, locking him into a rigid instrument of vision (in fact, into a movie) which controls not only what he sees but what he feels. The always remarked absence of qualifiers (adjectives, adverbs) is the simplest and surest sign here. Such an attempt—and one does feel and resent it often, in Flaubert and Joyce—is essentially the dream of achieving perfect empathic response, of making the reader become the story, or the story's emotional center at any given moment: Emma Bovary, Gabriel Conroy. And it is the dream not only of a few geniuses but of a large percentage of readers of fiction—the hunger for literally substitute life. Doomed of course, for the sane at least. But while Hemingway attempts as unremittingly as anyone to control his reader—to station him precisely in relation both to the visible and invisible actions of the story and to the author himself, and finally to trigger in him the desired response (again, to both story and author)—his strategy is entirely his own, and is in fact his great invention (the pure language itself being older than literature). Look at the famous opening of *A Farewell to Arms*—

> In the late summer of that year we lived in a house in a village that looked across the river and the plain to the mountains. In the bed of the river there were pebbles and boulders, dry and white in the sun, and the water was clear and swiftly moving and blue in the channels.

—As classical as Horace—in the sense of generalized, delocalized, deprived of native texture. What size house and what color, built how and of what? What village, arranged how around what brand of inhabitants, who do what to live? What river, how wide and deep? What kind of plain, growing what; and what mountains? Later—considerably later—he will tell you a little more, but very little. If you have never traveled in northern Italy in late summer—or seen the film of the book—you'll have no certainty of knowing how the earth looks above and beneath the action, in this or any other of his works. Or, in fact, how anything or anyone else *looks*. But by the audacity of its filterings, it demands that you lean forward toward the voice which is quietly offering the story—only then, will it begin to yield, to give you what it intends. And the gift will be what you *hear*—the voices of imagined characters speaking a dialect which purports to be your own (and has now convinced two generations of its accuracy). His early strategy is always, at its most calculated, an oral strategy. If we hear it read, it seems the convincing speaking-voice of this sensibility. Only on the silent page do we discover that it is as unidiomatic, as ruthlessly intentional as any *tirade* of Racine's. For behind and beneath all the voices of actors (themselves as few in number as in Sophocles) rides the one real voice—the maker's. And what it says, early and late, is always this—"This is what I see with my clean keen equipment. Work to see it after me." What it does not say but implies is more important—"For you I have narrowed and filtered my gaze. I am screening my vision so you will not see all. Why?—because you must enact this story for yourself; cast it, dress it, set it. Notice the chances I've left for you: no noun or verb is colored by me. I require your senses." What is most important of all—and what I think is the central motive—is this, which is concealed and of which the voice itself may be unconscious: "I tell you this, in this voice, because you must share—*must* because I require your presence, your company in my vision. I beg you to certify my knowledge and experience, my goodness and worthiness. I mostly speak as *I*. What I need from you is not empathy, identity, but patient approving witness—loving. License my life. Believe me." (If that many-staged plea is heard only intermittently in Hemingway's work after 1940—broken then by stretches of "confidence"—I'd guess that the cause would be the sclerosis consequent upon his success, the success of the voice which *won* him love, worship, a *carte blanche* he lacked the power to use well. Goethe said, "Beware of what you want when young; you'll get it when old." And the memory of the famished face of the deathbound Hemingway, quilted with adoration and money, is among the saddest and most instructive memories of Americans over twenty-five; his last gift to us.)

I've suggested that a final intention of Hemingway's method is the production of belief in the reader—belief in his total being and vision. Remember that he always spoke of the heavy role of the Bible in his literary education. The role has been generally misunderstood; seen as a superficial matter of King James rhythms, the frequent use of *and*, narrative "simplicity." But look at a brief though complete story from *Genesis* 32—

> In the night Jacob rose, took his two wives, the two slave girls and his eleven sons, and crossed the ford of Jabbok. When he had carried them all across, he sent his belongings. Then Jacob was alone, and some man wrestled with him there till daybreak. When he saw that he could not pin Jacob, he struck him in the pit of his thigh so that Jacob's hip unsocketed as they wrestled. Then he said "Let me go; it is daybreak."
> Jacob said, "I will not let go till you bless me."
> The man said, "What is your name?"
> He said "Jacob."
> The man said, "You are Jacob no more but Israel—you have fought gods and men and lasted."

Jacob said, "Tell me your name please."

He said, "Why ask my name?" and departed.

So Jacob called the place *Penuel,* face of God, "For I have seen God's face and endured"; and the sun struck him as he passed Penuel, limping.*

—and then at Erich Auerbach's description of Old Testament narrative:

> . . . the externalization of only so much of the phenomena as is necessary for the purpose of the narrative, all else left in obscurity; the decisive points of the narrative alone are emphasized, what lies between is nonexistent; time and place are undefined and call for interpretation; thoughts and feelings remain unexpressed, are only suggested by the silence and the fragmentary speeches; the whole, permeated with the most unrelieved suspense and directed toward a single goal . . . remains mysterious and "fraught with background."

There is, give or take an idiom, a profound likeness between the account of Jacob's struggle and any scene in Hemingway; and Auerbach might well be describing Hemingway, not the Bible. I have already implied the nature of the likeness, the specific hunger in Hemingway which was met by Biblical method. Both require our strenuous participation, in the hope of compelling our allegiance, our belief. Here are three passages chosen at random from a continuous supply—the opening of "A Very Short Story":

> One hot evening in Padua they carried him up onto the roof and he could look out over the top of the town. There were chimney swifts in the sky. After a while it got dark and the searchlights came out. The others went down and took the bottles with them. He and Luz could hear them below on the balcony. Luz sat on the bed. She was cool and fresh in the hot night.

a moment from Thomas Hudson's Nazi-hunt in the Cuban keys:

* Translation by Reynolds Price.

They called to the shack and a woman came out. She was dark as a sea Indian and was barefooted and her long hair hung down almost to her waist. While she talked, another woman came out. She was dark, too, and long-haired and she carried a baby. As soon as she finished speaking, Ara and Antonio shook hands with the two women and came back to the dinghy. They shoved off and started the motor and came out.

and—curiously analogous to Jacob's ordeal with "some man"—the almost intolerably charged and delicate exchange between Frederic Henry and his friend the young Italian priest who has visited him in the hospital with a gift of vermouth:

"You were very good to come, father. Will you drink a glass of vermouth?"
"Thank you. You keep it. It's for you."
"No, drink a glass."
"All right. I will bring you more then."
The orderly brought the glasses and opened the bottle. He broke off the cork and the end had to be shoved down into the bottle. I could see the priest was disappointed but he said, "That's all right. It's no matter."
"Here's to your health, father."
"To your better health."

Given the basic narrative strategies of the Old Testament and Hemingway, only the tone of the motives is different —in the third-person Old Testament the voice is plain command; in Hemingway, a dignified pleading: *Believe!* and *Please believe.* Believe what? *The thing I know.* What do you know? In one case, the presence of the hidden hand of God; in the other, that his life is good and deserving of your witness, will even help your life. Then, why believe? In one case, simply and awfully, so that God be served; in the other, so that the voice—and the man behind it—may proceed through his life. That is the sense in which both styles are almost irresistibly kinetic. And the reason why they have been two of the most successful styles in the history of literature.

Why did it fail him then?—his work, the literal words in their order on the page. In one sense, it succeeded too brilliantly—won him millions of readers willing to exert the energy and certify the life, some of them willing even to alter their own lives in obedience to what they, understandably though ludicrously, took to be injunctions of the work (there are certainly injunctions, though not to noise and bluster). But for nothing—or too little. In the only sense that can have mattered to him, his vision and its language failed him appallingly. It won him neither the relatively serene middle working-years of a Conrad or a Mann nor the transcendent old age of a Tolstoy, a James, Proust's precocious mastery of a silly life. Nor did it, with all its success in the world, allay even half his daily weight of fear. Immense time and energy were thrown elsewhere in flagging hope—sport, love, companions, drink, all of which took dreadful cuts of their own. Maybe it's permissible to *ask* why the words failed him; but to dabble in answers if one did not at least share a long stretch of his daily life and witness the desperate efforts in their long mysterious complexity is only a game, though a solemn game which can be played more or less responsibly and one which can no longer harm him or the work.

I've indulged already in the early pages of this with a guess, from the gathering evidence of his last four books, about his submerged subject which he found and attempted to float too late, when the search itself—or flight from the search—had dangerously depleted his senses and, worse, prevented the intellectual growth which might have compensated. But the words themselves? and the vision and needs which literally pressed words from him?—were they doomed from the start to kill him? A language fatally obsessed with defending the self and the few natural objects which the self both loves and trusts? A vision narrowed, crouched in apprehension of the world's design to maul, humiliate? Insufficiently surrendered to that design? Whatever the answers (and I'd guess that each is a mysterious *Yes*), it's clear that he was never capable of the calm firm-footed gaze of the godlike Tolstoy, who at twenty-six was producing from his own military experience, in a story called "The Wood-Felling," narrative so sure of its power as to be a near-lethal radiation—

> The wounded man lay at the bottom of the cart holding on to the sides with both hands. His broad healthy face had completely changed during those few moments; he seemed to have grown thinner and years older, his lips were thin and pale and pressed together with an evident strain. The hasty and dull expression of his glance was replaced by a kind of bright clear radiance, and on the bloody forehead and nose already lay the impress of death. Though the least movement caused him excruciating pain, he nevertheless asked to have a small *chérez* with money taken from his left leg.
> The sight of his bare, white, healthy leg, when his jack-boot had been taken off and the purse untied, produced on me a terribly sad feeling.

Yet Hemingway's work—its damaged tentative voice, for all its large failures, its small ignorances and meannesses—did a great deal, for him and us. Beyond carrying him through an after all long life and conveying an extraordinary, apparently usable portion of that life's texture of pleasure and pain to millions of contemporary strangers, it has left live remains—a body of fourteen volumes which, in my guess, will winnow to eight and then stand as an achievement, a vision, so far unexcelled in American letters, certainly by no one in his own century.* For what?—the intensity of their gaze, however screening, at a range of men and dangers which, with the inevitable allowances for private obsession, are as broadly and deeply representative as any but the great masters' (we don't yet possess one); for the stamina of their search, however veiled, through four decades for the demands and conditions and duties of human goodness in relation to other men, beasts and objects, and finally God; and then (strongest but most unprovable, most primitive and mysterious) for the language in which

* My own list, now, would be—*The Collected Stories, The Sun Also Rises, A Farewell to Arms, Green Hills of Africa, For Whom the Bell Tolls, The Old Man and the Sea, A Moveable Feast, Islands in the Stream.*

the search externalized itself, his optics and shield, weapon and gift. Gift to whom?

Me, as I've said, who have responded over twenty-five years to what I took to be an asking voice with what I now see was apprenticeship, neither exclusive nor conscious and quickly renegade but clearly the gravest homage I can offer. Useless to him but profound nonetheless. The profoundest—for I also see that I loved his voice and studied its shapes, not for its often balked and raging message but because I, balked and enraged, shared the motives at which I've guessed and, stranger, its two subjects: freedom and virtue. Polar heights, inaccessible maybe to climbers more intent on self-protection (footholds, handholds) than on the climb itself, the route and destination.

Gift also to all other living American writers, as obsessed as he with defense of what the self is and what it knows, any one of whom seems to me more nearly brother to him —in need and diet, dream and fulfillment, vision and blindness—than to any other artist in our history, or anyone else's (and, oddly, our avatar of Byron, the proto-American artist). Like it or not, our emblem and master whose lessons wait, patient and terrible.

Gift especially to the young. For it is almost certainly with them that his life now lies. It is easy enough to patronize Children's Classics—Omar, Mrs. Browning, Wolfe, lately Hesse—but any writer's useful survival is in heavy danger when the young abandon him entirely; it is only on them that he stands a chance of inflicting permanent damage (are Milton and Dante effectively alive? can they yet be saved in some form they'd have agreed to?— not by schools, apparently). In all Hemingway's work, until *The Old Man and the Sea* and *Islands in the Stream*, the warnings, if not the pleas, are for them; the lessons of one master, diffidently but desperately offered—*Prepare, strip, divest for life that awaits you; learn solitude and work; see how little is lovely but love that.*

—Half the lesson of the desert fathers, and given in language of the desert, bleached, leached to essence. The other half—an answer to *Why?*—is withheld until the last, and then only muttered. Surely there are young people now, readers and writers—children when he died—to whom he is speaking his dark secret language of caution and love, help and beggary, in the lean voice of an infinitely delicate, infinitely suffering thing. No shield, no help at all of course, to him or us (he never said it would be); yet more—a diamond point that drills through time and pain, a single voice which moves through pain toward rest and presses forward shyly with its greeting and offer, its crushing plea, like that of the hermit Paul when St. Antony had tracked him through beasts and desert and begged for instruction:

Behold, thou lookest on a man that is soon to be dust. Yet because love endureth all things, tell me, I pray thee, how fares the human race: if new roofs be risen in the ancient cities, whose empire is it that now sways the world; and if any still survive, snared in the error of the demons.

The Writer at the End of the Bar

Howard Moss

DATED at forty-five? Not yet,
You sly, old Phoenix in leather boots.
Infancy, with its double takes,
Is your seismograph, and its earthquakes.
Tell me, what are you writing now—
My Damaged Nerves: The Great Shakes?

Dumbshows count, not words. You are
Silent, maimed. Slumped at a bar,
What's left to learn in its mirrored length
That isn't already mirrored at length
In your life? Is it true you are
Writing *Oh, God, Give Me Strength—*

The Weak Shall Inherit Each Other?
They'd better; they don't inherit the earth.
Sometimes they don't—or can't or won't—
Even inherit each other. So
Why revise *The Prodigal Sons:
No Deposits and No Returns?*

Get up, get out. Night's dark and cheap.
Hell is a place that's never filled.
Maybe that's where you'll sleep tonight,
Writing in dreams, as the sleeve unravels
Your latest non-best-seller,
Down in the Dumps And Other Travels.

An Old Woman and Her Cat

Doris Lessing

HER NAME WAS Hetty, and she was born with the twentieth century. She was seventy when she died of cold and malnutrition. She had been alone for a long time, since her husband had died of pneumonia in a bad winter soon after the Second World War. He had not been more than middle-aged. Her four children were now middle-aged, with grown children. Of all these descendants one daughter sent her Christmas cards, but otherwise she did not exist for them. For they were all respectable people, with homes and good jobs and cars. And Hetty was not respectable. She had always been a bit strange, these people said, when mentioning her at all.

When Fred Pennefather her husband was alive, and the children just growing up, they all lived much too close and uncomfortable in a Council flat in that part of London which is like an estuary, with tides of people flooding in and out: they were not half a mile from the great stations of Euston, St. Pancras, and King's Cross. The blocks of flats were pioneers in that area, standing up stiff, grim, gray, hideous, among many acres of little houses and gardens, all soon to be demolished so that they could be replaced by more tall gray blocks. The Pennefathers were good tenants, paying their rent, keeping out of debt; he was a building worker, "steady," and proud of it. There was no evidence then of Hetty's future dislocation from the normal, unless it was that she very often slipped down for an hour or so to the platforms where the locomotives drew in and ground out again. She liked the smell of it all, she said. She liked to see people moving about, "coming and going from all those foreign places." She meant Scotland, Ireland, the North of

England. These visits into the din, the smoke, the massed swirling people, were for her a drug, like other people's drinking or gambling. Her husband teased her, calling her a gypsy. She was in fact part gypsy, for her mother had been one but had chosen to leave her people and marry a man who lived in a house. Fred Pennefather liked his wife for being different from the run of the women he knew, and had married her because of it, but her children were fearful that her gypsy blood might show itself in worse ways than haunting railway stations. She was a tall woman with a lot of glossy black hair, a skin that tanned easily, and dark strong eyes. She wore bright colors, and enjoyed quick tempers and sudden reconciliations. In her prime she attracted attention, was proud and handsome. All this made it inevitable that the people in those streets should refer to her as "that gypsy woman." When she heard them, she shouted back that she was none the worse for that.

AFTER HER HUSBAND died and the children married and left, the Council moved her to a small flat in the same building. She got a job selling food in a local store, but found it boring. There seem to be traditional occupations for middle-aged women living alone, the busy and responsible part of their lives being over. Drink. Gambling. Looking for another husband. A wistful affair or two. That's about it. Hetty went through a period of as it were testing out all these hobbies, but tired of them. While still earning her small wage as a saleswoman, she began a trade in buying and selling secondhand clothes. She did not have a shop of her own, but bought or begged clothes from householders, and sold these to stalls and the secondhand shops. She adored doing this. It was a passion. She gave up her respectable job and forgot all about her love of trains and travelers. Her room was always full of bright bits of cloth, a dress that had a pattern she fancied and did not want to sell, strips of beading, old furs, embroidery, lace. There were street traders among the people in the flats, but there was something in the way Hetty went about it that lost her friends. Neighbors of twenty or thirty years' standing said she had gone queer and wished to know her no longer. But she did not mind. She was enjoying herself too much, particularly the moving about the streets with her old perambulator, in which she crammed what she was buying or selling. She liked the gossiping, the bargaining, the wheedling from householders. It was this last—and she knew this quite well, of course—that the neighbors objected to. It was the thin edge of the wedge. It was begging. Decent people did not beg. She was no longer decent.

Lonely in her tiny flat, she stayed in it as little as possible, always preferring the lively streets. But she had after all to spend some time in her room, and one day she saw a kitten lost and trembling in a dirty corner, and brought it home to the block of flats. She was on a fifth floor. While the kitten was growing into a large strong tom, it ranged about that conglomeration of staircases and lifts and many dozens of flats, as if the building were a town. Pets were not actively persecuted by the authorities, only forbidden and then tolerated. Hetty's life from the coming of the cat became more sociable, for the beast was always making friends with somebody in the cliff that was the block of flats across the court, or not coming home for nights at a time so that she had to go and look for him and knock on doors and ask, or returning home kicked and limping, or bleeding after a fight with his own kind. She made scenes with the kickers, or the owners of the enemy cats, exchanged cat lore with cat lovers, was always having to bandage and nurse her poor Tibby. The cat was soon a scarred warrior with fleas, a torn ear, and a ragged look to it. It was a multicolored cat and its eyes were small and yellow. It was a long way down the scale from the delicately colored, elegantly shaped pedigree cats. But it was independent, and often caught itself pigeons when it could no longer stand the tinned cat food, or the bread and packet gravy Hetty fed him, and it purred and nestled when she grabbed it to her bosom at those times she suffered loneliness. This happened less and less. Once she had realized that her children were hoping that she would leave them alone because the old rag-trader was an embarrassment to them, she accepted it, and a bitterness that always had wild humor in it only welled up at times like Christmas. She sang or chanted to the cat: "You nasty old beast, filthy old cat, nobody wants you, do they Tibby, no, you're just an alley tom, just an old stealing cat, hey Tibs, Tibs, Tibs."

The building teemed with cats. There were even a couple of dogs. They all fought up and down the gray cement corridors. There were sometimes dog and cat messes which someone had to clear up, but which might be left for days and weeks as part of neighborly wars and feuds. There were many complaints. Finally an official came from the Council to say that the ruling about keeping animals was going to be enforced. Hetty, like the others, would have to have her cat destroyed. This crisis coincided with a time of bad luck for her. She had had flu, had not been able to earn money, had found it hard to get out for her pension, had run into debt. She owed a lot of back rent, too. A television set she had hired and was not paying for attracted the visits of a television representative. The neighbors were gossiping that Hetty had "gone savage." This was because the cat had brought up the stairs and along the passageways a pigeon he had caught, shedding feathers and blood all the way; a woman coming in to complain found Hetty plucking the pigeon to stew it, as she had done with others, sharing the meal with Tibby.

"You're filthy," she would say to him, setting the stew down to cool in his dish. "Filthy old thing. Eating that dirty old pigeon. What do you think you are, a wild cat? Decent cats don't eat dirty birds. Only those old gypsies eat wild birds."

One night she begged help from a neighbor who had a car, and put into the car herself, the television set, the cat, bundles of clothes, and the pram. She was driven across London to a room in a street that was a slum because it was waiting to be done up. The neighbor made a second trip to bring her bed and her mattress, which were tied to the roof of the car, a chest of drawers, an old trunk, saucepans. It was in this way that she left the street in which she had lived for thirty years, nearly half her life.

She set up house again in one room. She was frightened to go near "them" to reestablish pension rights and her identity, because of the arrears of rent she had left behind, and because of the stolen television set. She started trading again, and the little room was soon spread, like her last, with a rainbow of colors and textures and lace and sequins. She cooked on a single gas ring and washed in the sink. There was no hot water unless it was boiled in saucepans. There were several old ladies and a family of four children in the house, which was condemned.

She was in the ground floor back, with a window which opened onto a derelict garden, and her cat was happy in a hunting ground that was a mile around this house where his mistress was so splendidly living. A canal ran close by, and in the dirty city water were islands which a cat could reach by leaping from moored boat to boat. On the islands were rats and birds. There were pavements full of fat London pigeons. The cat was a fine hunter. He soon had his place in the hierarchies of the local cat population and did not have to fight much to keep it. He was a strong male cat, and fathered many litters of kittens.

IN THAT PLACE Hetty and he lived five happy years. She was trading well, for there were rich people close by to shed what the poor needed to buy cheaply. She was not lonely, for she made a quarreling but satisfying friendship with a woman on the top floor, a widow like herself who did not see her children either. Hetty was sharp with the four children, complaining about their noise and mess, but she slipped them bits of money and sweets after telling their mother that "she was a fool to put herself out for them, because they would never appreciate it." She was living well, even without her pension. She sold the television set and gave herself and her friend upstairs some day trips to the coast, and bought a small radio. She never read books or magazines. The truth was that she could not write or read, or only so badly it was no pleasure to her. Her cat was all reward and no cost, for he fed himself, and continued to bring in pigeons for her to cook and eat, for which in return he claimed milk.

"Greedy Tibby, you greedy *thing*, don't think I don't know, oh yes I do, you'll get sick eating those old pigeons, I do keep telling you that, don't I?"

At last the street was being done up. No longer a uniform, long, disgraceful slum, houses were being bought by the middle-class people. While this meant more good warm clothes for trading—or begging, for she still could not resist the attraction of getting something for nothing by the use of her plaintive inventive tongue, her still flashing handsome eyes—Hetty knew, like her neighbors, that soon this house with its cargo of poor people would be bought for improvement.

In the week Hetty was seventy years old came the notice that was the end of this little community. They had four weeks to find somewhere else to live.

Usually, the shortage of housing being what it is in London—and everywhere else in the world, of course—these people would have had to scatter, fending for themselves. But the fate of this particular street was attracting attention, because a municipal election was pending. Homelessness among the poor was finding a focus in this street, which was a perfect symbol of the whole area, and indeed, the whole city, being half fine converted tasteful houses, full of people who spent a lot of money, and half dying houses tenanted by people like Hetty.

As a result of speeches by councillors and churchmen, local authorities found themselves unable to ignore the victims of this redevelopment. The people in the house Hetty was in were visited by a team consisting of an unemployment officer, a social worker, and a rehousing officer. Hetty, a strong gaunt old woman wearing a scarlet wool suit she had found among her castoffs that week, a black knitted tea cosy on her head, and black buttoned Edwardian boots too big for her, so that she had to shuffle, invited them into her room. But although all were well used to the extremes of poverty, none wished to enter the place, but stood in the doorway and made her this offer: that she should be aided to get her pension—why had she not claimed it long ago?—and that she, together with the four other old ladies in the house, should move to a "home" run by the Council out in the northern suburbs. All these women were used to, and enjoyed, lively London, and while they had no alternative but to agree, they fell into a saddened and sullen state. Hetty agreed too. The last two winters had set her bones aching badly, and a cough was never far away. And while perhaps she was more of an urban soul even than the others, since she had walked up and down so many streets with her old perambulator loaded with rags and laces, and since she knew so intimately London's texture and taste, she minded least of all the idea of a new home "among green fields." There were, in fact, no fields near the promised "home," but for some reason all the old ladies had chosen to bring out this old song of a phrase, as if it belonged to their situation, that of old women not far off from death. "It will be nice to be near green fields again," they said to each other over cups of tea.

The housing officer came to make final arrangements. Hetty Pennefather was to move with the others in two weeks' time. The young man, sitting on the very edge of the only chair in the crammed room, because it was greasy and he suspected it had fleas or worse in it, breathed as lightly as he could because of the appalling stink: there was a lavatory in the house, but it had been out of order for three days, and it was just the other side of a thin wall. The whole house smelled.

The young man, who knew only too well the extent of the misery due to lack of housing, who knew how many old people abandoned by their children did not get the offer to spend their days being looked after by the authorities, could not help feeling that this wreck of a human being could count herself lucky to get a place in this "home," even if it was—and he knew and deplored the fact —an institution in which the old were treated like naughty and dim-witted children until they had the good fortune to die.

But just as he was telling Hetty that a van would be coming to take her effects and those of the other four old ladies, and that she need not take anything more with her than her clothes "and perhaps a few photographs," he saw what he had thought was a heap of multicolored rags get up and put its ragged gingery-black paws on the old woman's skirt. Which today was a cretonne curtain covered with pink and red roses that Hetty had pinned around her because she so liked the pattern.

"You can't take that cat with you," he said automatically. It was something he had to say often, and knowing what misery the statement caused, he usually softened it down. But he had been taken by surprise.

Tibby now looked like a mass of old wool that had been matting together in dust and rain. One eye was permanently half-closed, because a muscle had been ripped in a fight. One ear was vestigial. And down a flank was a hairless slope with a thick scar on it. A cat-hating man had treated Tibby as he treated all cats, to a pellet from his airgun. The resulting wound had taken two years to heal. And Tibby smelled.

No worse, however, than his mistress, who sat stiffly still, bright-eyed with suspicion, hostile, watching the well-brushed tidy young man from the Council.

"How old is that beast?"

"Ten years, no, only eight years, he's a young cat about five years old," said Hetty, desperate.

"It looks as if you'd do him a favor to put him out of his misery," said the young man.

When the official left, Hetty had agreed to everything. She was the only one of the old women with a cat. The others had budgerigars or nothing. Budgies were allowed in the "home."

She made her plans, confided in the others, and when the van came for them and their clothes and photographs and budgies, she was not there, and they told lies for her. "Oh, we don't know where she can have gone, dear," the old women repeated again and again to the indifferent van driver. "She was here last night, but she did say something about going to her daughter in Manchester." And off they went to die in the "home."

Hetty knew that when houses have been emptied for redevelopment they may stay empty for months, even years. She intended to go on living in it until the builders moved in.

It was a warm autumn. For the first time in her life she lived like her gypsy forebears, and did not go to bed in a room in a house like respectable people. She spent several nights, with Tibby, sitting crouched in a doorway of an empty house two doors from her own. She knew exactly when the police would come around, and where to hide herself in the bushes of the overgrown shrubby garden.

As she had expected, nothing happened in the house, and she moved back in. She smashed a back windowpane so that Tibby could move in and out without her having to unlock the front door for him, and without leaving a window suspiciously open. She moved to the top back room and left it every morning early, to spend the day in the streets with her pram and her rags. At night she kept a candle glimmering low down on the floor. The lavatory was still out of order, so she used a pail on the first floor as a lavatory, and secretly emptied it at night into the canal which in the day was full of pleasure boats and people fishing.

Tibby brought her several pigeons during that time.

"Oh you are a clever puss, Tibby, Tibby! Oh you're clever, you are. You know how things are, don't you, you know how to get around and about."

The weather turned very cold; Christmas came and went. Hetty's cough came back, and she spent most of her time under piles of blanket and old clothes, dozing. At night she watched the shadows of the candle flame on floor and ceiling—the window frames fitted badly, and there was a draft. Twice tramps spent the night in the bottom of the house, and she heard them being moved on by the police. She had to go down to make sure the police had not blocked up the broken window the cat used, but they had not. A blackbird had flown in and had battered itself to death trying to get out. She plucked it, and roasted it over a fire made with bits of floorboard in a baking pan: the gas of course had been cut off. She had never eaten very much, and was not frightened that some dry bread and a bit of cheese was all that she had eaten during her sojourn under the heap of clothes. She was cold, but did not think about that much. Outside there was slushy brown snow everywhere. She went back to her nest thinking that soon the cold spell would be over and she could get back to her trading. Tibby sometimes got into the pile with her, and she clutched the warmth of him to her. "Oh you clever cat, you clever old thing, looking after yourself, aren't you? That's right my ducky, that's right my lovely."

And then, just as she was moving about again, with snow gone off the ground for a time but winter only just begun, in January, she saw a builder's van draw up outside, a couple of men unloading their gear. They did not come into the house: they were to start work next day. By then Hetty, her cat, her pram piled with clothes and her two blankets, were gone. She also took a box of matches, a candle, an old saucepan and a fork and spoon, a tin opener, and a rat-trap. She had a horror of rats.

About two miles away, among the homes and gardens of amiable Hampstead, where live so many of the rich, the intelligent, and the famous, stood three empty, very large houses. She had seen them on an occasion, a couple of years before, when she had taken a bus. This was a rare thing for her, because of the remarks and curious looks provoked by her mad clothes, and by her being able to appear at the same time such a tough battling old thing and a naughty child. For the older she got, this disreputable tramp, the more there strengthened in her a quality of fierce, demanding childishness. It was all too much of a mixture; she was uncomfortable to have near.

She was afraid that "they" might have rebuilt the houses, but there they still stood, too tumbledown and dangerous to be of much use to tramps, let alone the armies of London's homeless. There was no glass left anywhere. The flooring at ground level was mostly gone, leaving small platforms and juts of planking over basements full of water. The ceilings were crumbling. The roofs were going. The houses were like bombed buildings.

But in the cold dark of a late afternoon she pulled the pram up the broken stairs and moved cautiously around the frail boards of a second-floor room that had a great hole in it right down to the bottom of the house. Looking into it was like looking into a well. She held a candle to examine the state of the walls, here more or less whole, and saw that rain and wind blowing in from the window would leave one corner dry. Here she made her home. A sycamore tree screened the gaping window from the main road twenty yards away. Tibby, who was cramped after making the journey under the clothes piled in the pram, bounded down and out and vanished into neglected undergrowth to catch his supper. He returned fed and pleased, and seemed happy to stay clutched in her hard thin old arms. She had come to watch for his return after hunting trips, because the warm purring bundle of bones and fur did seem to allay, for a while, the permanent ache of cold in her bones.

NEXT DAY she sold her Edwardian boots for a few shillings —they were fashionable again—and bought a loaf and some bacon scraps. In a corner of the ruins well away from the one she had made her own, she pulled up some floorboards, built a fire, and toasted bread and the bacon scraps. Tibby had brought in a pigeon, and she roasted that, but not very efficiently. She was afraid of the fire catching and the whole mass going up in flames; she was afraid too of the smoke showing and attracting the police. She had to keep damping down the fire, and so the bird was bloody and unappetizing, and in the end Tibby got most of it. She felt confused, and discouraged, but thought it was because of the long stretch of winter still ahead of her before spring could come. In fact, she was ill. She made a couple of attempts to trade and earn money to feed herself before she acknowledged she was ill. She knew she was not yet dangerously ill, for she had been that in her life, and would have been able to recognize the cold listless indifference of real last-ditch threatening illness. But all her bones ached, and her head ached, and she coughed more than she ever had. Yet she still did not think of herself as suffering particularly from the cold, even in that sleety January weather. She had never, in all her life, lived in a properly heated place, had never known a really warm home, not even when she lived in the Council flats. Those flats had electric fires, and the family had never used them, for the sake of economy, except in very bad spells of cold. They piled clothes onto themselves, or went to bed early. But she did know that to keep herself from dying now she could not treat the cold with her usual indifference. She knew she must eat. In the comparatively dry corner of the windy room, away from the gaping window through which snow and sleet were drifting, she made another nest—her last. She had found a piece of polythene sheeting in the rubble, and she laid that down first, so that the damp would not strike up. Then she spread her two blankets over that. Over them was heaped the mass of old clothes. She wished she had another piece of polythene to put on top, but she used sheets of newspaper instead. She heaved herself into the middle of this, with a loaf of bread near to her hand. She dozed, and waited, and nibbled bits of bread, and watched the snow drifting softly in. Tibby sat close to the old blue face that poked out of the pile and put up a paw to touch it. He meowed and was restless, and then went out into the frosty morning and brought in a pigeon. This the cat put, still struggling and fluttering a little, close to the old woman. But she was afraid to get out of the pile in which the heat was being made and kept with such difficulty. She really could not climb out long enough to pull up more splinters of plank from the floors, to make a fire, to pluck the pigeon, to roast it. She put out a cold hand to stroke the cat.

"Tibby, you old thing, you brought it for me then, did you? You did, did you? Come here, come in here." But he did not want to get in with her. He meowed again, pushed the bird closer to her. It was now limp and dead.

"You have it then. You eat it. I'm not hungry, thank you, Tibby."

But the carcass did not interest him. He had eaten a pigeon before bringing this up to Hetty. He fed himself well. In spite of his matted fur, and his scars and his half-closed yellow eye, he was a strong healthy cat.

At about four the next morning there were steps and voices downstairs. Hetty shot out of the pile and crouched behind a fallen heap of plaster and beams, now covered with snow, at the end of the room near the window. She could see through the gap in the floorboards down to the first floor, which had collapsed entirely, and through it to the ground floor. She saw a man in a thick overcoat and muffler and leather gloves holding a strong torch to illuminate a thin bundle of clothes lying on the floor. She saw that this bundle was a sleeping man or woman. She was indignant—*her* home was being trespassed upon. And she was afraid, because she had not been aware of this other tenant of the ruin. Had he, or she, heard her talking to the cat? And where was the cat? If he wasn't careful he would be caught, and that would be the end of him. The man with the torch went off and came back with a second man. In the thick dark far below Hetty was a small cave of strong light, which was the torchlight. In this space of light two men bent to lift the bundle, which was the corpse of a man or a woman like Hetty. They carried it out across the dangertraps of fallen and rotting boards that made gangplanks over the water-filled basements. One man was holding the torch in the hand that supported the dead person's feet, and the light jogged and lurched over trees and grasses: the corpse was being taken through the shrubberies to a car.

There are men in London who, between the hours of two and five in the morning, when the real citizens are asleep, who should not be disturbed by such unpleasantness as the corpses of the poor, make the rounds of all the empty rotting houses they know about, to collect the dead, and to warn the living that they ought not to be there at all, inviting them to one of the official "homes" or lodgings for the homeless.

Hetty was too frightened to get back into her warm heap. She sat with the blankets pulled around her, and looked through gaps in the fabric of the house, making out shapes and boundaries and holes and puddles and mounds of rubble, as her eyes, like her cat's, became accustomed to the dark.

She heard scuffling sounds and knew they were rats. She had meant to set the trap, but the thought of her friend Tibby, who might catch his paw, had stopped her. She sat up until the morning light came in gray and cold, after nine. Now she did know herself to be very ill and in danger, for she had lost all the warmth she had huddled into her bones under the rags. She shivered violently. She was shaking herself apart with shivering. In between spasms she drooped limp and exhausted. Through the ceiling above her—but it was not a ceiling, only a cobweb of slats and planks—she could see into a dark cave which had been a garret, and through the roof above that, the gray sky, teeming with incipient rain. The cat came back from where he had been hiding, and sat crouched on her knees, keeping her stomach warm, while she thought out her position. These were her last clear thoughts. She told herself that she would not last out until spring unless she allowed "them" to find her, and take her to hospital. After that, she would be taken to a "home."

But what would happen to Tibby, her poor cat? She rubbed the old beast's scruffy head with the ball of her thumb and muttered: "Tibby Tibby, they won't get you, no, you'll be all right, yes, I'll look after you."

Toward midday, the sun oozed yellow through miles of greasy gray clouds, and she staggered down the rotting stairs, to the shops. Even in those streets where the extraordinary has become usual, people turned to stare at a tall gaunt woman, with a white face that had flaming red patches on it, and blue compressed lips, and restless black eyes. She wore a tightly buttoned man's overcoat, torn brown woolen mittens, and an old fur hood. She pushed a pram loaded with old dresses and scraps of embroidery and torn jerseys and shoes, all stirred into a tight tangle, and she kept pushing this pram up against people as they stood in queues, or gossiped, or stared into windows, and she muttered: "Give me your old clothes, darling, give me your old pretties, give Hetty something, poor Hetty's hungry." A woman gave her a handful of small change, and Hetty bought a bun filled with tomato and lettuce. She did not dare go into a cafe, for even in her confused state she knew she would offend, and would probably be asked to leave. But she begged a cup of tea at a street stall, and when the hot sweet liquid flooded through her she felt she might survive the winter. She bought a carton of milk and pushed the pram back through the slushy snowy street to the ruins.

Tibby was not there. She urinated down through the gap in the boards, muttering, "A nuisance, that old tea," and wrapped herself in a blanket and waited for the dark to come.

Tibby came in later. He had blood on his foreleg. She had heard scuffling and she knew that he had fought a rat, or several, and had been bitten. She poured the milk into the tilted saucepan and Tibby drank it all.

She spent the night with the animal held against her chilly bosom. They did not sleep, but dozed off and on.

Tibby would normally be hunting—the night was his time —but he had stayed with the old woman now for three nights.

EARLY NEXT MORNING they again heard the corpse-removers among the rubble on the ground floor, and saw the beams of the torch moving on wet walls and collapsed beams. For a moment the torchlight was almost straight on Hetty, but no one came up: who could believe that a person would be desperate enough to climb those dangerous stairs, to trust those crumbling splintery floors, and in the middle of winter?

Hetty had now stopped thinking of herself as ill, of the degrees of her illness, of her danger—of the impossibility of her surviving. She had cancelled out in her mind the presence of winter and its lethal weather, and it was as if spring were nearly here. She knew that if it had been spring when she had had to leave the other house, she and the cat could have lived here for months and months, quite safely and comfortably. Because it seemed to her an impossible and even a silly thing that her life, or rather, her death, could depend on something so arbitrary as builders starting work on a house in January rather than in April, she could not believe it: the fact would not stay in her mind. The day before she had been quite clear-headed. But today her thoughts were cloudy, and she talked and laughed aloud. Once she scrambled up and rummaged in her rags for an old Christmas card she had got four years before from her good daughter.

In a hard harsh angry grumbling voice she said to her four children that she needed a room of her own now that she was getting on. "I've been a good mother to you," she shouted to them before invisible witnesses—former neighbors, welfare workers, a doctor. "I never let you want for anything, never! When you were little you always had the best of everything! You can ask anybody, go on, ask them then!"

She was restless and made such a noise that Tibby left her and bounded onto the pram and crouched watching her. He was limping, and his foreleg was rusty with blood. The rat had bitten deep. When the daylight came, he left

Hetty in a kind of a sleep, and went down into the garden where he saw a pigeon feeding on the edge of the pavement. The cat pounced on the bird, dragged it into the bushes, and ate it all, without taking it up to its mistress. After he had finished eating, he stayed hidden, watching the passing people. He stared at them intently with his blazing yellow eye, as if he were thinking, or planning. He did not go into the old ruin and up the crumbling wet stairs until late—it was as if he knew it was not worthwhile going at all.

He found Hetty, apparently asleep, wrapped loosely in a blanket, propped sitting in a corner. Her head had fallen on her chest, and quantities of white hair had escaped from her scarlet woolen cap, and concealed a face that was flushed a deceptive pink—the flush of coma from cold. She was not yet dead, but she died that night. The rats came up the walls and along the planks and the cat fled down and away from them, limping still, into the bushes.

Hetty was not found for a couple of weeks. The weather changed to warm, and the man whose job it was to look for corpses was led up the dangerous stairs by the smell. There was something left of her, but not much.

As for the cat, he lingered for two or three days in the thick shrubberies, watching the passing people and beyond them, the thundering traffic of the main road. Once a couple stopped to talk on the pavement, and the cat, seeing two pairs of legs, moved out and rubbed himself against one of the legs. A hand came down and he was stroked and patted for a little. Then the people went away.

The cat saw he would not find another home, and he moved off, nosing and feeling his way from one garden to another, through empty houses, finally into an old churchyard. This graveyard already had a couple of stray cats in it, and he joined them. It was the beginning of a community of stray cats going wild. They killed birds, and the field mice that lived among the grasses, and they drank from puddles. Before winter had ended the cats had had a hard time of it from thirst, during the two long spells when the ground froze and there was snow and no puddles and the birds were hard to catch because the cats were so easy to see against the clean white. But on the whole they managed quite well. One of the cats was female, and soon there were a swarm of wild cats, as wild as if they did not live in the middle of a city surrounded by streets and houses. This was just one of half a dozen communities of wild cats living in that square mile of London.

Then an official came to trap the cats and take them away. Some of them escaped, hiding till it was safe to come back again. But Tibby was caught. He was not only getting old and stiff—he still limped from the rat's bite— but he was friendly, and did not run away from the man, who had only to pick him up in his arms.

"You're an old soldier, aren't you?" said the man. "A real tough one, a real old tramp."

It is possible that the cat even thought that he might be finding another human friend and a home.

But it was not so. The haul of wild cats that week numbered hundreds, and while if Tibby had been younger a home might have been found for him, since he was amiable and wished to be liked by the human race, he was really too old and smelly and battered. So they gave him an injection and, as we say, "put him to sleep."

American Girl

Pamela Hadas

I CALL it my diamond solitaire,
Although it's emerald as grass
(Is that why you stare?)
And the object is to amass

As many points as I can.
The points on the diamond are marked
With chalk and bags of sand
Against the green. I am marked

By a madness of numbers.
I play nine parts
And lead nine lives. I'm limber;
I live by short stops, false starts

And a crowd of angels: base men,
Outfielders, catchers, pitchers, umpires . . .
Of course, it's all in my mind—
I play in a league of desires.

Why are you so blank? It's as if you
Had never seen a game like this before.
It's a kind of melodrama. Hiss. Boo.
Cheer. I'm going to try it once more.

I run in circles around this square,
The object being to get home,
And home, as if I could care,
Is the trampled bag I started from.

But how can I teach you anything?
Love me, love me. That's my only game.
I'll be your living doll. I'll sing
And I'll dance. I'll love my shame.

I call it my diamond solitaire,
Or my cold emerald merry-go-round.
I've outgrown it. I'm sick of this fair
I've run into the earth's fair ground.

The Perfect One

Steven Orlen

MY FRIEND tells me I don't understand women,
a good question to ask myself in private.
Consider my suicides, my wives, who gave birth
to me daily. Under their wings I was slick
and charming. They were the coddlers who kept me.
To the shadows of their breasts, I brought my grief.
But the man, the elusive one, hid his eyes and slept.

Consider the advice my mother gave me
wheezing on her knee: "Never marry a girl
who can't sing in your sleep." I never did.
I couldn't find her. I lay awake.
"A boy takes wives by being forcefully inept,
a man steps into a woman's life by being blunt."
But mother's gone the way of most perfection
and father turned out to be right after all.

When I was crazy, I touched a tree,
and asked it what it was, beyond itself.
I think I suffered a long time without knowing.

*   *   *

In the mornings a lady comes to rouse me.
She is not my lover, she is not my mother.
She is the future and she is desperate to please me.

When she hands me my toothbrush, I tell her:
"Wait, you are the Perfect One, I can see
right through you." In the next bed my father writes:
"Everything will happen in its time . . ."

I had a dream last night in which
she came for me. "I'm not ready," I said,
but she was all smiles like the bark of a tree.

As I grew smaller, she grew more perfectly large.
Then she found it, my birthmark, and entered
my body through that one remaining hole without teeth.
"Get out," I told her, "you're just like me!"

She smelled like death as I breathed her out.
All of this is written in the book my father wrote.

Suspension Points . . .

Meyer Liben

As I passed my money to the stationer for the news-paper, it flashed across my mind (with the speed of a meteor, though less dramatically) that I could, if I so wished, spend a good part of the rest of my life describing this act, in its immediacy (I could add information about the money I gave, the change I received, in which hand I held the money, and how I folded and held the paper), its historical antecedents, all its ramifications, both fore-ground and background, to say nothing of tributary and peripheral elements.

There is the act itself, now in its more abstract quality, of exchanging money for a commodity. What belonged to him now belonged to me. He profited materially (must be a forty or fifty percent markup, or why should he bother with it?), I gained possession of an object of which I could make various uses—read it, use under the kindling in a fireplace, roll up and swat people or flies with, spread on the floor after washing same, work into airplane or other interesting shapes, use in collages the way the cubists used to do (but that's not my line of activity), clip out interesting items for own future use or to send to interested friends, make confetti with, line garbage cans with, could even (though I've never done this) save the paper, day after day, and then sell to a scrap-paper man, thus retriev-ing some part, however infinitesmal, of the original pur-chase price.

This buying of a paper is an act expressive of the history of the exchange of objects, an act old as mankind and whose analysis is no doubt almost as old (in the sense that it would probably have to be done before being thought about), moving through history down to the times of Adam Smith, Ricardo, Marx, Weber. . . . Can you imagine the time I'd have to spend learning and relearning the history and the analyses of theories of exchange in the spheres of economics, sociology, political science? And then summarizing all that material?

And then there is my partner in the transaction I started with. We are not friends, but I know him quite well, in the way that you get to know quite well people whom you have been dealing with steadily over many years. I know how long he's been in this spot, what he did before he was here (he was a car dealer, and before that a salesman for a hardware company in the Southwest), and I know his wife, who sometimes helps in the store. I've followed the history of their children as they've grown, and as much as I know about him he knows about me. Over the course of years these exchanges of nonintimate confidences—another kind of exchange!—can add up to a good deal of information, knowledge, even insight.

And his physical description, and that of his wife, and of their children (from the few glimpses I've had of them over the years). And the character analyses, and behavior patterns, and the description of the store itself—its size, layout, decor, and how all that has changed over the years.

The fact is that I knew this store before the stationer moved in, know something of the history of its previous occupants, their businesses and families, and the history too of the building in which the store is located, for it so happens that I once, at a social gathering, met the real estate agent who handled that building, a man with a strong memory as well as a keen historical interest and imagination, who told me what he knew about the building going back decades—who had built it, some of its better-known occupants, who had occupied the various store-fronts, a veritable treasure-trove of information about the building, and naturally, about the neighborhood too, in which he had grown up, and about which he knew a great deal, combining interest with daily experience and reading. All this I remember, and could set down pretty much as he told it to me, for I am blessed, or cursed, with a photographic memory, and the flow of associations, particularly when I am in a certain kind of reflective, even slightly gloomy mood, leads me to a recall approximately total. And there is a good deal to be said about the agent himself —I heard about him from others, the complex deals he'd been involved in, but I won't even go into a summary of all that.

And I could describe in detail (only space, time, and disinclination forbid it) the individuals who were in the store at the time I bought the newspaper, not the clerks whom I've already mentioned as part of those I could describe, but the other customers. There were five such customers, three of them strangers, one of them an acquaintance, and the fifth a man I knew by sight, a well-known publisher who lived in the neighborhood, and who had in his hand some half-dozen magazines, to make himself *au courant*, no doubt, with the newest developments in the business and literary worlds, which have so many points of intersection. (Or maybe he was going on a long journey.) Yes, I could describe this publisher, what I knew of his life, his firm, the nature of his publishing activities, the authors he's published, his successes and failures. I could describe the three strangers, one a lanky, perfectly-groomed man who seemed to be waiting to speak to the proprietor, another a child trying to decide what candy bar to choose among all the candy bars—and I could describe too all those candy bars, their shapes and tastes, the history of their prices and wrappers and so on; the third a young woman of great beauty, with the imperiousness that sometimes comes with such beauty (it showed in the movements of her head), and an abiding sadness (yes, it is possible to tell in a glimpse what abides), perhaps bitterness, which did not flaw that beauty but cast a kind of shadow over it, and I could speculate on the causes of this sadness or bitterness, in the way of family upbringing, problems of character, of love and marriage, a veritable panorama of possibilities thronged my imagination as I glimpsed this young woman, who was browsing among the paperbacks. And I could describe those paperbacks—I have browsed among them myself— to give an idea of what people are reading, to analyze popular taste, to explain how it is that among the mediocre and trashy books there are always a few works of genuine merit, to examine the prices, to write indeed a history of paperback publishing on the basis of the selection in this store, in front of which books stood the young woman I've already mentioned, the third of the strangers in the store at the moment that I picked up my newspaper.

And the acquaintance! I haven't forgotten him. He lives in the neighborhood, we had once met in the apartment of a mutual friend, and though neither one of us was seeing much of that mutual friend, we never failed to ask one another about him, what he was doing and so on. This mutual friend is a man who made a pile of money in corporate law, gave up the law, and spent a good deal of his time traveling the world in search of coins, the possession of which was for him a passion bordering on mania. No wonder neither my acquaintance nor myself hardly ever saw him. He was always in the suburbs of Rome, or on the isle of Crete, and indeed one of the invariable subjects of discussion between my acquaintance and myself was the whereabouts of our friend. "I got a postcard the other day from Ankara." "I heard he was in Labrador." I don't think either one of us *ever* saw this mutual friend anymore, but he was responsible for the continuance of this acquaintanceship, that and other things, for we discovered that we had other interests in common—horseracing and local politics, for instance—and these are subjects of inexhaustible interest. The history of racehorses and horseracing! The psychology of gambling! The complexities of big-city life! That's just for starters (you have to be careful, by the way, in the use of exclamation points. Too many of them create a factitious interest, and that is one step away from boredom).

I don't believe I mentioned where I was coming from and where I was going. I'm sure I haven't mentioned it. I was coming from home and was on my way downtown, by subway, on matters of business. My stop at the stationer's was a way stop. Most stops between home and a destination are way stops. No? Home is not a way stop. To flesh out this account (to spirit it out too) I'd have to tell about home and family and about my business life, means of livelihood and so on. Well, this is obviously not material for a page.

You perhaps now more clearly see what I mean when I say that I could spend a good part (*good* meaning *long* here) of the rest of my life, to give the full story, foreground, background and middle ground, of my purchase of the newspaper (and the subway ride! The experiences down there! The history of urban mass transportation!) and I don't plan to do that. I plan, and am in the process of carrying out the task, to show how it is possible that the description of this simple act of exchange, if elaborated in all directions, could easily lead to so ample an expenditure of time.

Included in so comprehensive a survey and analysis would be a picture, in words of course, of my mood at that moment of exchange, my situation, place in the world, whatever it is that we have come to mean by the word *existential*, the meaning and bearing of a life as regards one's hopes and anxieties, as regards its importance, value, fulfillment, and in relation to other lives, to society, nature . . . Just imagine the complexity, intricate variety, of all these relationships (and so many others!), all these ways of explaining (curious how a single word, *explain*, is not sufficient to cover the meaning) just how it is and where it is that one has a place in the world—how he stands, falls, leans, and inclines, the various tensions, yearnings, advances, and withdrawals (this the incompletest list of all) which make up one's life at a given time. Why, you could use up dozens and dozens of pages just listing these existential stances, adding so many words after *tensions, yearnings, advances,* and *withdrawals.* . . . Those four dots tell it all.

Exclusion has its place in the scheme of things, and catalogues are forms of exclusion, just because they are incomplete.

I've neglected to mention the time and weather. It was a cold, blustery November morning, that's as exact as I'm going to be in these matters (I'm not going to say a word, except to state that I'm not going to say a word, about Time and Weather as concepts), but I do want to say a few incomplete exclusionary words about the newspaper I bought.

Indeed, finally (how do you like that for an arbitrary

exclusion?) the newspaper itself. I don't mean its physical dimensions and weight, though why shouldn't those characteristics be described any less than one describes the lineaments of a person or the appearance of a room? But its content, the total reading of which, unless you've learned one of those new methods of Speed Reading, would surely take a number of hours, and the summary of which, if you wish to include necessary and proper historical, grammatical, psychological, sociological, anthropological . . . (praise these suspension points, which make unnecessary the completion of all those lists, catalogues, itemizations, collections, numerations, etc. Though couldn't the *etc.* take the place of the suspension points?) would take up more space than time permits. I don't know how many words that particular issue of the *New York Times* (there, you see, I am not hiding anything) contained, but to give you an example of what would be involved in an adequate survey, let me just state that in this particular edition of the paper the name of a person was mentioned (two words, mark you, out of perhaps hundreds of thousands) who happens to be a man I know extremely well, we have had business dealings together, some of them of a quite fantastic, even profitable, nature, involving the purchase of mineral rights in certain countries (I cannot be more specific because some of these operations are still in progress, of a certain delicate international and diplomatic import), a man, as I've said, and I repeat myself for reasons of sentence clarity, that I know very well, to the fibers of his being (how more apt an expression that would be if we were engaged in the textile business), know him not only through our commercial connections but also on his own, as an individual, as a family man, as a political participant, as a man of the world, know his fraternal connections, his peccadilloes, his childhood and growing up, know a great deal about his parents, his lineage, the genealogy of the man, know him at home with his intimates, as a watcher of television, know his interests, his hobbies, his passions, his eccentricities, know his temperament, his character, the details of his psychoanalysis (he is in some ways an extraordinarily frank man but oh with such reservoirs of secrecy), know his qualities good and bad, know the clothes he favors, the books and women he prefers, know what he thinks of his friends, of himself, know the nuances of his behavior, as well as the grosser outlines of it (what stops you from going on with such a list?) and he represents (I haven't gotten away from my subject at all) just two words—first and second name—in this newspaper of how many hundreds of thousands of words (lucky it's not a Sunday paper), the one I bought as an exchange commodity and about which I've said so little, when you consider its makeup, from news in its various categories, local to national to international to extraterrestrial (soon the moon correspondent will have more glamor than the foreign correspondent), not forgetting business, sports, finance, real estate. . . . (what *is* the proper number of suspension points?), its various departments, with their analyses of literature, politics, theater. . . . (the suspension points have it all over *etc.* because of the physicality, the ideographical extension), its advertisements, from the minutest classified to the full-page spread for products, causes. . . . , its prophecies in the way of weather, the outcome of horseraces and other sporting as well as political events. . . . , but I really haven't had a chance to read it, just glanced at it. . . . (the suspense in these suspension points).

Twentieth Anniversary Love Poem

Thomas Williams

My WIFE is entered, my calves are her stirrups.
No, I am driving this salty car past banks of old snow
Strange that in dreams I am always a man of twenty-six,
craggy in March, as hard as cracked china.
veteran, free lance, uncommitted, the war over.

My children grow into their own age, they become
veterans, free lance, committed to aliens.
My son is at times hard, strange, staring beyond.
My daughter grows toward her wounds; she was born
printed with diagrams for the amateur.

I once knew a pretty nurse, sweet Syringia.
Knocked up by a salesman of pharmaceuticals,
she wasted after the D&C from dreaming of tiny lips
and a warm tongue at her breast like the piston of a pump.

In March the deer have had a winter of hunger,
the does are heavy with their twin fawns,
and the crust supports the running dogs.
The deer are weak, but the dogs are fed in kitchens.

My wife groans, rising in the stirrups. I am her beast
and we canter where we are, coming from nowhere.
No, she watches as from a throne of old judgment
the bottle of beer that is snug in my crotch.
I am driving this salty car, feeling her heels
on my calves, my veins in the turning engine.

"Our roots are not legs to run from the ax blow, the saw,
the sapsuckers' gimlets. Our only escape is growth,"
say the wordless hemlocks. "With the dense patience of
wood
we encircle the ax cut, we grow over our wounds."

At the exit ramp's curve a pigeon, stunned by a car,
flutters in the salty dust, listing to starboard
while a crow walks around him, fussily, carefully,
aiming his pick at the eyes, yet avoiding the touch
of even those feather-soft, fluttering wings.

At the Suicide Club they always bore you with methods.
How they go on and on with their pills and gas,
their bridge abutments, their seventh-story windows,
their shotguns fired by a toe and a loop of string,
their tailpipes fitted with vacuum cleaner hoses;
let them pout and despair in their murmurous garages.

Battered and poised, veterans at taking and giving,
this union keeps moving and breathing here in sad March;
it is startled again and again by the shadows of joy
out of the dark doubleness always upwelling.

I am driving this salty car past banks of old snow,
and for richer or poorer my calves are her stirrups,
her light heels printed for life on my calves
bent with ease and with pleasure and now forever set.
In sickness and in health we encircle our wounds, our
    welcomes.

We grow them into us.

Ransome at Sublimity

Donald M. Monroe

Chapter 1: IS THERE AN ART TO BEING AGNES?

" A GGH," *shouts Agnes, "grab some Kleenex. Your stuff's running out of me all over the floor."*

I first met Agnes at the Art and Architecture Department picnic at the beach. She was sliding down an eighty-foot mountain of sand drinking wine from a canteen. Later, she gave her piece of bread to four scrawny kittens someone had abandoned in the park and she scared four Boy Scouts away from her campsite by making faces at them, because they had been chasing the kittens through the woods. That night she cried about it.

"They'll be all right," I said.

"No they won't," she said. "No they won't."

Agnes types my letters for me.

I write:

Dear Edward,

Enjoying your sabbatical? How're things over in Belfast? Is the killing and destruction as bad as it reads in the papers? My neighbors have a flock of noisy domesticated peacocks that keep me awake all night. Say hello to May from Agnes and me.

Agnes types:

Dear Edward,

Enjoying your sabbatical? My neighbors are a flock of noisy, domesticated peacocks that keep me awake all night. Say hello to May from Agnes and me.

I let it stand. Agnes knows me better than I do. Fuck politics.

Chapter 2: ON THE NATURE OF DREAMS

AGNES, I DREAMED my father died. I went home to clean the barn.

In it, mice had jumped into an iron pot of garden sulphur. Five of them. Their bodies lay in the form of a cross, chemically burned, or as if by napalm or an atomic blast. Above them, flower pots, umber as the faces of Indians who touched and drew roots and herbs, food and magic from this ground a hundred years ago, line the shelves of the tack room like skulls.

These pots are filled with fur pulled by the mice from a threadbare Chinese rug stored beneath; and now these threads, made soft by their chewing, shelter a smell (years after their small deaths) toxic as the rot of larger corpses: like battlefields of the dead, though fainter; a suggestion of youth or the war.

And in this small barn, beneath a home-fire-brigade water pump (the black hose of which crumbles in my hand), beneath my father's old white civil defense hard hat with the emblem on it, which he carried to meetings once a week (too old for the killing itself), beneath also a non-combatant gas mask in which, where the nose of a man should go, mice have gathered another small home; beneath all of this I discovered what seemed at first only a pine cupboard with a brass handle at each end.

I dragged it squealing across the brown floor, down two steps into the sun, and I saw that it had once been painted carnival yellow with red piping. Inside, the shelves were bright as they must have been forty years ago, the small cupboard new; though the outside had faded even locked away in the dark barn.

The top of this picnic-buffet is oak, and can, I discovered, be lifted off. Beneath it, on a hidden molding, someone about six years old has written in pencil, "ELISabETH." My mother cannot remember any friends or relatives with that name. In the summer, my mother explained, my two uncles would carry the cupboard among the trees and the women would fill it with sturdy china and steel tableware, and on certain special, warm evenings the family would walk down the yew alley from the porch like a processional, with hot dishes wrapped in white cloths; and they would sit, the ten of them, around the stump-and-beam table and pretend to have come miles to this woods beyond the garden. The children played the barn was their ruin; the indifferent, munching sheep became unicorns, and the broken sulky, a chariot.

Chapter 3: ON THE NATURE OF THE MUSEUM

1. I WILL PUT OUT MY CIGARETTE BEFORE I LEAVE THE MUSEUM.

2. I WILL TURN OFF THE HOTPLATE BEFORE I LEAVE THE MUSEUM.

3. I WILL MAKE SURE ALL THE DOORS AND WINDOWS ARE LOCKED BEFORE I LEAVE THE MUSEUM.

4. I WILL TURN ON THE BURGLAR ALARM BEFORE I LEAVE THE MUSEUM.

While Edward Shackleton is on sabbatical, I am Acting Director of the Museum. Mrs. Beremy is the office secretary. She was also, I think, the Museum's first accession.

"Mrs. Beremy?"

"Yes?"

"Let's take down that goddam sign."

"Mr. Grove put that sign up," she says, "in nineteen twenty-seven." Mr. Grove has been dead for fifteen years now.

"Do you smoke?"

"No, Mr. Ransome."

"Then why is it necessary to remind you to put out your cigarette? And you're the one who always closes up. You know about the alarms."

"That sign's been there a long time, Mr. Ransome."

"It's had a long, happy life," I say, taking it from the wall. "Let its passage be easy."

"I like that sign!" she says. "But Mr. Shackleton didn't like it either."

The "either" sounds ominous, as if Edward had suddenly disappeared after objecting to the sign.

"You know," she says, "maybe we ought to wait until Mr. Shackleton comes back. After all, he *is* the Director."

"Five," I murmur, carrying the sign toward the trash. "I will put a gun to my head before leaving the Museum."

"What did you say, Mr. Ransome?"

She waited weeks to get even. Then one morning she walked into my office and laid a paper on my desk.

"The University Press sent this back. It was supposed to go in the *Monthly Newsletter,* under 'Recent Accessions,' but they think there's been some mistake."

She turned and walked away. I looked down.

> 1 white shirt
> 4 cl.   "
> 2 sheets
> 2 pl. cs.
> 7 hanks.

NO STARCH PLEASE

J. Ransome

Chapter 4: ON THE POSSIBILITY OF AESTHETIC IMPROPRIETY

AGNES, my drawing student Eva McKenna rides her bicycle down by the campus. She wears jeans, a bright green sweater, and her long hair is the color of dark red earth, or of some of the old bricks in my parents' garden wall. I am driving my car. I wave at her as I pass. She recognizes me and waves back. Somehow, I alone in my car, she on her bike—it is the closest we may ever come, going the same direction. Closer than in class, surrounded by all the others.

"McKenna," I said to her one day after class. "What a beautiful name."

"Married it and divorced it!" she said. She is funny and free of bitterness.

"But you kept the name?"

"Better than my old one."

"And what was that?"

"Stickel. 'Eva Stickel is a pickle, Eva Stickel is a pickle.' I got so sick of my name when I was a little girl I used to think maybe it was something I got for being bad."

"Were you?"

She laughed.

"Yes."

"Would it be all right," said Eva McKenna one day that spring, "if I missed your class for about a month? My daughter has to have heart surgery and I need to take care of her."

"Certainly."

Eva McKenna, you go to the very best corner I keep hidden in the back of my mind. Agnes Day is there, and several other women. I think you will like them. The first went there when I was five. I had been sick and was recovering at my great-aunt's small cottage in Carmel. The first day I was allowed outside was in March, cold and sunny. On the porch of the house next door was a woman who must have been, I now realize, about ten years older than your twenty-eight. She had long brown hair and long hands and she was drawing an acacia which stood in her front yard. "She's a real Countess," my great-aunt said. "She escaped, with no money." I stood in the yard, looking at her over the coreopsis. She must have heard our murmuring above the light wind, for she turned and looked at me, longer than just a glance; then, as if nothing had happened, she continued drawing. I went back into the house and lay down. I never saw her again, yet I remember her face better than any I have ever seen. Go with her, Eva McKenna; I believe I have always known at once those I could love.

Chapter 5: ON THE CORRECTION OF AESTHETIC IMPROPRIETY

"AGGH," *shouts Agnes, "grab some Kleenex. Your stuff's running out of me all over the floor."*

I love only Agnes Day. She taught me how to walk on

the beach at night, to hear each wave winding higher in pitch as it nears the sand. Then, in the morning, beneath the swell of a dune, she laced a vine with flowers, half buried it, and thrust a daisy upright in the center.

"There," she said.

"What is it?"

"You don't know?"

"No," I said.

"It's an elf trap."

"An elf trap."

"Yes, you see the elf's attracted by the daisy and when he steps in the noose to get it, you trap him."

"Ah-*ha*."

Later that day, beside a stream so clear the water seemed only a glaze on the pebbles beneath, she made me a fishing pole. I had found some leader hooked on a rock. She broke off a sapling, tied the leader to it, and to the leader she attached a sprig of blackberries.

"There," she said.

"But what can I do with it?" I said.

"You can fish."

"But what will I catch with berries?"

"An Ondine," she said. "Spirit of the water."

And so I caught her, or she, me, and I learned to throw on seasons with a free hand, to eat full, cold winter crab and parsleyed sole in warmer months. And life seemed to go as slow and magically as swimming beneath the sea, one's breath held—my own breath held that life would not sweep out of her fragile, coved body like a tide.

"Aggh," shouts Agnes, "grab some Kleenex. Your stuff's running out of me all over the floor."

"Let it."

"But it'll make a spot on your rug."

"Let it!"

"Oh, come here, you. . . ."

Chapter 6: IN THE MUSEUM

WOULD IT BE *all right if I missed your class for about a month? My daughter has to have heart surgery and I need to take care of her.*

Certainly.

Drawing class meets on Tuesday afternoon. Eva McKenna has been absent for a week, taking her daughter to surgery. On Monday, in another state, at another university, four students were shot to death by National Guardsmen. My students are setting up their drawing equipment. I am sitting on the window ledge. Through the window, I can see fifty or so people walking silently down Chandler Street past the Humanities Building three blocks away, a daylight vigil.

"Want to hold class today?" I say. I'm surprised how very flat and tired my voice sounds. "Do you want to?" No one answers or gestures, only a few look up. Everyone is very, very quiet.

"You know what?" says Mr. D. quietly, from the back of the room. "I feel like when Kennedy got shot." I say nothing and nod. Mr. D. looks around, his features a faded fresco on the dusty air. No one is going to speak. I think to myself: Mr. D., Eva McKenna, the Greenberg girl—they teach my class. I only read aloud from their eyes.

"Let's talk about the war," says Mr. D.

"What," I say, "do you want to say about it?"

"Do you know how many people were killed in it yesterday?" he says louder. "Not *us* and *them* figures, but how many *people?*"

"How many people died here in town yesterday," I say, sliding down from the window ledge.

"What do you mean?"

"I mean, how many people died here in town yesterday? Ten? Twelve?"

"That's different," he says. "I'm talking about killing."

"Ten or twelve people died here in town yesterday . . ."

"But we can *stop* the war and we can't stop people getting old and dying."

Good. He's getting mad at me.

"How about some more comments?" I say. I glance around. Everyone is very, very quiet. What is there to say? We are all so much the same.

"Come on," I say. "I'll show you something."

I'm out in the hall before people start trailing along. Mr. D. catches up with me.

"Where we going?" he says.

"The Museum."

It's closed. I use my key. We go in. It was built in 1912 to house a large collection of Oriental art donated to the University. We walk to the second floor, past cabinets of jade urns, past ebony thrones, past scrolls, hangings, and the implements of war. Then, in a side room, we arrive at the tomb statues, half a dozen of them, in a small glass case. Beneath each is a card stating the fragment's age, where it came from, and the words "Anonymous Modeler."

"See," I say. "Same guy did all of them."

Mr. D. snorts, then looks puzzled.

"He's dead," I say. "The 'Anonymous Modeler' has been dead from eight to twelve hundred years. Even the corpses from the graves these things were on have been gone for a thousand years. *But here are the works.*"

Mr. D.: "*Sure, but of course it wasn't even just one guy and we don't even know their names and it was just chance all this stuff wasn't smashed.*"

Perfect quiet for a real, full second.

"Good. Now, you think about that."

I turn and walk away.

Stopping by the Art Department, I open my mailbox. There are two ads from textbook companies, which I throw in a trash can down the hall. A note from the department chairman about fouled-up registration which I look at while opening the door to the stairwell. And going down the stairs, I see the unfamiliar return address, the strange handwriting on the envelope. I rip it open. Out the basement door, beneath the serriform clouds: the single sheet is yellow, torn from a small notebook.

Dear Mr. Ransome,

My daughter died Friday morning. The surgery went well but there were complications.

I guess no more drawings for a while.

Eva McKenna

Chapter 7: ON THE NATURE OF
JOHN BLACK'S FARM AT
SUBLIMITY, OREGON

THE SAME DAY. Night, and a full moon. I should be writing
a letter to Miss McKenna explaining how sorry I am to
hear about her daughter dying—no, not that I am sorry
to hear about it, but that I am sorry it happened. That her
daughter died. *I am sorry that your daughter died.* Elaborate that. I don't feel like writing the letter. I don't feel
like doing anything. I get in my car and drive out toward
John Black's place. He teaches what I teach.

John lives on a small farm twelve miles out. I drive up
the Coast Highway about six miles and turn off to the
right, up Orchard Road, negotiating a rather steep hill. At
the top of that hill, on one side of the road, stretch fields
enough to make ten families rich (if no sons want to move
to town), fields gray in the cold light. The road is gravel
with deep ruts, though not rough enough to need a jeep.
I bounce a little. Only ten miles an hour, the gravel crunch-
ing underneath. I stop for some reason.

After I get out, I think for a moment: my car's in the
middle of the road. But, hell, nobody drives out here and
there are only a couple of houses and you can see miles.
I think, too, of leaving my headlights on, but don't. I open
the trunk and take out a big bottle of wine, drink some,
and stick it back among the old clothes, hatchet, flashlight,
beat-up charred pans, roll of toilet paper, rain slicker,
yellow newspapers, couple of prestologs, sleeping bag, tarp,
rope, copy of Russell's *History of Western Philosophy,* and
a transistor radio that hasn't worked for three or four years.

Nothing. Silence. I sit on the hood. I have been outside
a half hour and I can see pretty well: the valley, its colors
dying for rain, muted toward the perfect dark, the black
at the base of trees, hidden in grass, far off.

I get back in and start the engine. I do not turn on the
headlights. It is as if I can see in the dark—no, not see in
the dark—I can see the dark itself and what it does not
cover, see how far it goes. And hear the darkness at the

edge of the road, beside the wheels; for there *is* darkness there, a fall of two hundred feet or so, down through jack pine. The gravel is thicker at the edge of the road and as I approach the drop I can hear the heavier rock hitting the underside of the car.

Strange, not to give a good goddam about going over the edge here; or, perhaps, this is a car-driver's thought. Surely my great-grandfather drove a wagon at night, guided only under the moon, the ruts as intelligible as runes beneath an archeologist's fingers; and perhaps Indians walked on the trail which became this road, without fear—how silly even to think of it—of falling into the shallow valley.

Up ahead I see a curve where John's driveway is, turn toward the house, sound "shave-and-a-haircut" on the horn.

I take the wine out of the trunk. The house itself seems a darker dark than the road outside, though there are lights at the windows and loud rock, music almost thick enough to float on, washing from the front door.

"Hey, come on in!" says John.

Here are people. About ten. Mr. D., my painting and drawing student, is here. He nods at me. So are a bunch of other people I know, men and women. They are sitting around on the big braid rug, passing a pipe. I go sit down next to Mr. D. after he motions me over.

"Give me a pull on that, will you?" he says. I hand him the bottle. I get the pipe and pass it on without using it. "Go ahead," he says.

"Maybe later."

"No, go ahead."

I look at him very seriously. I whisper, loud as I can, "I'm afraid of getting busted."

Somebody's voice on the other side of the room says, "Ransome's drunk out of his mind."

Mr. D. looks at me very seriously. He says, "But Mr. Ransome, don't you see? If we get busted, so will you, just for being here."

"But," I say, "it's the *principle* of the thing." I smile. He smiles. And we both start laughing.

After a few minutes he says, "That Kent State shit, that's bad shit." I watch him. "Man I don't think you got," he says, "I don't think you got what I meant today." He studies me. "See, I meant, if we don't . . . *change* . . . we're going to kill our fucking selves and everybody else."

I can't say anything.

"See," he says, "that's all I meant. I don't think you understand. It's people dying man, dying, you know?"

I look away. John comes over and crouches down. (John calls Agnes "Supermind" because she speaks so many languages, loves her like he was her brother. She calls him "The Devil's Cherub" because he's a little fat. John's wife is Chinese and her name is Victoria.)

"You look deader than usual," John says. "What happened?"

"Nothing."

"Here, take a joint and go up on the roof. Nice night out there." He slaps me on the shoulder like a friendly bear.

"I think I *will* go out and walk around a little."

"Good. Make some noise when you come in so we know it's you."

"Okay."

"I'm getting paranoid," says John .

"Me too." I stand up. "Here," I say to Mr. D., handing him the wine. "See you later." I stick the joint in the cuff of my sweater.

The screen door closes behind me. I don't want to go up on the roof. I don't want to go home. I don't want to go anyplace. I laugh at myself. I'll sleep around here, I think; get out my sleeping bag and sleep around here.

There is a barn about a hundred yards behind the house. Before John bought it, the place was a working farm. That is where I will sleep, in the barn. I open the trunk of my car and grab the bag—and something else, a pencil and my tablet. I will write to Miss McKenna.

Chapter 8: DEFECTS THAT MILITATE AGAINST JOHN'S FARM AT SUBLIMITY

DEATH. Death here. The smell of dead sheep which, living, greased the fold beneath where I will sleep. A faint smell of birds. Even their skeletons have flown to purer air. Nothing here was born after I was, even the dust.

I unroll my sleeping bag. A few feet away is a work-bench with no tools, some child's perhaps. Between the handle of the small vise and the top of the workbench is a skein of cobwebs. The windows are opaque with dirt. Moonlight enters only around two jagged, splintered panes near the roof. I lie down and there is not one sound moving anywhere around me.

Here is where I should write to Eva McKenna but I can't because I feel too tired. (I must be too tired because I can't think of a thing to say.) So, I will go to sleep.

Hours later, through my sleep, John's first yell is a mumble. The second one's clearer:

"Wake up, you mother!" John's laughing between shouts. "Wake up up there!" He pounds on the wall. "What the fuck you doing to my barn?"

"Shut up. I'm asleep. Go away."

Other voices: "What's happening? Oh, nothing. He's freaked out in the barn. No shit?"

"I'm asleep, goddamit! Go away!"

"Hey, leave him alone John, he sounds mad."

"Shit, he's not mad, he's just *irritated*. Ransome, you mother, don't light any matches up there because this thing's condemned and I don't care if you burn yourself up but I don't want to lose this barn. You hear me?"

"Go fuck your wife!"

"You go fuck my wife!"

"Everybody else maybe, but not me!"

"Come on people, let's go back to the house. He's okay."

"You sure he's okay?"

"Oh, hell yes. It's when he shuts up I start worrying about him."

Chapter 9: LOFT

IT IS GROWING lighter. Here is where I will begin.

Dear Eva McKenna, now I know why I paint. The sun is almost coming up and the boards over my head in the barn where I have slept have become a dozen differing shades of brown, like a section of the earth, dug into deeply. This barn, I think, was built from other barns or other, earlier buildings, for each board shows a different age, a different degree of dark weathering. How could words explain this? Have we enough in the names of colors; and what of the mixtures? Let me, then, call all these slowly brightening strips, these solid ribbons of wood, brown. *Brown.* I think I could paint it, the dim, rich colors above my head, but instead I will give you only, as I can give only at the moment, the word: *brown. Brownnnnnnnn. Brown.*

Dear Eva McKenna, I don't know why I or anybody else is crazy enough to paint. It doesn't do a damn thing for your health and it isn't real. Throw away all your equipment and go sleep in a barn.

(Love. Love? *Love?* We do not act, or write letters, on love. It would be too hurtful. We must be kind. *Oh, let me be kind, to not leave someone I may not love for someone I may love . . . to be as good as the hot muffins Agnes makes on Saturday morning . . . to not thunder off on some sudden infatuation. I left another woman to come to Agnes on just such an intuition . . . and it was right.* Life makes no sense. *I promise to be kind.* Life must be, at least, kind.)

I remember how, in a loft, the loft of a warehouse, a flop, two doors from the Rescue Mission, that I was awakened in the night by sounds like the shrieks of braked freights; that, barely awake, I became aware that they were the sounds of a man. And finally, that they were my own sounds; and I felt arms and hands beneath my own arms and hands and was carried upward and away to a room nearby that was very white. From a window in that room came, after days of perfect silence, the sounds of the big trains starting up slowly once again. I can remember those first sounds well and now I realize that it is no accident that they resemble the sounds of your name: Eva McKenna Eva McKenna Eva McKennaEvaMcKennaEva-McKennaEvaMcKenna.

Somebody going out of his head is supposed to see his penis turn into a serpent; what really drives a man crazy is finding his penis has turned into a monkey wrench, which he proceeds to throw into the best-ordered aspects of his life.

Agnes, I love you.

Dear Eva McKenna, somewhere in space all deaths are past facts. I am told that if the sun were to burn out, shattered as the Mazda bulb above my head in this barn has been shattered, by some random or aimed shot, if the sun were to cease giving light, we would not know it for an unimaginable length of time. And so too, I would say, for each of us a sun has already flamed and died somewhere. This darkness walks toward us, slow as the speed of light.

Dear Eva McKenna, cosmology is no cure for death, neither is painting. In fact, it is not even my own death itself I fear so much as the suggestion of it, like pissing blood. . . .

Chapter 10: THE PRICE OF SUBLIMITY

THE PHONE RANG. I took off my coat then answered it.

"Where have you been?" said Agnes.

"John Black's barn."

"John's barn?" I don't think she believes me.

"I took my sleeping bag up in the loft of John's barn. Then he came in and woke me up shouting at about three and I couldn't go back to sleep and about five I went to the all-night and had some eggs and coffee."

"But why would you sleep in his barn?"

"I was thinking."

"I still don't understand."

"I can't explain it. I'm tired."

"You slept in John's barn."

"No, I went out and screwed fourteen different women." I sound unpleasant but it is only the tiredness.

"All right, all right." She believes me about the barn now. "I was up all night. I didn't know where you were."

"Why didn't you call John or Bill? You could have figured I would have been at one of their places."

"Oh. . . ." Sigh.

"Oh, I'm sorry. I understand. You don't want to be calling around for me in the middle of the night like some distraught housewife. Look, I'm terribly tired. I have to try and sleep now. I have to."

"I'm worried about you."

"I understand. It was terrible of me not to call and let you know where I was. I'm terribly sorry." *Dear Eva McKenna, I'm terribly sorry . . .*

"Well, I still can't understand this."

"We'll talk about it later." *I'm terribly sorry to hear of your daughter's death . . . I'm terribly sorry to hear of your loss . . . I . . .*

"All right. Try to go to sleep."

"Really, I'm terribly sorry." *I am terribly sorry about the loss of your . . . I am terribly sorry to learn of . . . I am terribly sorry to . . .*

"Jack, are you crying?"

"Yes."

Chapter 11: ON THE NATURE OF DREAMS, PART TWO

WHEN I FELL ASLEEP I dreamed I was looking from my parents' dining room window into the large, sunken rose garden. I was ten. It had been raining for several days. The brick wall around the back of the garden was dark red between patches of brown moss. The grass was thick and uncut, as it was late fall. It was a dark day, though the darkness made the green lawn seem bright against the dark green boxwood borders. Down in the rose garden, twenty yards from me, two people were throwing a plastic ball, like a beach ball, back and forth. One was my student, Eva McKenna, the other her daughter, who, as I had guessed, had red hair like her mother's. And as they threw the ball back and forth, the mother lightly to the child, the child with effort, laughing, I realized that Eva McKenna's daughter must be named Elizabeth.

"Elizabeth," I said, knocking on the window. "Elizabeth, come inside, it's raining out." And it was raining. Elizabeth's hair, like her mother's, clung in ropes of burnt umber. With my tapping, the child turned and, hesitating for her mother's approval, she walked toward me, across the grass and up the brick steps.

I smiled at her and she at me, and she flattened her hand against the window. I, on the other side, placed my hand over it and felt the chill glass slowly warming.

Chapter 12: ON THE CORRECTNESS AND NECESSITY OF THE PERFECTLY IMPROPER

"Here!"

"No," says Agnes.

"Right here!"

"It's not right. Not on your parents' property."

"Ohhh . . ."

"Oh," she says, touching me, "we just did yesterday and we'll be home again tomorrow. Just . . . not here."

We had carried glasses of brandy, glasses with pictures of horses on them, horses going over hedges after hounds and foxes, carried these glasses into the arboretum. And suddenly we had been sitting on the rough grass of the hillside, looking at the mountains sixty miles across the valley, and I had wanted to make love to her.

"Just not here," she says.

"Yes, but that's just it." I look at her. "It has to be here. Now."

Now. All this happened a year ago. The picnic-buffet is still in the barn, which I cleaned. Eva McKenna's daughter is dead and in the ground. The arboretum has been sold and cut into small lots.

Dear Miss McKenna,

What can I say?

Jack Ransome

Oh, Agnes, I say: it must be here. Now.

Chapter 13: FRAGMENTS AND THE WHOLE

EVA, I HAVE TRIED to paint a picture of you and the effort has died in embers the color of your hair. You have lost your child and I have lost only, sadly, an idea: the idea of yourself, of myself perhaps and the Indians, the house, the ground; nothing lost to me as real as your child, her thin legs running through the mind's unburnt fields. I cannot scorch that blight. I cannot even offer you my transient hands. There is no difference in fidelity to the dead or to the living. Someone loves me, someone (at least one) loves you. Only the moment finds my lover alive, your loving child gone.

The darkness is walking toward us. And this light. .

Directions to the Nomad

James Welch

PAST the school and down
this little incline—
you can't miss it.
Tons of bricks and babies
blue from the waist down.
Their heads are cheese
and loll as though
bricks became their brains.

What's that—the noble savage?
He's around, spooked and colored
by the fish he eats,
red for rainbow, blue
for the moon. He instructs stars,
but only to the thinnest wolf.

When you get there
tell the mad decaying creep
we miss him. We never
meant it. He'll treat you right,
show you poems
the black bear couldn't dream.
One more thing—if he tries
to teach you mountains
or whisper imagined love
to the tamarack, tell him
you adore him,
then get the hell out, fast. .

The Counterintellectuals

Peter Steinfels

I

WHEN Edmund Burke sat down in 1790 to denounce those responsible for the French Revolution, still in its early and less fearful period, he turned at once to the intellectuals of his day, the French *philosophes* and their English admirers. "Literary caballers, and intriguing philosophers . . ." Burke wrote, "political theologians and theological politicians"; "petulant, assuming, shortsighted coxcombs of philosophy"; "cold hearts and muddy understandings." However familiar the rhetoric may sound today, it would be a mistake to associate Burke with that garden variety of anti-intellectualism which rises to talk of "impudent snobs" and "nabobs of nihilism." Burke was himself an intellectual, or as he would have said, a political Man of Letters; and his true heirs are partisans in the bitter disputes which currently divide American intellectuals.

Indeed, the foremost critics of intellectuals have generally been other intellectuals—true ones, like Burke, and not the "marginal intellectuals, would-be intellectuals, unfrocked or embittered intellectuals, the literate leaders of the semi-literate" whom Richard Hofstadter pointed to as the characteristic spokesmen for popular anti-intellectualism. Nor have the internal feuds and contentions of the intellectual community been random and unpatterned; from Burke to de Tocqueville to Weber to Raymond Aron and others in our own day, there is a continuity of complaints and themes. The community of intellectuals has been beset not simply by brawls and vendettas but by recurring bouts of civil war. Since the French Revolution, the intellectuals have never ceased to be shadowed by the *counterintellectuals*.

I define counterintellectuals as the party of public thinkers that opposes the typical adversary role that intellectuals play in public life. Quite likely the counterintellectual will do so in the name of defending intellect; he demands more, not less, sophistication and expertise. He does not usually deride the potential of the intellectual party, but rather perceives this potential as being largely for mischief. He warns against the intellectual's politics in general, and he stands guard against its errors in particular.

The medium-sized literature generated in the attempt to formulate a satisfactory definition of "intellectual" has tended to strain out the political factor. When Seymour Martin Lipset defines intellectuals as those "who create, distribute, and apply culture, that is, the symbolic world of man, including art, science, and religion," he makes no specific mention of politics. One might therefore think of a self-conscious group which now and then, wisely or foolishly according to one's point of view, takes time out from the business of being intellectuals to drop into the political fray. The truth is, though, that the political fray was there from the first and that the intellectuals as a self-conscious group were forged in the heat of it. In a sense, and this is the sense which disturbs the counterintellectual, the term "intellectual" has always implied a politicization of the intellect, and almost always on the side of dissent and opposition. We see "intellectuals" when men from certain lines of activity join together on a public issue or when their products—paintings, writings, philosophies—themselves become public issues. Remove the heightened political context, as history does from time to time, and the category swiftly dissolves into its component parts of writers, professors, scientists, lawyers, artists, civil servants, and so on. As Hofstadter insists, "The modern idea of the intellectuals as constituting a class, as a separate social force, even the term *intellectual* itself, is identified with the idea of political and moral protest."

It was in France, gripped in the hysteria of the Dreyfus Affair, that the term "intellectual" emerged in its present meaning. On January 13, 1898, George Clemenceau's journal *L'Aurore* published Zola's *J'Accuse*. The following day a petition appeared: "The undersigned, protesting against the violation of legal procedures at the trial of 1894 and against the mysteries which have surrounded the Esterhazy affair, continue to demand a new trial." Below this simple declaration was a list of names: Zola himself, Anatole France, Marcel Proust, Léon Blum, and others from France's literary and scientific elites. Above the text was the headline: "Manifesto of the Intellectuals."

As a noun describing a certain social type, "intellectual" had occasionally been used before; but it was the political crisis that pumped blood into these syllables. Within a day of the Manifesto's appearance, the literary critic Ferdinand Brunetière was overheard denouncing the elitism implied by the new term; it was "one of the most absurd eccentricities of our time . . . that writers, scientists, professors, philologists, should be elevated to the rank of supermen." Brunetière's remarks were nothing compared to the savage attack by the novelist Maurice Barrès. He called the Manifesto a "Who's Who of the Elite." "All these aristocrats of thought . . . who would be ashamed to think like ordinary Frenchmen." Barrès went on to compare "these self-styled intellectuals . . . these stunted geniuses, these poor poisoned intellects" to guinea pigs and lobotomized dogs which must be infected or mutilated for reasons of scientific progress. A few days later, Jean Psichari, dean of studies at the Ecole des Hautes Etudes and the son-in-law of Ernest Renan, sent an open letter to *Le Temps* asserting that "intellectuals" have the right to engage openly in political affairs. The Dreyfus Affair, then, which instructs us of the political circumstances surrounding the emergence of the new term, should also remind us that if the "intellectuals" were united, the intellectuals were not, and one of the things which divided them was precisely the public role which the new term designated.

To be sure, the two parties were primarily divided by the question of the Captain's guilt or innocence and by all the issues of individual rights, justice, social stability, and national strength which the Affair had accumulated; that is, they were divided along the ancient fault of Left/Right. If quarrels over the intellectuals' role spring from such an obvious source, why clutter the discussion with further subtleties? Indeed, the literature on intellectuals is already burdened with a great number of dichotomies; men of action and men of ideas; anti-intellectuals and intellectuals; bureaucratic intellectuals and independent ones; scholars and intellectuals; technocrats and ideologists; mandarins and intelligentsia; experts and men of letters.

Counterintellectualism corresponds to some of these categories—but to none of them exactly. The counterintellectual is more apt to be a conservative and a technocrat than a radical and a man of letters, but what of the conservative man of letters or the radical technocrat? The concept of counterintellectualism is not an all-inclusive substitute for all the other ways of looking at conflicts among intellectuals. Yet it does, I believe, provide an important perspective on the controversies which today, more than ever, divide the intellectual community.

II

THE COUNTERINTELLECTUAL CASE centers on a much noted characteristic of the intellectuals, variously described as their independence; their distance from political power; their relative detachment from great class and institutional interests (except, add the counterintellectuals, from their own); their lack of attachment, even, to a professional or scholarly discipline. The intellectual takes pride in this independence. It allows him, he feels, to see what others do not; it qualifies him for his role as society's conscience. The intellectual is marginal; and it is this marginal position which Karl Mannheim hoped might permit intellectuals to transcend the limits of ideology. But for the counterintellectuals, this very independence is precisely what disqualifies writers, artists, professors, and clergymen from stepping out of these limited occupations and into the politically charged role of "intellectual."

Alexis de Tocqueville made the classic statement of the counterintellectuals' case in his analysis of the effect of the *philosophes* on the French Revolution:

living as they did, quite out of touch with practical politics, they lacked the experience which might have tempered their enthusiasms. Thus they completely failed to perceive the very real obstacles in the way of even the most praiseworthy reforms, and to gauge the perils involved in even the most salutary revolutions. . . . As a result, our literary men became much bolder in their speculations, more addicted to general ideas and systems, more contemptuous of the wisdom of the ages, and even more inclined to trust their individual reason. . . .

Our revolutionaries had the same fondness for broad generalizations, cut-and-dried legislative systems, and a pedantic symmetry; the same contempt for hard facts; the same taste for reshaping institutions on novel, ingenious, original lines; the same desire to reconstruct the entire constitution according to the rules of logic and a preconceived system instead of trying to rectify its faulty parts. The result was nothing short of disastrous. . . .

Starting from the intellectual's distance from political power and practical life, the counterintellectual critique can move in a number of directions. It may stress the intellectual's incompetence and his capacity for inadvertent mischief: he bumbles onto the stage of history with florid speeches and pretentious manifestoes; his own plans are ineffective but he may set into motion what he cannot, through lack of will or ingenuity, control. Or the critique may stress the intellectual's treacherousness, his elitism, and his authoritarian tendencies. The absence of power, poisoning him with resentment, renders him hungry for the taste of rule. In this case, he is no bumbler, but is immensely successful at noisily inflaming opinion or silently tunneling the bedrock of traditional values. He is an intriguer, not a dreamer; and for all his inexperience of power, a ruthless seeker of its substance.

The intellectual's detachment from power, then, renders him innocent in the ways of the world—or a Machiavellian. He lacks force of will; he is a fanatic. He is bloodless; he is bloody-minded. He is sentimental and humanitarian; he is cold and ruthless. He is soft. Or hard. In any case, he is rootless, volatile, and untrustworthy.

The trunk of the counterintellectual case swiftly

branches into a number of themes. Burke catalogued many of them in explaining the causes of the French Revolution: "Along with the monied interest, a new description of men had grown up, with whom that interest soon formed a close and marked union; I mean the political Men of Letters. Men of Letters, fond of distinguishing themselves, are rarely averse to innovation." To compensate for the decline in "favours and emoluments," Burke went on, which had set in since the reign of Louis XIV, the Men of Letters caballed together, contriving to control public opinion and occupy "all the avenues to literary fame." They plotted the destruction of Christianity. Their "resources of intrigue" and "violent and malignant zeal" overcame "the desultory and faint persecution carried on against them." They

> pretended to a great zeal for the poor, and the lower orders, whilst in their satires they rendered hateful, by every exaggeration, the faults of courts, of nobility, and of priesthood. They became a sort of demagogues. They served as a link to unite, in favour of one object, obnoxious wealth to restless and desperate poverty.

Status anxiety, fascination with the exotic, monopoly of the media, baseless complaints of repression, elitism disguised as social concern, radical chic—for 180 years, counterintellectuals have elaborated the themes that Burke announced. But certain additions have been made to the canon. A major one dwells on the idea of secular religion. In an era when traditional religious beliefs are declining, the intellectual has inherited—or seized—the mantle of the theologians and preachers. He may supply the masses with secular dogma—ideology—to fill the place once occupied by traditional religion. He may bless or curse the rulers of society. Above all, the intellectual himself is most in need of this ersatz religion and apt, therefore, to outdo even his priestly predecessors in fanaticism, excommunication, and heresy hunting. This criticism may be informed with the sense that all religion is now anachronistic; simply by employing religious terminology in connection with intellectuals, it casts doubt on their modernity and good sense. Or the counterintellectual may warn that it is the *displacement* of hopes and longings from the realm of the sacred to that of the secular which makes them so explosive.

Other counterintellectual themes draw on the lore of psychology. A recurrent one is that the intellectuals suffer from a sort of masochism which drives them to provoke public retribution. Another theme is that of boredom: the intellectuals make trouble just so things will be a little less dull. A sub-theme is sexual boredom, or even impotence. The intellectuals get their kicks by identifying with youth, revolutionaries, and purveyors of violence. Finally, the intellectuals are considered so unnaturally susceptible to attacks of guilt as to unhinge their judgment and produce self-destructive behavior.

III

IN THE TWENTIETH CENTURY, the counterintellectual case has been made by writers as disparate as Charles Péguy, Harold Lasswell, and George Orwell, each, of course, in his own particular version. In the very influential *Capitalism, Socialism and Democracy*, Joseph Schumpeter devoted ten pages to a "Sociology of the Intellectuals"— as succinct and even sly an example of contemporary counterintellectualism as one could want. According to Schumpeter, the intellectual is a Frankenstein's monster created by modern capitalism. Having given him the printing press and a mass audience of the newly literate, it can neither control him (thanks to the freedom stemming from bourgeois *laissez-faire*) nor sufficiently reward him (the expansion of higher education creates an intellectual proletariat). The ungrateful monster, nursing his own anticapitalist resentment, penetrates the labor movement, political parties, and civil bureaucracies so as to unite all hostility to capitalism in a fatal challenge to the system. (The more realistic intellectuals, Irving Howe pointed out in 1954, "might have smiled a doubt as to their capacity to do *all that*.") Raymond Aron, admirer of de Tocqueville, has carried on the master's critique, most notably in *The Opium of the Intellectuals*. The secular religion theme, reflected in Aron's title, was prominent in *The True Believer* by Eric Hoffer, whose popularized counter-intellectualism seems to have teetered its way through a number of books toward old-fashioned anti-intellectualism.

Daniel Bell presented a sophisticated elaboration of the counterintellectual critique when, in *The End of Ideology*, he distinguished between "scholars" and "intellectuals":

> The scholar has a bounded field of knowledge, a tradition, and seeks to find his place in it, adding to the accumulated, tested knowledge of the past as to a mosaic. The scholar, qua scholar, is less involved with his "self." The intellectual begins with *his* experience, *his* individual perceptions of the world, *his* privileges and deprivations, and judges the world by these sensibilities.

Since business civilization refused intellectuals high status, according to Bell, they rejected it: "There was a 'built-in' compulsion for the free-floating intellectual to become political. The ideologies, therefore, which emerged from the nineteenth century had the force of the intellectuals behind them. They embarked upon what William James called the 'faith ladder' . . ."

In a brief passage Bell thus blended the themes of unrequited ambition, status anxiety, unbalanced psyches, and secular religion into a description which he insists is not meant to be "invidious." He has, however, bestowed upon his "intellectual" the mentality of a child; more important, since the ideologies with which the intellectuals are linked are now "exhausted," the intellectual is an anachronism, or perhaps a vestigial social organ, like the appendix, significant only because of an unfortunate tendency to become inflamed.

But it is probably not in major theoretical statements that counterintellectualism has its greatest effect. It is in the tradition's "trickle-down" of images and generalizations to articles, reviews, and columns, incidental passages and footnotes in books. I am not an assiduous note-taker; but a random run through recent publications, even without dipping into the better newspaper and magazine columnists, provides many typical examples.

The radical professor, according to a portrait published in *Commentary*, "is a man who has wandered through life, never testing himself outside the university, never quite growing up. His emotional life is barren. He is envious, resentful. . . . His status is threatened. . . . He is an elitist at heart but represses this realization . . . it pleases him to avenge his secret old elitist dream; he has helped rub the rabble in the faces of those privileged few still up there enjoying the power and the glory. . . . He cannot bear to be left out of a magic circle where power, glory, and virtue reside, if briefly; and in the rebellion . . . he is free to deny his own unmanly fraudulence. . . ."

Talking of the "surprising conquest of the mass media" by the intellectuals during the sixties, Nathan Glazer and Daniel Moynihan declare, with Burkean vigor, that "the intelligentsia, as it so often has, lusted after the sensational and the exotic. The hard work of politics and social change bored it."

When New York intellectuals turn to politics, write Irving Kristol and Paul Weaver in *The Public Interest*, "their general purpose, in such cases, is to wreak as much mischief as possible so that American society will bore them a little less."

As for intellectuals' obsessive talk of persecution and repression, "one hears it wherever fashionable folk gather," states Walter Goodman in *Commentary*. "Cocktail-party conversation in liberal circles starts from the understanding that those who are out to get us are well along in the process, and proceeds to further calamities."

"What, then, are we to think," asks Anthony Hartley, ". . . of the intellectuals who repeat with a pleasant shudder that 'power comes out of the barrel of a gun,' or talk of Molotov cocktails over their martinis? . . . That liberal America (or perhaps merely fashionable America) should fall for all this is something of an intellectual disgrace. . . ."

(Cocktail parties are to contemporary counterintellectuals what coffeehouses and salons were to Burke. Intellectuals are virtually never heard saying anything except at cocktail parties, although why the counterintellectuals so dutifully attend all these parties is never explained. The people and ideas being discussed at such gatherings are inevitably "fashionable"; no counterintellectual has ever attacked an unfashionable idea, or found a fashionable one worth defending.)

"Anti-communism is now unfashionable among the American intellectual elite (which is not to say that it might not become fashionable again at some later date) . . ." writes Andrew N. Greeley in a *New Republic* article on the failure of the antiwar movement. He concludes: "There seems to be some extremely important payoff in being alienated from the larger society, indeed, even in suspecting the 'fascist mass' is out to get you. One cannot escape the impression that some commentators are eagerly awaiting an 'era of repression' so that they can experience the same kind of 'subpoena envy' they experienced in the McCarthy era."

Zbigniew Brzezinski, in *Between Two Ages,* analyzes "middle-aged admirers of the militants, who—though most often physically passive—outdid themselves in their efforts to drink again at the fountain of youth by vicarious identification with youth's exuberance." Brzezinski quotes Leopold Labedz on the "revolutionary Establishment of New York and London" which practices "alienation at fifty thousand dollars a year" and "thrilled with revolutionary prospects, and displaying the characteristic *Salon-Maoismus,* contributes to the orgy of snobbery attendant upon the current Utopian wave." In the same book Brzezinski repeats the theory that today's political militants and their intellectual leaders "frequently come from those branches of learning which are most sensitive to the threat of social irrelevance. Their political activism is thus only a reaction to the more basic fear that the times are against them, that a new world is emerging without either their assistance or their leadership."

Lewis Feuer provides an academic paper on "the evidence and sources of intellectuals' authoritarianism." He demonstrates this phenomenon by (a) remarking the "impressive tradition of philosophical Utopias" which all share "the same vision of the rule of the scientific intellectuals"; (b) citing the intellectuals' claim that "the pen is mightier than the sword" and Keynes' belief that the power of ideas exceeds that of vested interests; and (c) quoting several incriminating Chinese proverbs, such as, "Without leaving his study, a Bachelor of Arts may understand the affairs of the empire." If this universal propensity were not bad enough, modern conditions "have bred in intellectuals a more acute authoritarianism." Intellectuals are frustrated because their thinking does not culminate in action, which "from the biological standpoint," Feuer informs us, is "a psychological anomaly." This frustration may be turned inward as self-aggression "in movements as diverse as monasticism and beatnikism." Or if "the desire for action is not subdued . . . the intellectual then tends to dictatorial, impatient, and ruthless modes of action."

Science marches on: "From a psychological standpoint . . . the intellectual can be said to have something about him of the feminine." And as Feuer hauls out the image of "the bookish boy" treated by his rough companions as a "sissy" and, later, proving his manhood through bitter engagement in the struggle of ideas, the counterintellectual impulse reaches the border of self-parody. The merits of the other articles, reviews, and books from which I have plucked quotations vary widely, but most make at least a plausible argument for something. The point, though, is the way the traditional images and assertions, the ancient refrains, steadily recur. A sturdy plant, counterintellectualism; even the adverse weather of "radicalization" only makes it thrive the more.

IV

IT THRIVES, in part, because it is more than a tradition of polemics; it is a tradition firmly rooted in certain academic disciplines, one that serves the needs of a pivotal group of intellectuals.

Burke and de Tocqueville are both associated with the formation of sociology. So, too, of course, is August Comte, who also bemoaned the fact that crucial political issues had fallen into the hands of the intellectuals. "Any man who can hold a pen," he complained, "may aspire to the spiritual regulation of society, through the press or from the professional chair, unconditionally, and whatever may be his qualifications." Robert A. Nisbet, in *The Sociological Tradition*, notes how this conservative distrust of intellectuals "became translated into a 'sociology of the intellectual' that was to persist from Comte to the present day." The founding fathers of sociology meant to give a constructive reply to the destructive work of the French Revolution; indeed, writes Nisbet, "It may be said with no exaggeration that de Tocqueville, Marx, Le Play, Durkheim, Weber, Simmel, Michels, and Mosca . . . all wrote as though the Jacobins were looking over their shoulders." And when the Jacobins faded into history, the Bolsheviks replaced them. Though the majority of sociologists today may be considered in the party of the "intellectuals"—statistics on their support of antiwar activities indicate as much—the counterintellectual doctrine has gone hand in hand with the influential sociological theories inspired by the anti-communist, anti-ideological mood of the 1940's and 1950's.

It may seem odd to find the counterintellectual tendency in Comte, who, after all, envisioned a future society directed by an intellectual elite of sociologists (led by Comte); but in fact this apparent contradiction reveals the heart of the dispute. The *philosophes* had bungled the job of reconstructing society, just as later on the revolutionary socialists did. The task should therefore be taken over by properly trained scientific scholars. One elite was to be replaced by another; and in this conviction Comte has been followed by numerous more moderate sociologists and political scientists. The intellectuals are amateurs; the sociologists and political scientists are professionals; and counterintellectualism functions to sanction the professionals and discredit the amateurs.

Richard Hofstadter has suggested that anti-intellectualism was apt to emerge in response to the two roles in which intellectuals impinged upon the public: as ideologue and as expert. But he did not consider the conflict *between* these roles, which has turned out to be a major source of counterintellectualism. Along with those academic disciplines claiming special competency in the professional management of society, there exists a sizable community of expert intellectuals—in and around government, foundations, unions, and corporations—for whom counterintellectualism is an important buttress. It contrasts the intellectual's lack of special competence with the expert's supposed capacity to measure consequences and thus act responsibly. At the least, counterintellectualism bathes the expert in a glow of prestige which helps assure new recruits to take his place. But even more important for the expert, counterintellectualism maintains his legitimacy against the attacks of the traditional intellectuals during periods of political turmoil. A young scholar, Michael W. Miles, has shrewdly characterized this conflict in the United States today. Couched in rather mechanistic and reductionist terms, his own description adopts the counterintellectual manner dished out, however, with a more even hand:

> The "technocrats"—the true believers in technology—are not necessarily specialists; they are themselves often intellectuals who from their staging areas in the academic bureaucracies make forays into the larger marketplace of ideas. They have developed a characteristic sales formula in which a "hard-nosed" realism bordering on reaction is combined with sudden displays of reformist zeal. Both of these tactics are shocking and contribute to notoriety and sales. . . . The "action intellectuals" have been challenged in the 1960's by re-emergent Left-wing intellectuals for shares of the market and the ideological leadership of the new middle class.

This insurgence of the Left-wing intelligentsia—aided by the political failures of the Establishment as well as by their more attractive style of treating current public issues —has been met by a rising tide of counterintellectual polemic. As Miles observes, this competition is "ultimately a deadly serious business, indicators of which are their theoretical postulation of each other's liquidation as a stratum and their infighting in the public prints, intellectual communities, and academic bureaucracies."

V

ALONG WITH ENJOYING a secure abode in certain academic disciplines and in the community of experts, counterintellectualism has, since World War II, been endowed with all the apparatus with which an "ism" makes its way in the intellectual world: magazines, money, conferences, a network of mutually supportive advocates, who came this time not from the Right but from the Left. The story, by now, is well known: the ideological warfare of the late thirties produced a group of fiercely anti-Communist, Left-wing intellectuals—democratic socialists, ex-Communists, and ex-Trotskyites for the most part. Well-drilled in Marxist texts and socialist history, blooded in the tribal wars, they were already trained and in motion when the Cold War put their skills at a premium and promoted them to the center ring. Daniel Bell, a major figure in this group, has mapped the headwaters of the new political current: *"Partisan Review, Commentary,* and *The New Leader,* the three magazines, and the writers grouped around them, that originally made up the core of the American Committee for Cultural Freedom." The neo-orthodox realism of Reinhold Niebuhr ("the father of us all," in George Kennan's often quoted view) linked the group to the religious world; and the American Committee for Cultural Freedom was an offshoot of the Paris-based Congress for Cultural Freedom which in 1953 began sponsoring, among magazines spread from Germany to India, the Anglo-American monthly *Encounter.*

The story is well known because in 1967 it was revealed that the Congress and *Encounter* had been receiving funds from the C.I.A. This stimulated a good deal of understandably anxious discussion about the "cultural freedom" and intellectual independence these organs were ostensibly established to defend. Attention was centered on the question of how much criticism of America was voiced by the Congress and its brood of magazines, a question complicated by the C.I.A.'s sophisticated recognition that a certain diversity of opinion was needed to maintain the credibility of the organizations it infiltrated and supported. Other questions about the common outlook of these publications—not limited to the beneficiaries of the C.I.A.—took second place.

Encounter, for example, projected a consistent attitude not only toward communism and the West, but also toward intellectuals. A certain figure hovered menacingly in the background—the fellow-traveler, the naïve do-gooder, the Popular Fronter. For a journal flying the banner of intellectual freedom, *Encounter* had very little faith in intellectuals—an untrustworthy lot, it seemed, always ready to sell out society to Jean-Paul Sartre. The second issue recounted the catastrophes, starting with World War I, which had destroyed Europe's faith in progress and led to an age of nihilism. The editorial absolved "the people" from responsibility for this development and instead pointed at the intellectuals. "But if intellectuals today have no right to accuse the people, there is a class of people whom they can and must judge—themselves," as though that alternative thoroughly exhausted the possibilities. The editorial ended with an appeal for intellectuals to burn with the "will to question"; but *Encounter* left the impression that it was, above all, the intellectuals, and especially those of Leftist persuasion, who needed to be questioned. The very same issue contained an exposition by Arthur Koestler of the laws of "political libido" ("twentieth century man is a political neurotic"), according to which the radicalism of intellectuals was a form of extended adolescence, with either incestuous, nymphomaniac, or masochistic overtones, depending upon whether one was a sectarian, a petition signer, or a militant. The next issue included the text of a talk—introduced as a sequel to Koestler's article—on the "Neuroses of the Indian Intelligentsia."

The first, slight shift of American intellectuals to the Left in the late fifties and early sixties was met in *Encounter* with an amused disdain. *Dissent* was declared to have "acquired a decided *chic.*" The small shoots of the New Left as well as the Leftward orientation initiated by Norman Podhoretz at *Commentary* were reported by Irving Kristol in a "Letter from New York," which opened with the ritual counterintellectual exorcism:

At three successive cocktail parties I have heard various men of letters roundly proclaim that they have lapsed into socialism. . . . I call this development to your attention so that you'll know what is *chic* with us. . . . For at least some of the middle-aged (to put the matter delicately), socialism seems to be a moral equivalent for adultery—a last desperate flight from the respectability that comes with rising incomes and falling hair. . . .

A few years later, in 1965, Kristol was ascribing the teach-ins and antiwar activity to the boredom and resentment of students and junior faculty, and reiterating the theme of amateurs versus professionals. Psychologists, mathematicians, chemists, and philosophers, he reported, had been prominent in teach-ins, while the experts on Asia, communism, and international affairs were notable by their absence. "They have too great an appreciation of the mess we are in. . . . Besides, practically all of them have contacts in Washington, and they know that, had they a new, good idea about Viet Nam, they would get a prompt and respectful hearing." Kristol concluded with a warning about backlash—which was also the drift of a widely cited article the following year on public opinion and the war by Seymour Martin Lipset. One might or might not deplore the war personally (and one was not very clear about which it was), but there was little, except for guarding against excessive criticism, that sensible men could do about it.

Such articles were not without valid observations, but their underlying premise was the contrast between the intellectuals' political illusions and the "real world." The world of power, especially American power—where a good, new idea would always get a prompt and respectful hearing—was treated with sympathy and even solemnity ("If America fails in Vietnam, she will owe it to her virtues as well as her errors"). The intellectuals, meanwhile, had to be spooned regular doses of *The God That Failed*, and if big gods like communism grew a little tiresome in their failure, then little gods like the Third World, Castro, C. Wright Mills, the peace movement, and even pornography would have to do. Failing gods seldom being in short supply, *Encounter* and its like-minded publications left many an idol in shards. It was, however, a very selective iconoclasm, one that seldom questioned, much less attacked, the reigning idols of America and the "free world." It was a regimen suited to domesticate the intellectuals' critical instincts, to harness them in the traces of a deferential and prematurely gray realism.

Each of these journals was distinctive, although there were several cases of editors who progressed from magazine to magazine. *Commentary*, in particular, broke ranks during the early sixties, adopting a more quizzical, and at times, even radical view of American society and of American foreign policy. (*Commentary*, of course, has since returned to the fold.) But these magazines had in common a sense of moral urgency about the issue of anti-communism which they never displayed on issues like McCarthyism or the war in Vietnam, their attention in these instances being largely focused on the dangers of moral urgency

The editors and contributors of these journals have been extremely talented. *Encounter* and *Commentary* were once acclaimed, with some justice, to be the two best-edited periodicals in the English language. *The New Leader* and *The Reporter* provided high quality background reporting unavailable elsewhere. *The Reporter* eventually folded, but *The Public Interest*, a well-written, well-edited, and influential quarterly forum for the "experts," has since appeared. Counterintellectual themes find ready acceptance in other publications spawned by the Congress for Cultural Freedom, such as *Survey*, and in journals like *Dissent, Foreign Affairs, The American Scholar, Harper's,* and *The New York Times Magazine*.

This is not meant to hint darkly of a counterintellectual conspiracy, a media monopoly, or academic-bureaucratic cabal. What does exist is simply a solid counterintellectual "establishment," with an academic base, an avid demand from the community of experts, and a network of outlets, well situated to channel its ideas and slogans to the general public.

VI

INSOFAR AS counterintellectualism merely reflects an attempt to understand the behavior of intellectuals by probing behind their own declarations and examining the social and material conditions in which they labor, it is unexceptionable. What is questionable is how well the counterintellectual critique, in its common elaborations, has succeeded in this effort. My own opinion is that many of its historical statements are false; its psychological assumptions—about compensation, guilt, and the like—dubious; its imagery hackneyed. It is, by and large, a Higher Folklore, a bag of old bones as well as old treasures. Occasionally, it is only a genteel form of anti-intellectualism. More often, its generalizations deflate quickly once they are removed from the realm of universal axiom to a more or less "testable" proposition. Does Bell's distinction between scholars and intellectuals fit the reality of the Dreyfus Affair when the ranks of the Dreyfusard intellectuals were filled with *universitaires?* Does it fit Marx, de Tocqueville, Burckhardt, Weber, Raymond Aron, Jean-Paul Sartre, Sidney Hook, Daniel Bell? Don't the same people switch back and forth from their scholar role to their intellectual role? Are these switches accompanied or precipitated by drastic changes in status and personality?

Or take the statement of Lionel Trilling, "The characteristic error of the middle-class intellectual of modern times is his tendency to abstractness and absoluteness, his reluctance to connect idea with fact, especially with personal fact." Well yes, of course. But compared to whom? In the past ten years, have American intellectuals tended to abstractness and absoluteness, and been reluctant to connect idea with fact, any more than have politicians, generals, diplomats, and policemen? I suspect that the data, if they don't wipe out this great truth altogether, will shrivel it into a much more minor one. (I set aside the prior question of why a tendency to abstractness and absoluteness is, necessarily and always, an "error.")

Like folklore, with its well-known toleration for contradictory maxims, counterintellectualism proves itself extremely malleable. If the intellectuals' status is low, they are resentful; if it is high, they are worried about keeping their position, or their appetite for honors is whetted, or they are elitists, or they are bored. Charges of status anxiety, resentment, boredom, and elitism are flexible and often impossible to verify; one can manipulate them at will.

Counterintellectual "truths" can be turned inside out without the seams showing. If Bell asserts that intellectuals characteristically spin their abstractions out of their "self," making personal experience the criterion for the world, Trilling asserts that intellectuals escape their personal experience by latching onto unconnected abstractions. The professor who wrote on the *New York Times* Op-Ed page that "Pessimism has always been intellectually fashionable" could just as well have written "Optimism has always been intellectually fashionable"—I doubt whether many readers would stop and wonder about the truth of the matter in either case. The operative word, in any case, is neither pessimism nor optimism but *fashionable*. Since fashionableness is such a strong element in the intellectual stereotype, it matters little how you fill in the blank spaces.

What is perhaps most curious about counterintellectualism is the character of its spokesmen. Commonly they are individuals who pretend to a skepticism about folklore and conventional wisdom, who would scrutinize all unverified assertions and sweeping generalizations. They deride arguments that explain political leaders in terms of personal aggrandizement ("sellout") or Sunday supplement psychology ("repressed") or hyperbolic labels ("fascist"); yet are not nearly so fastidious about applying the same procedures, usually in better prose, to intellectuals and militants.

The counterintellectual spokesman, in fact, is caught in a dilemma. He, too, is an intellectual; and insofar as his criticisms are valid, most of them turn back upon himself and his sympathizers. To start with the petty items, there is no evidence that the counterintellectuals are any more attracted to Trappist austerity, less concerned about personal advancement, or harder pressed for wealthy backing than the intellectuals. When certain New York intellectuals became involved in the city school strike several years ago, it was remarked with some relish that they sent their own children to private schools; so, it turns out, do the counterintellectuals who were doing the remarking. When Daniel Moynihan proposed that Washington correspondents are a new breed of Ivy League elitists, part of Washington's social elite "with all the accouterments one associates with a leisured class," someone took the trouble to check the Washington social register, wherein was found, among relevant parties, only Joseph Alsop —and Daniel Moynihan. Several scholars have commented on the irony of the theories, proposed by Bell, Lipset, and others, which explain McCarthyism and other turbulent political movements as reflections of status anxieties; clearly it has been the status of those constructing the theories which is manifestly threatened, whether in the case of McCarthyism, the New Left agitation on campuses, or the antiwar movement's attack on academic-government connections.

In terms of their relationship to power, the counterintellectuals fall into two groups. Some served the government directly and extensively. Among these are men with long careers showing no disastrous and many beneficial accomplishments. The story of others, however, is summed up in the unfortunate metaphor chosen by Theodore H. White in the 1967 *Life* article on how "the new actionintellectuals have transformed the ivory tower." "For them," wrote White, "it is a forward observation post on the urgent front of the future—and they feel it is their duty to call down the heavy artillery of government, now, on the targets they alone can see moving in the distance." The metaphor became a literal statement in Vietnam; the ivory tower was transformed into a forward observation post, and scholarly discipline, expertise, professionalism, and practical experience did not seem to abate but rather magnify that subservience to abstraction and that cruel absolutism which was supposed to characterize the intellectuals without power. It was these men who could not "connect idea with fact, especially with personal fact."

Then there are the counterintellectuals at one remove from power. Have they been correspondingly fascinated with it—as their own critique would suppose? The anticommunist counterintellectuals have displayed something less than a "will to question" when it came to the crimes of their own government, the follies of the experts, or even their own sources of income. They protested McCarthy faintly, protested the war in Vietnam occasionally, but protested the protesters unremittingly. In the July, 1967, issue of *Foreign Affairs,* Irving Kristol wrote a remarkable article on "American Intellectuals and Foreign Policy." "What we are witnessing," he assured his readers, "is no mere difference of opinion about foreign policy, or about Viet Nam. Such differences of opinion do exist, of course." Intellectuals may talk about the war in Vietnam—"for credibility's sake." But the real issue was the "sociological condition and political ambitions of the intellectual class, for the intellectual, lacking in other-worldly interests, is committed to the pursuit of temporal status, temporal influence, and temporal power with a single-minded passion that used to be found only in the highest reaches of the Catholic Church." Kristol went on to explain that intellectuals always oppose their nation's foreign policy, since foreign policy, being less susceptible to ideology, renders them less important. He repeated most of the cardinal points of counterintellectualism, explained that the United States was an "imperial power" and could do nothing about it, but that the anachronistic refusal of the intellectuals to accept this fact of life would make our role much more difficult. Most important, a new intellectual "mass"—as distinguished from the elite who commute to Washington— had emerged, "full of grievance and resentment." While the burdened policy-maker could use intellectual and moral guidance in carrying out his imperial responsibilities, what he was destined to get was only the irresponsible acts of a disaffected intellectual class trying "to establish a power base of its own." What a great relief it must have been to the burdened policy-makers to know that all the public fussing had nothing to do really with the war in Vietnam but only reflected the political ambitions of undereducated and outdated assistant professors! But is not the author of this article also implicated in the counterintellectual critique? Is his brave and majestic version of America's foreign policy possibly affected by his distance from power or his own self-interest? Is he, like other intellectuals, in hot pursuit of temporal status, influence, and a power base—except that he has chosen the route of the courtier rather than the *frondeur?* Is his argument not an ideological exercise serving to render more important his own party of intellectuals, whose status had been threatened by their moral and political failures in Vietnam? Needless to say, among members of the foreign-policy-making elite, who had evidently been seriously disturbed by an opposition intellectuals had not demonstrated in the midst of any other twentieth-century war, Kristol's new, good idea about Vietnam—for that is what it was—received a prompt and respectful hearing. In fact, it was circulated and cited for months. Dare one even suggest that, in these circles, it was *fashionable*?

VII

WHEN ONE NOTES that the counterintellectual critique applies with equal plausibility—or implausibility—to the counterintellectuals as well, the game takes on an aspect of making faces in a house of mirrors, and is increasingly played for less fun and profit. Should the counterintellectuals abandon their tradition? They are not, of course, likely to do so. But, also, I think that they should not. Despite their hostility, it remains true that counterintellectuals have done a large measure of the intelligent theorizing about intellectuals, and any writer who wishes to treat the subject seriously will touch upon counterintellectual themes and insights. More important, at its best, counterintellectualism plays, for the intellectuals, the role of an intelligent conservatism. It is an antidote for the nonsense which the intellectuals are always capable of producing. It forces the intellectuals to sharpen their wits and check their facts and, sometimes, shut their mouths altogether.

As important as consideration of the merits of the counterintellectual tradition is the simple recognition that *it is a tradition*. Certain conclusions follow: The first is that the contemporary counterintellectual's frequent pose of standing alone against the tide of intellectual conformity is not only fanciful but also self-deceptive. By exaggerating the intellectuals' monolithic strength and underestimating the resistance to their ideas, one justifies a narrow concentration on criticizing the intellectuals while remaining blind to dangers from other quarters. Elliot Cohen's famous remark in *Commentary*, in the middle of the 1952 Presidential campaign, that Senator McCarthy's "only support as a great national figure is from the fascinated fears of the intelligentsia," is one example. So too the French anti-communist pacifists of the thirties, disgusted by the rallying of intellectuals behind the militant anti-Nazism of the Popular Front, imagined that France was being brainwashed into provoking a war with Germany. They believed themselves to be unfashionable iconoclasts when they attacked the intellectuals' efforts to stiffen the country's resistance to Nazism, never noticing how little in fact the country was in a mood for resistance. Left-wingers and anti-Nazi themselves, they were nonetheless too fixated on their quarrel with the other intellectuals to have qualms about the wide acceptance of appeasement and even the peculiar allies their pacifism was collecting on the Right.

The fact that counterintellectualism is a tradition should also compel the counterintellectual to a further self-consciousness, a greater critical reflection on his own outlook. The existence of a tradition means that ideas can be picked, ready-to-wear, off the racks. Just as the Left intellectual has an abundant store of stock phrases and notions to tempt him from the hard work of thinking things through anew, the counterintellectual themes are similarly available in the dime stores of the mind. In truth, one doesn't really have to attend those cocktail parties; one can simply read other counterintellectual critics and grasp at a passing fact now and then to verify their clichés.

Left-wing intellectuals are repeatedly urged to reflect on the unexpurgated past of their own enthusiasms, the fatal deformations, the unpleasant underside, the plentiful ambiguities and ironies. What is sauce for the goose should be sauce for the countergoose. The counterintellectual tradition can lay claim to a good number of wise and honorable men, from de Tocqueville to Orwell; its themes have also been voiced by humbugs and hacks, skirmishers in the unending struggle of established power to remain exempt from scrutiny and criticism. Like some doctrines favored by the intellectuals, counterintellectualism has proved capable of transmutation into fascist and authoritarian forms as well as moderate and pluralist ones.

What counterintellectuals might do, however, is recognize their tradition for what it is; and contemplate it with that full measure of irony and that awareness of complexity and ambiguity which they often counsel for others. The best of their tradition is not without reproach. Burke raged for Holy War against France; de Tocqueville forgot his speculative generosity in the face of a challenge to bourgeois property and acquiesced in the massacre of French workers; Weber urged German renewal through imperialism and trumpeted war propaganda. The characteristic error, as Lionel Trilling might say, of counterintellectuals has been to avert their critical gaze at key moments—and particularly from themselves. "An intellectual is someone whose mind watches itself," was Camus' now familiar definition. A counterintellectual has too often been someone whose mind preferred to watch other minds.

Paintings from the Slaughterhouse:
A Slide Show of Hogs

Cynthia Macdonald

THIS IS a quick sketch: at first there was only about
Two minutes to catch each hog, to render it.
I tried to get the details of a hoof, a head,
The mammary glands as they went past. (Next slide,
   please.)
Two pigs, snout by snout, an interesting balance
Of flesh, curves and holes . . . It was so slippery—
Blood—that I had trouble with my footing.

> He wears a black Bulgarian suit
> To paint in, carries blood secrets
> In his lunch box and his
> Paints in a brown Jocasta bag.
> (The slaughterhouse has no cafeteria.)

After a week or so, I relaxed and began to relate
To the hogs. You can see the warmer quality.
(Next) An interesting perspective: the head
Below me and the hind legs stretching up
To where the steel hooks pierce them.

> His mother is always sick,
> Calling for him, moaning his
> Name through bubbles of saliva
> Which make him think that she
> Is dying. She has survived many deaths.
> (He is not an employee, therefore ineligible for
> Blue Cross.)

These took longer, up to six minutes; time I gained
By following the subject pig around the moving circle of

The conveyor track on which it hung. After a while
The workers got to know me and sometimes slowed the
   track.
(Next) Some critics haven't liked the reds
I used to catch this sow in oil on paper.

> He sits in a field, dreaming
> Of his sister as he paints
> The flowers: they are his sister's
> Parts. Bees nuzzle her breasts.
> (The slaughterhouse is closed on Sundays.)

But after friendliness, demands on me began. The men
Wanted drawings, not sketches of the parts,
But the entire pig or even groups. They didn't realize
It took perhaps a week to get one that I thought
Was right. (Next) I love the angle
Of the crotch and did a series of them. They have
For me a quality which is voluptuous.

> When he cannot paint, he folds
> Paper into white cranes to bring
> His family better fortune. He has
> Tin boxes filled with cranes
> Stored in his closet.
> (The lard cans are a useful size and come with lids.)

Heads: round-headed pigs, the kind they use
For head cheese. The men were angry when I wouldn't
Give them finished drawings, began to hide the heads
In the machinery. But I discovered how to get some
From the freezer. They were heavy; I embraced them;
An armful, I can tell you (Next). Full-length
Body: some have said it has a quality of Venus.

> He casts horoscopes, skewering people
> To their stars, telling them what
> They are and will become, and
> What he is: Leo with Aries rising.
> He is dark-haired in his Lion House.
> (Yellow helmets are required for anyone within the
> plant.)

The veterinarian wanted me to draw him beside a hanging
Carcass. When I wouldn't—the hogs were difficult enough

Without injecting humans—he threatened to declare me
A sanitary risk. The fear that I might have to stop
Before the subject was exhausted shows, I think,
As frenzy in the paint (Next), this one (Next)
And this (Next). A melting quality: the pigs
Dissolving in the fire through which they're put to stop the
   blood
And singe the hair off. You know I am a vegetarian.

> He sleeps. The walls of his room
> Turn to flame. His mother wakes him
> From his screaming and brews
> Him garlic tea to ward off evil.
> (Albino pig skin is saved for burn skin-grafts.)

Many pigs, more fully drawn and painted. One day
The circling overhead conveyor belt went wild,
Then stopped, releasing them: pigs whirling
Through the air, landing all around us. One crushed
The foreman's leg. I used the time of porcine chaos
To do this group: limb over limb, reds mingling,
Snout merging into snout, body within body, and yet
Each one distinct: a fugue of pigs.

> He is lying in the snow, painting it,
> Licking it, washing the red from
> His pictures with snow, freezing his pulse
> Until it slows to a less painful measure.
> He has decided to paint snow scenes.
> Occasionally, a little blood throbs in the corner

The Death of the Russian Novel

George Blecher

PART I: COMPARISONS. Select the paragraph or paragraphs which come closest to a complete answer.

*　　*　　*

There is something about the Russian Novel which keeps bothering me. There it stands, bigger than life, twice as vivid and twice as energetic, and it jabs its fingers in my ribs, slaps me on my back, breathes in my face, and asks me embarrassing questions about why I live the way I do. I don't know how to answer. But I have the sense that the answer is not in the soot on my windowsill. The answer is not in the deranged man masturbating on a fire escape across the street. The answer is not in war, overpopulation, racism, or any other catch-phrase. The answer is not anything with an animal's name. Perhaps part of the answer is the lack of animals.

*　　*　　*

Rudensky touched the young stallion's flank and felt a shiver run up and down its hide. "You don't like a human's touch," he thought. "That's all right, that's good. I don't ask you to like me. All you have to know is that I'm going to be your master." He put his hand to the horse's muzzle but it flared its nostrils and jerked away, pulling its teeth back in a high-pitched whine. Rudensky waited patiently until the horse calmed down. "Good boy, good boy," he murmured. Then he touched the muzzle again, more gently this time, and blew into the horse's ear. Quickly, deftly, with the grace of an acrobat, he was in the stirrup swinging himself into the saddle. The horse was caught off-guard for a second, just enough time for Rudensky to find his seat, and then it groped high at the air with its hooves, its eyes hurt and furious at being outfoxed. Rudensky laughed and set his knees into the horse's side. "Now you know who's the clever one!" he shouted.

*   *   *

Maybe food is the key to the answer. Lilly cooks a tender veal cutlet and covers it with a fine, delicate cream sauce. I should be pleased. But after I take a few bites, enough to satisfy my first hunger—just at the time when eating should be a pleasure—it becomes a duty instead. I can't taste the sauce. She says it's the best she's ever made, the most subtle. But I can't taste it.

The whole table glittered with old, heavy silverplate. At one end, lying regally on a bed of parsley, was a magnificent sturgeon smothered in fresh dill and sliced lemons. Surrounding the fish like courtiers to a queen were heaping bowls of herring, pearl onions, pyramids of red and black caviar. Toward the center were the main courses: a whole candied ham, glazed and dressed with pineapple rings like a clown's motley; a huge, dripping side of veal and a platter of steaming snipe, cooked in the French style with oranges and wine, lying on a bed of wild rice. At the far end were the desserts: a high frothy pudding called *fromage de neige* (a specialty prepared by the French cook Anton Gregorovitch had hired for this most special of occasions), and fresh fruits from all corners of Russia: apples from Petersburg, grapes from Georgia, tangerines from the shores of the Black Sea.

The guests gasped with surprise as they entered the room. They had known that Anton Gregorovitch was not a poor man, but they'd had no idea that he possessed either the wealth to afford such a feast or the generosity to serve it.

"Incredible!" said Brozhanin the banker out loud. His amazement spoke for the whole company.

Anton Gregorovitch folded his hands and smiled ingenuously. "Thank you, my friend. It does look rather appetizing, doesn't it?"

While they sat in their places waiting to be served, the guests raved about the luxury and expense of the meal, but as soon as the servants filled their plates they forgot their decorum and attacked the food like hungry animals.

❀　　❀　　❀

Maybe the answer is loneliness. At least I always come back to that. I'm always coming back to loneliness no matter what I do.

❀　　❀　　❀

Fyodor Petrovitch was the second clerk in charge of the Province of Vlosk in the Office of Provincial Records. He lived in a small, bare, unheated room off the Nevsky Prospect, on a dingy side street where the sun rarely chose to shine. He was a very solitary old man, this Fyodor Petrovitch: in the evenings he sat by himself in his room, drinking weak tea from his samovar and reading back issues of the illustrated magazines his landlady had already discarded. From time to time he went to a little cafe, but he didn't like the rough company there and he usually sat by himself in a corner, drinking as many vodkas as he needed to make the room fog before his eyes. Before he passed out, he would sometimes raise his fist and shout once or twice: "The bastards! When will they learn to treat the common man with respect?" and then his head would sink to the table. When the proprietor noticed him he'd call, "Hey, old man, this is no hotel I'm running!" But Fyodor Petrovitch was dead to the world. Soon one of the rough coach-drivers would grab him and send him flying out the door. He would climb back to his room by instinct and habit, like a dog finding its way home in the dark, and he'd pass out again on the bed. There he'd sleep until Monday.

Well, one day Fyodor Petrovitch was going by a store which specialized in antique jewelry. Among the many items in the window was a large cameo brooch he'd never noticed before: a portrait of the most exquisite young woman he'd ever seen, a shy young countess (or so Fyodor Petrovitch imagined) with large eyes and her hair swept over a long, swanlike neck. For weeks he passed the store, hoping that the brooch would be gone and he would be free of his strange obsession, for such is what it had become. He thought about her constantly, in every waking moment and in his dreams as well. Her face even floated before his eyes when he did his figures: a seven would remind him of the curve of her neck, and in a nine he would recognize the roundness of her cheek.

One icy morning when he passed the shop, he noticed that the brooch was gone. Immediately he broke into a sweat colder than the freezing wind. He ran into the store and seized the clerk. "It it sold? Did you sell it?" he demanded.

"Sell what?" said the clerk.

"The brooch! The one with the girl's head on it!"

"Oh, that one," said the clerk slyly, smiling to himself. (He had noticed the look in Fyodor Petrovitch's eye every time he passed the shop, and he'd decided to trick the old man.) "Someone is very interested in it," he said. "However, I could let you have it for, say . . . a hundred rubles?"

A hundred rubles! It was almost everything he'd saved in all his years at the Office of Provincial Records! But he knew he had to have the brooch; a voice said to him, "You will die without it."

So he ran home and cut open his straw mattress, then ran back to the clerk. He thrust the money triumphantly into his face. "There it is! A hundred rubles! Now give it to me!"

"Easy, easy, old man," said the clerk as he counted the money in an agonizingly slow fashion. "You certainly are anxious to have it, aren't you, old fellow?"

But when the clerk finally produced the brooch from a side drawer, Fyodor Petrovitch seized it out of his hand and ran out of the store.

A year passed. Fyodor Petrovitch went to work as usual, and every day he came home and climbed the steps to his room. Nothing at all seemed to have changed in his humdrum life. But he was never seen again in the little cafe; instead he spent even the weekends in his room, and it was rumored that he had sworn off vodka forever. Then one day in the middle of the week he neglected to come to work. The Chief Clerk, a kindly soul, assumed he'd had an attack of his usual arthritis. But after three or four days his landlady noticed a strange smell as she passed his door. She knocked, but there was no answer. Finally she called the porter, and when there was again no answer, she ordered him to take the hinges off.

They found Fyodor Petrovitch dead, lying on his mattress with a peaceful, contented smile on his lips. His hands were held close to his chest. When they pried them open, they found a large cameo brooch pressed tightly against his heart.

*   *   *

There are times when I'm completely in love with Lilly: when I remember how beautiful her breasts can look in leotards; when I ask her how in God's name she can put up with me, and she answers, "Are you crazy? You're the warmest man in the world!"; when she gets up in the middle of the night and paints a whole canvas, then tumbles, happy and exhausted, into my arms; when she turns her body in a certain shy way and I realize that no woman can make me as happy as she.

But I get distracted. Sometimes anyone with a cute behind or a glint in her eye can make me stop in my tracks and hate myself. The times I've been unfaithful, well, they were times that seem to recede into anecdote before I know it. The second meeting is always a disappointment. She is just a woman too, this second one, and love is as complex and difficult as ever, no matter how hard I try to simplify it.

*   *   *

Maria Petrovna sat on the velvet couch, her coal-black eyes burning defiantly at Alexy. Like a connoisseur examining a painting, he studied the milk-white skin above her breasts; her smooth, tapering arms; her waist, still narrow as a schoolgirl's; and her rich, thick chestnut hair. She would marry him, that was clear. She didn't know it, of course, and neither had he until this moment, but now, as she looked at him with a hate as pure and clear as the crystal chandelier above her head, Alexy knew there was no escaping her: only such a woman could be his wife!

*   *   *

The fear of death rivets me to the sidewalk. I start falling and spinning, and I have to grab hold of something and breathe through my mouth until it passes. Yet it doesn't change my life at all; it doesn't make me live better.

Sometimes I sit down with myself and say, "Look, you're thirty now. At best, you've got fifty years more. But what are you doing with it? You drag yourself from day to day, you spend most of your time wanting, wanting, but what you have is never any good and what you don't have is marvelous. Why don't you eat your cutlet, man? Eat it with pleasure and joy. Love your wife. Make your babies. Love your friends and have the courage to tell those who seek to diminish you that they are the devil and you want no part of them. Courage, man, courage and appetite!"

*   *   *

Arkady Simonovitch was dying. The pillows were piled high around him, and the doctors hovered nearby with spoons of bitter, amber liquid which they kept dangling in front of his nose. He waved them away like flies. Enough, he thought, enough, enough! He had lived seventy-seven years, had fathered five legitimate children and God knows how many bastards, and now he was being treated like a sickly child. No, he'd had enough of it. Let the world be taken over by the New Generation, the Weak Ones. Let them see how difficult it was to be a man!

He looked at his youngest son, Gregor. He was staring out the window at the tall, waving oaks, one hand on his hip and the other cradling his chin. A dandy, scowled

Arkady Simonovitch, nothing but a dancer at balls! But in spite of himself he had to admire the handsome lad: the cut of his suit was good, the material was selected with a certain fineness of taste, and perhaps with his inheritance and a little cleverness, he would get along quite nicely.

By his bedside sat Varvara, his youngest daughter. She was too plump and matronly for such a young woman, and she read too many books, qualities which would not serve her well in finding a man. Yet Arkady Simonovitch admired her too. She brought back to him his wife Lubskaya, the same patience and intelligent irony in her eyes. Underneath her matronliness there was strength, and with strength even the plainest of women could make herself attractive.

So it was not so hard to die after all, he thought.

Arkady Simonovitch coughed loudly. The doctors turned their heads, but he closed his eyes and ignored them. He had settled most of the business of his life, financial and otherwise, and what there was left could be taken care of by the priests and accountants. He thought back to an afternoon like this one, bright and chilly, the sun a brittle diamond in the autumn sky. He was a young man, out hunting in the woods, when he heard a woman laugh; he looked around and saw in among the trees a peasant girl. She was far more desirable than the spindly-armed schoolgirls he suffered to dance with at balls; this one's breasts were like young melons in her blouse, and her eyes sparkled gaily. She had been washing her feet in a stream, but when she saw Arkady Simonovitch, she grabbed her sandals and bounded away like a roe-deer.

"Hello," he called out, "why are you running?"

"Because you come too close, Arkady Simonovitch!" She peered at him from behind a tree, her eyes smiling.

"But I don't want to hurt you!" he said.

"I know that, Arkady Simonovitch. But if you caught me, what *would* you want to do to me?"

He tried to come closer, but she darted behind another tree. "At least tell me your name," he called.

"My name is Never Enough!"

"Never Enough? That's a strange name."

"No, it isn't. It suits me perfectly. No matter how much

you get of me, it's Never Enough. Now good-bye, Arkady Simonovitch. Don't forget me!"

And she lifted her skirts to him, exposing her thighs, and ran away. He tried to find her, but the woods grew too dark to see, and he went home, aroused and fuming with desire.

"Never Enough!" Arkady Simonovitch thought to himself. He felt a smile come over his lips. "I'll find you," he said, "and when I do, *then* you'll know what I want of you!"

When the sun started to fill the room with the long, purposeful rays of late afternoon, the doctors noticed that Arkady Simonovitch was dead.

PART II: THE DEATH OF THE RUSSIAN NOVELIST: COMPARE AND CONTRAST. Read the following incidents carefully. Note how people choose their own ways of dying. Compare and contrast them to modern examples.

Alexander Pushkin, a man who was afraid of getting old, died in a duel with a young baron over his wife's honor. (She was a beautiful but empty-headed girl who would probably have been better off with the baron than with Pushkin; Pushkin knew it too; but the possibility of a duel came at just the right time, when his financial and artistic troubles were piling up around him, and a duel must have seemed so dazzlingly simple in the midst of his more dreary and prosaic problems.)

At any rate, they went out on a freezing cold morning to the outskirts of Moscow. The snow was up to a man's waist, and the sky must have been a blue so deep it was almost purple. The snow was completely fresh—it took the seconds an hour to trample down a proper dueling-area—and the field itself must have reflected some of the blue of the sky, making it look the color of icebergs. Trees with a thin coating of ice tinkled like wind-chimes. A splendid, unforgettable day!

When the signal was given, the baron strode quickly to the line (he was an excellent shot and Pushkin, for all his bravado, was not so hot), took aim, and shot Pushkin in the stomach. A terrible moment. What had happened to the purity of the day, the sharpness of colors? Now everything had become business again. Seeing Pushkin fall, the baron started to walk away. But Pushkin shouted, "Wait! Give me a chance!"—words which must have hit the young baron right in the pit of *his* stomach. According to the etiquette of dueling, however, he had no choice: he had to stand. But if he had been a reckless enough young man to pursue the wife of a poet whose bad temper was famous throughout Russia, at least he was not a complete fool; so he turned sideways to avoid a shot in the heart. Pushkin raised himself on one elbow and took aim—for two full minutes, some say. There it was, the father taking sweet revenge on the son: for isn't it likely that during those two minutes the baron thought to himself, "What right has he got to be angry at me anyway? He's just jealous that I'm younger than he is." And Pushkin must have thought, "I'm going to shoot that little bastard right in the balls."

Finally Pushkin pulled the trigger, and the baron collapsed in the snow.

The day was suddenly bright again. "Bravo!" shouted Pushkin.

Then he fell into blackness.

*　　*　　*

At the age of eighty-two, Tolstoi woke up one night and decided to escape from his family. He packed a knapsack and left a note saying that he was going away to seek Truth. At eighty-two, to seek Truth! How he must have driven his wife Sonya crazy with all that Truth-seeking! Well, when she read the note the next morning, she must have known what he was up to. She must have felt a panic that turned her body into one strummed nerve. For she and Tolstoi had been at each other's throats for years; he was growing weaker and his secretary was stealing from his diaries and selling the material to the papers; and now their youngest daughter Sascha babied and coddled Leo with an intimacy he'd never allowed his own wife. So she knew when she read the note that things had gotten too much for him; he had gone away to die in peace.

Those days before he collapsed in a little railroad station

in the middle of nowhere seemed to Tolstoi the most glorious in his life. He was free again, finally free. Of course he wasn't any more or less free than he had ever been, but for Tolstoi illusion was all. He would have made a great salesman, that Tolstoi; he could convince himself of anything. Even when his life started to sputter out in the station, he was dreaming. He talked about getting well and continuing his pilgrimage, of signing over all his lands to Sonya and starting all over again. It was no wonder that when she showed up, he wouldn't let her into his sickroom. She was Reality, and Reality was Death.

When he was a boy, Tolstoi's oldest brother Nikolai told him about a green carved stick buried in the woods of their parental estate, Yasnaya Polyana. (What poet ever put together those wonderful sounds!) There were magic words inscribed on this stick which contained the secret of universal love; with it, evil could be banished from the face of the earth, and all men would become brothers. The little boy Leo cried every time Nikolai told him this story, and he cried whenever he thought about it the rest of his life. Picture the eighty-year-old in a peasant's shirt, his long lion's face marked with a perpetual scowl, sitting in his garden and crying. When he died, they brought him back to Yasnaya Polyana and buried him in the woods where the green stick was hidden.

*   *   *

Chekhov's death was almost too Chekhovian; but then so were his later plays a little overripe with melancholy and the erosions of time. With his young actress-wife, he took a vacation to the Black Forest, though the vacation was a sham: both of them knew he was dying. It was like being in a play. They sat each evening talking or reading to each other, pretending they were like any other couple. The lights were dim, their voices hushed, the trees creaked outside their windows. Both of them were professionals; they were each other's loving audience as well as actors in the same play. The pale but healthy girl sitting by a lamp and reading Shakespeare; the middle-aged newlywed Chekhov lying on his couch with his wispy beard and glowing tubercular eyes—it is not hard to picture them on stage. If they hadn't been actors, it might have been depressing or heartbreaking to go through with this charade. But not these two—make-believe and reality had finally become congruent. They were the leading characters in the final Chekhov play.

On one of those nights Chekhov called from his couch for champagne. "It's been a long time since I've had champagne," he said, paused for an actor's two heartbeats, and drained the glass. A little while later, he whispered, *"Ich sterbe!"*—something a Wagnerian hero might utter on stage. He turned his back, the last exit, and passed away.

As was fitting, his death had two more acts. The first came on the train which carried his body back to Moscow. Somewhere along the way it got mixed up with a shipment of oysters; when the workmen unpacked the crates, they found ninety-nine crates of oysters and one crate of Chekhov. And there was more coming. The same train carried a Russian general who had also died abroad. Both funeral processions pulled up next to the train station. By accident the two coffins were exchanged, and until the mistake was discovered, Chekhov was led through the hot, dusty streets of Moscow by a full military marching band and a red-faced policeman high on a white horse.

Gorky, who was there, thought it was a terrible affront to the great writer. Poor Gorky. He never did have a sense of humor.

❊　　❊　　❊

Ernest Hemingway, a man who was afraid of getting old, spent all his life trying to find the ideal duel to fight. He fought everything he could find: bulls, lions, his fears, his wives, Gertrude Stein; he even read all his critics and went a couple of rounds in his head with each of them. Looking at it one way, a fight or a duel provides company for a lonely man. When someone bares his teeth, points a gun, or swings an evil fist at your gut, at least you know he cares. A duel is a dazzlingly simple moment of human contact. But Hemingway never found the duel he was looking for. No one loved or hated him enough to make him feel wanted. On that morning in his pine-paneled den with the chill, impersonal barrel filling his mouth, he must have felt so lonely, so utterly alone. Isn't it possible that if he'd let himself bawl like a baby and at least feel the loneliness, someone upstairs would have heard and come down to save him?

❖ ❖ ❖

E. M. Forster died at the venerable age of ninety-one. The papers said that he died in his sleep, just like that, no fuss or fury, he just went to bed one night and let himself be taken away. But then he had never been the sort of man to make a fuss. For several decades he'd been content to live in a little apartment in Cambridge, listening to his gramophone or talking quietly to friends. The few interviews he granted portrayed him as a reserved, somewhat untrusting man, unwilling or unable to reveal very much of himself to strangers—even reverential ones.

That is a strange kind of man to be a novelist. Self-revelation, not of facts but of deepest fantasies, is part of the novelist's business. And I thought I knew a lot about this man through his books: I knew the magnitude of his sentiment, I knew his small prejudices, I knew about his sense of the mystery beneath the ordinary. So at what point did he decide to close up? Why did he choose to live the rest of his life like a ghost? What great fear told him, nay *demanded,* that he never publish another work of fiction the last forty-six years of his life?

❖ ❖ ❖

Like many Russian novelists, Jack Kerouac, a man of Tolstoian appetites, died in St. Petersburg. But what a St. Petersburg! The America he had crossed so many times (the ghost of which now lay somewhere under the new superhighways) had shrunk to a wretched, sweltering place in Florida where the old and unloved go to roast in the sun like barbecued chickens.

There was a logic to it. There always is. When he died, he was prematurely old. He had lost his fantasy. He felt neglected, unloved. It was so sad to watch him resurrected briefly on television the year before he died. Do you remember how handsome he used to look on his first book-jackets? Now he was pudgy and sullen. He sat before the TV cameras, swiveling in his chair, denouncing his past friends, his past illusions, squinting at the bright lights, his arms moving dreamily with the sluggish grace of an alcoholic. Movingly, shamelessly, he complained that the present was shit.

After his death some of his friends wrote poems about him. These poems tended to be too long and almost incoherent. He had gotten through to his friends; he had made them feel guilty, but the source of the guilt wasn't clear. No one could say exactly why he died.

PART III: PERSONAL EXPERIENCE. Use the following stories as examples for your own reflections on the general topic of the exam.

I have a friend who used to remind me of people in Russian novels. On the surface he seemed colorless, but underneath his soul was Russian.

We were both graduate students one winter in Paris, and we shared a chilly, expensive apartment in a little street near the Pantheon. At the beginning he seemed like the most proper guy you'd ever want to meet: he wore dark suits, horn-rimmed glasses, attended his classes with a sense of duty, and kept his hair short. I didn't like him at first—his agreeability annoyed me, and the routine of his life seemed insanely dull. But then I started noticing a laugh he had. It was the most poignant, tinkling laugh I'd ever heard. It was like a little girl's giggle, high and melodic, and he seemed so relieved and happy when he laughed that he made me happy too. I realized how shy he was. His eyes would glimmer like those of a child who's been left out of a joke; when you laughed with him, it was like accepting him, allowing him to be close to you.

There was something Russian about the way he brought girls home with him almost every night. Mostly they were foreign students, tall, lost girls whom we nicknamed "*La Suédoise*," "*L'Allemande*," "*L'Italienne*," to tell them apart.

He'd spend hours sitting with them by the gas heater in the living room. They'd move their hands furiously, complaining about Paris, French men, their landladies, anything they could think of. And he sat listening attentively, his chin in his pale palm, smiling and soaking up their troubles like a kind uncle. It wasn't love he inspired in them; it was trust. So when he tried to make love to them a date or two later, they reacted as if he'd broken an unspoken agreement. Later they called up and apologized, explained how upset they'd felt that evening, but they never became his lovers. Whether they knew it or not, they had come to Paris looking for danger and excitement, and to them he appeared as pure as Sir Galahad.

As the year wore on and Paris turned gray with the winter, more of the Russian came out in him. He began to disappear for days at a time. He never announced his departures or explained where he'd been. Sometimes I'd run into him in the long subway tunnels of Châtelet. There he was at the other end of the long tiled tube, coming toward me in his tweed coat and Brooks Brothers scarf. We'd get closer and closer, I'd start to smile a greeting, but then I noticed that he didn't know who I was. I'd call him back: "Hey, where are you going?" "Oh," he'd say, and that shy, silver laugh would dance out of his mouth.

In the coldest part of the winter, he fell in love. She was a strange girl, the one he picked—dark, slight, nervous as a cat, quick-witted, and something of a nag. But he was ecstatic. He moved her into the apartment a week after he met her, and she'd cook for all of us. At least outwardly, he began to relax a little. He took off his tie and rolled up his sleeves. He talked more, cracked quiet little jokes, tried to become one of the boys; he even took to smoking cigars.

But after only a few weeks of this curious bliss she disappeared. One morning he woke up and she was gone without a note. He was frantic. He paced around the room: "Goddamn, goddamn, where did she *go?*" But then I saw him change again; the most Russian of all his selves emerged. All the stealth in his mind, all his capacity for intrigue, gathered inside him and focused on one end: to find her. He became a brilliant and methodical detective. With his hands in his pockets, his body stiffened against an imagined wind, the eyes behind his glasses small and suffering, he scoured the neighborhood. He spoke to everyone: the concierge, the shop-keepers, the street-sweepers, even the bus-drivers on the line which passed our building. Finally he found her, don't ask me how. But he had her address in a bleak city in the north of France. He went to bring her back. A week later he returned alone—not bitter, not angry, just limp and exhausted. He told me this story.

She was married, appropriately enough, to a psychiatrist. One of her neighbors told him with a trace of green-eyed envy that she left whenever she got bored, and her husband never failed to take her back. My friend stood outside her house in a gray, pouring rain, trying to decide what to do. He was soaked, he was shaking with chills. That morning he'd hid behind a tree as she went out for groceries. Her face was hidden by a kerchief, and she wore a frumpy housecoat: why had he come all this way for a little French housewife? Fantasies whirled through his head. Should he go in and rescue her? Did he really want her? What would he do when he saw her? What would she do when she saw him? Would she look past him like some blank-eyed movie schizophrenic? (But these are things that I might think, not he; after all, he was a man of decision, of dark, snaking inner drives. No, more likely if he thought anything, he thought of their nights together. His new strength, her flirtatiousness! And that moment must have been the worst for him. For he was terrified he would never be that happy again.)

He knocked on the door. The husband, a sharp-nosed man with rimless glasses, answered. Panic. He had thought she was alone. But my friend, the man of decision, had that contingency covered too. In a soft, steady voice he stared into the husband's eyes and lied: he was an American soldier whose car had broken down in the rain. Could he come in and use the phone?

She saw him. She stood in the hallway and saw him. He looked at her for only a moment, then ducked his head, but that moment was to reverberate in his mind for months afterward like a witch shrieking through a child's dreams. He started to speak, but his laugh, that lost, silvery laugh, caught in his throat instead and made him almost faint.

He groped for the door behind him and plunged into the rain.

In a way, there is a happy ending. He's married now, has a sparkling little boy, a partnership in a law firm, a future. He still laughs his laugh occasionally, but it is a ghost of the former one. He conceals the Russian from himself. The Law is not Russian. Honesty is not Russian. Justice is not Russian. Only the laugh which catches in the throat is Russian.

         ✿   ✿   ✿

I have another friend who reminded me of Stavrogin in *The Possessed*, though perhaps he was more like Kirilov, a lesser character, the revolutionary incurably bound to a vision of the ideal world the real world wants no part of.

He was a very heavy, light-skinned black, built like an ex-tackle but with the shy, clumsy gestures of an adolescent. I knew him one winter when we were both floating around Europe looking for something to keep us occupied. Remember that this is eight years ago, before we were all made members of the Youth Culture and the Movement. We were in-between eras, and we had nothing but our nervous itches to keep us company. I met him in Rome in front of American Express: "Hey, baby, can you turn me on tuh-to a thousand lire? Just enough to get me straight, my man." His eyes flickered away from me and back with distrust, as if even *he* didn't believe his own con. I guess that was why he interested me; he seemed complex, self-doubting, as lost as I was. So I took out my wallet and gave him the gaudy bills. "Yeah, cool," he said, and extended his hand for me to pat. It was big and soft, a giant pudding of a hand.

Rome was a deserted place that winter. The Via Veneto was empty, the Spanish Steps glowed in the winter sunlight like dried bones, and the only people in the streets were a few homosexuals out cruising, an occasional forlorn whore, and ambitious but aimless kids like this guy and me. So we ran into each other several times. Sometimes I'd treat him to a plate of spaghetti, but more often we'd sit for a while in a deserted cafe and have a cup of sweet coffee until his restlessness (or maybe it was his guilt) took over, and he left, saying he had to meet his man.

There were times when he got nervous and abstract. The world became too much for him. He'd sit in the cafe dropping lump after lump of sugar into his cup until the surface tension broke and the coffee spilled onto the marble table top. His big hands would clench and he'd speak in his frantic, feverish stutter: "You th-think you can understand what we go through? You really do? My brothers are dying in Alabama and Mississippi and Indochina and the Dominican Republic and you're sitting on your ass in Rome digging the *ragazze*. You couldn't understand if your puh-pecker depended on it. But I sympathize with you because the grays b-been brainwashing you for years and you not expected to know. They been killing my brother for centuries. What is he? Just some stupid nigger, right? It's okay, it's cool. Shit on him, kill him, he digs it, he don't even bleed."

He would picture some rice paddy in a land which was still just a strange word (you see, he really did *believe* in Brotherhood!), and his eyes would cloud with tears. "So fucking stupid!"

"What is?"

"The colored cats! Why do they go and kill their own brothers? Them little black-pyjamaed cats in Viet Nam are their brothers, and they're too dumb to know it. They didn't do nothing to us; it's the white people who's the enemy! So why do the colored cats go there and shoot those people who could be their brothers in the Revolution? Why don't they turn around and shoot the fucking lieutenants?"

During the next year I ran into him in three or four different cities. It was always the same: he talked about making a revolution, the evils of capitalism and imperialism, and since he'd started to read hungrily, his tirades now bristled with impressive and guilt-making statistics. One time I met him in Copenhagen. It was a balmy, lax, fragrant summer, and I was having a great time. The girls smiled when they saw someone a little out of the ordinary, and the group of Americans and Englishmen who had been floating around the continent looking for a purpose now had one: to make love to as many soft, smiling girls as we could lay our hands on. So when I saw his ponderous body coming down the street like a walking conscience, I felt guilty. He made my girl-chasing seem like imperialism.

I sat down with him in a cafe overlooking a lake where swans floated on placid waters. I asked him how long he was staying.

"Not long, man. I'm on my way to Sverige. The only decent socialist country in the world. This place is just a satellite of Uncle Sam, the imperialist warmonger."

When he went into his usual speech, I got nervous. "Agreed that society is cruel and inhuman," I said. "Agreed that it should all be changed. But what are you going to do until it happens?"

"I'll be a hairdresser," he said.

"A what?"

I could see how threatened he felt. "Don't bug me, man. You're just a mocky intellectual from New Yoke. You think you can hype me like Mr. Shapiro hypes my people in Harlem."

"But you're smart, you speak five languages, why don't you go back to school so you can *do* something?"

"Fuck that, man. You got no right to talk while my people are dying."

Until the Revolution came, he floated from country to country. Not having any particular taste for women, in his way the most innocent, vulnerable, tortured person I'd ever met, all he could do was carry around his rage and tell it to anyone who would listen. After a while he settled in Sweden where he became active in a local expatriate chapter of SNCC. Once in a while I saw pictures of him in foreign newspapers, massive and wild-eyed, shouting into a microphone about racism in Europe. One year he wrote a passionate series of articles for a Stockholm newspaper. I hoped he was doing okay. But I knew better. Maybe it was his lack of humor, the suspicion which persisted in his eyes, his invincible innocence: but I knew that he would never find a place in the world. He was doomed to a loneliness so deep that even his imagined brothers would deny him. Maybe in some other age he could have been a martyr, smiling knowingly while the lackeys fanned the flames at his feet; but now it was clear that the second wave of the Revolution, the one which gets down to business, would roll right over him.

Soon there came rumors that the other people in the Movement didn't like him: he was *too* crazy, *too* tortured, *too* disorganized. A couple of years ago Bobby Seale stopped in Stockholm on a fund-raising tour. My friend suited up completely in black: black pants, black shirt, black boots, black gloves, and a black beret. He was about to be vindicated. He was about to be received into the arms of his revolutionary brothers. So imagine him before a mirror in a chilly room in a joyless city full of people who misunderstood or despised him, putting his three-hundred-pound body into the uniform of the Cause. Think of his hopes, the glow of expectation in his heart! He was completely happy then; he must have loved the world passionately for the first time in his life. A Russian moment, of course, totally Russian.

As Bobby Seale stepped off the plane with the wild, vindictive Swedish wind whipping the flaps of his coat, my friend stood at the foot of the stairs and snapped to attention. I have heard that Seale looked down on this man, this huge, unloved man in black, and said, "What the fuck is *that?*"

* * *

This one is the hardest to tell. When I try to picture how it happens, my mind fights me every inch of the way. But I have to try, I have to understand.

So look. There are mornings, occasional mornings, when life begins for me like a Russian Novel. I wake up with tears of joy in my eyes. I was dreaming something, what I can't remember, but the feeling itself lingers. I have the sense that *my life is mine,* no one else's, mine for the short time I'm allowed to keep it. Everything in the room seems to belong to me for the first time: the white walls, the green plants, the typewriter waiting on the table, they're all mine. I see Lilly sleeping next to me. Her dreams are angry ones, she's rocking furiously on her side, her eyes clenched tight. But I'm not afraid of her. I love her. I want to tell her to depend on me, to trust me, to find her safety in me, there's enough strength in me at this moment to keep both of us alive.

So I reach out and hold her. Her body is a warm nest. Slowly she turns over, opens her eyes, and smiles at me. Now remember that this is a beautiful girl as far as I am concerned—not cool and distant, but alive, sexy, as vital as that feeling I had when I woke up. We begin to kiss like strangers, like animals nosing at each other, tentative and hungry. We feel the mystery growing between us. When I finally slip inside her, it's like coming home. But when I'm riding high in the clutch of love, during the time when nature is telling us to open, open, open more and more until we are exposed as totally as babies, we start to close up and drift away from each other. Like Forster, like my friend in Paris, we recede into private securities, backwaters of ourselves. The feeling I had that my life was mine gives way to a feeling of empty isolation.

What happens blow-by-blow in this ritual of loneliness is not necessary to go into. Suffice it to say that we have lost each other in a moment of fear so deep it cannot be felt. And the morning which began so promisingly, as if it were the first morning of my life, has now become a familiar disappointment. The consciousness of that moment in time, all that I have, that moment in time, vanishes and blurs as it never did for Pierre or Natasha, for Stavrogin and each of the Karamazovs—as it might not have for the people who dreamed them either.

PART IV: THE PRESENT AND THE FUTURE. Write a heartfelt essay on the topic: "Are There Any Russians Left In Russia? Is Even Lenin Still A Hero? When They Close His Mausoleum For Repairs, Does The Cosmetics Expert Touch His Body With Love And Awe Or Does He Look At Him As Just Another Stiff? Is It Possible That The Russians Aren't Russian Anymore? Why Is Voznesensky A Lesser Poet Than Mayakovsky? Why Is Solzhenitsyn A Lesser Novelist Than Tolstoi? Why Do I Suspect That If I Went To Russia, I Would Still Come Back To New York, The City Of Separations?"

Choubouloute [*]

Daryl Hine

AN HORATION ODE FOR HOLLY STEVENS

This sand is basalt black as a negative,
The faces too are black, also negative,
     The pigs, the cocks, the arts, the beaches,
  Black as your hat or the ace of spades, black

As sin? as death? We're white as the sepulchers
One sees beside the paths, in the villages,
     With corrugated roofs and whitewashed
  Walls, where the black are at home in blackness.

Islands invite impermanent visitors,
Requests to go back home from the residents.
     If paradise were not an island
  How could the landlord be so exclusive?

The Caribs went and so did the Arawaks
Before them; then his Grace the Conquistador
     Came, bringing strange diseases, smallpox,
  Measles and syphilis, fatal imports.

The blacks in fact were later imported to
Supply the Creoles' lack, proletariat
     To cut the sugarcane, banana,
  Pineapple, manioc, with machetes,

Or fish the crawling, dangerous Atlantique.
Their masters, who espoused the philanthropy
     That philosophes enjoyed in eighteenth
  Century France, gave their cattle freedom.

Who knows where that might lead? lest Napoleon,
First Consul then as Emperor recognize

  [*] Choubouloute—*The Week in Martinique.*

Some freedoms mean a double standard,
Joséphine Bonaparte, Empress Upstart

Restored her fellow Créoles to slavery
As local girl made good in a fairytale,
    Until the onset of effective
Menopause led her to Malmaison where

La Citoyenne—society's sobriquet—
Resumed her role as rose-lover. History,
    Which "teaches little save statistics,"
Doesn't record if she missed her native

Savannah where today there's a monument
To this romantic schemer and courtesan
    Whose heart was Caribbean bullion,
Typical daughter of Fort-de-France, Ma-

rie-Joseph Rose Tascher de la Pagérie.
Pélé volcano muttered and fidgeted
    Until at last it had a breakdown
Filling the center of St. Pierre with

A flood of fireworks. Henceforth the capital
Of Martinique's a Mediterranean
    Provincial town, Tahitian village
Built on the ashes of buried Paris.

La Belle Époque deserved a catastrophe.
Preserved in lava like Herculaneum,
    Remembered as a place of Culture,
Literature and the Arts of Living,

The site of 1902 has been visited.
The Arawak, a genial, civilized
    Ceramic people, first were eaten
Up by the paleolithic Caribs;

The French, they say, will eat almost anything
That doesn't get there first, like a fer-de-lance;
    A mongoose though can kill his cobra
And is required to do so daily

In public. Any wonder the madwoman

Directed tous les blancs to return to their
    Pays natal, the Riviera?
    Grande Rivière is another landscape

Entirely: the bays in the permanent
Arrest of cliffs, the swell with its permanent
    Attack upon black rocks where pastel
    Fishermen's cabins attach the tideline;

And here took place (I think) the penultimate
Sublime and silly romanesque episode
    Of *Paul et Virginie*, the scene where,
    Rather than take off her pants, there perished

In sight of land the crinoline heroine.
Or was it on the isle of Réunion
    That Paul and Virginie were parted,
    Innocent savages, but of color?

Beloved Caesar preaches his negritude
To multicolored beautiful citizens
    Of France, the heirs of Pascal, Curie,
    Diderot, Debussy, Gauguin, Schoelcher;

And we, who came but brought no superior
Cuisine or language, culture or theory,
    And take away impressions, sand-fleas,
    Dysentery, souvenirs, rum and sunburn,

What were we looking for in geography?
The Island's shape reduced to a passenger
    From overhead the way the airplane
    Abendlandsuntergang circles homeward.

The Real Meaning of the Faust Legend

Alvin Greenberg

WHO IS THERE who isn't peddling himself to the devil in some way? There are those who do it according to the tradition: for knowledge and power. There are those who do it for fame and money. There are those who do it to maintain the status quo and those who do it for the sake of revolution. There are those who do it to keep their children fed, to quiet their own consciences, to make the sun rise tomorrow morning, or to torment their heirs. There are those who do it for what most of us might agree are sufficiently good reasons, and others whose reasons, well, leave something to be desired. Why do I do it? I do it for a .368 batting average.

Fame, you might say. Not hardly. I don't hit that for the Reds or the White Sox. Not even for Indianapolis or Louisville. I hit it for Muncie of the Three-I League. I never wanted the fame, believe me; I only wanted to hit .368. And not even that on a regular basis. I wanted it as a lifetime average. The nice thing about that is that it leaves a lot to chance: I might hit .318 one season, but I might also hit .427—as, in fact, I did three years ago. The logical question, of course, is how fame can fail to come to one who hits consistently up there where I do, but the answer is equally logical. I hit it for Muncie. In other words, I have had my chances higher up—have them most every spring, as a matter of fact. Muncie is a farm club, after all. So there I am down in Tampa or Sarasota every March, and people who know what I did at Muncie last year are watching me each time I take batting practice, and all those out-of-shape big-league pitchers who are sweating off their bellies doing laps around the outfield are just waiting for the first intersquad game. And with good reasons, too, because they know how good I'm going to make them look. I play on "B" teams in the Grapefruit League and end up hitting .187, so naturally when we break camp for the exhibition swing heading north, you know where I'm going.

EVERY YEAR, of course, my season gets interrupted at Muncie when somebody at Denver breaks a leg or goes into a two-month-long slump and the big brass decide to call up the leading hitter in the minors to fill the gap, but for the most part my stays in the lofty altitudes of Triple-A ball are mercifully short. I'm in a slump the day I suit up. I may have hit safely in the last thirty-two games for Muncie, with two or more hits in twenty of them, as is frequently the case, but suddenly I'm o for 18 before I trickle one between first and second that rolls dead before the right-fielder gets to it. Once I even got peddled to the Yankees in a stretch drive, but you don't want to hear about that one. Muncie is where I always end up.

And why not? There are people who think I must be on the verge of suicide, being able to hit the way I do at Muncie and then not making it at all anywhere further up the ladder, and my previous manager, who never hit more than .250 himself, was one of those who had the notion that all I needed to make it in the majors was confidence. But he was dead wrong. I *knew* I could hit .368, I had perfect confidence in my ability to do so; after all, I did it—or something close to it—every year, and how many ballplayers can say that, even in the minors? So Billy cost the parent club a good bit in psychologist and hypnotist bills with his silly theory, and then one summer cost himself a sizable measure of pain over his investment in double-up bets when I had a fat hitting streak in the beginning of August. I had gone five for eight in a Sunday doubleheader, including a pair of bases-loaded doubles in the second game, and had hit safely the last three times at bat, and on the bus home from Peoria Billy got on my back again about the confidence thing.

"No, Billy," I told him, "you're wrong, dead wrong. I've got so much confidence I'm willing to bet you I hit

.385 for the season. I'll pay you a hundred dollars for each point I hit below that and you pay me a hundred for each point above." He looked at me then and fell silent and took off his cap and scratched his head. He was obviously tempted—maybe only to see if I really had the confidence to shake hands on a bet like that—but the fact was that I was already hitting .379 and was on a pretty hot streak, so he thought better of it and shook his head no. And that was a good thing for him because I ended the season at .397. But I didn't want to let him off that easy.

"All right then, Billy," I said, because I wanted to show him just how wrong he was about his confidence theory. "How about a five-dollar bet that I get a hit first time up next game?"

Well, that was all right with him, especially since the next game, though at home, was against Des Moines, which was currently leading the league by a good twelve games and had a couple of hot young pitchers who were sure to be called up by the end of the month. That may have made a difference to Billy, but not to me. After Johnson and Feathers went down on called strikes in the first, I patted Billy on the shoulder and went up there and lined the first pitch over the third baseman's head and down into the corner for a stand-up double.

Sitting on the bench during the next inning, I asked Billy if he wanted to double up his bet on my next at-bat, giving him a chance to come out five ahead. He was paying more attention to the kid on the mound than to me, but he mumbled, "OK, why not?"

I didn't get a turn at the plate again till the last of the fourth with one out, because that kid hadn't allowed one out of the infield since my first-inning double, and maybe Billy wasn't even thinking about our bet by then because we were losing 4–0 and he had to get a scouting report in on the kid by noon the next day. This time I waited out a couple of pitches, till I was sure Billy was watching, and then lined one up the middle. Took off my cap and waved at Billy from first base and he just stood on the dugout steps and shook his head at me and that was where we both stayed while the next two guys fouled out to the catcher.

When I came up again in the last of the sixth, with two out and none on, we were seven runs behind, and besides me nobody had gotten to base except the catcher, Wiltz, who had walked the inning before. Billy was juggling relief pitchers and looking very sad, so I had to shake him a bit to get his attention. He looked irritated when he turned around; as far as he was concerned it wasn't anything but a hot, lost, miserable afternoon, and there wasn't much anyone could do about it at this point. What's more, it was dragging on endlessly, for in spite of the way we were being set down Des Moines had kept up enough action on the bases and in our bullpen so that the game was almost two hours old already. I just stayed calm though.

"Double up again, Billy?" I asked him.

"What's that?" he said, like he didn't even know what the name of the game was.

"It was five on my first at-bat," I reminded him, "and ten on my second. Want to go for twenty this time?"

"Shit," he said, squinting up at me, "that's five straight since Sunday, you can't keep that up against a kid like this, he's major-league stuff."

"We're on then?"

"Right," he said as I headed for the on-deck circle, "we're on."

I was first-ball hitting again and went with the pitch, which was a nice outside slider that I lined to right just beyond the first baseman's reach. And stayed on first base again while Kryzinski struck out for the third straight time.

By the time I came up to lead off the last of the ninth, Johnson had got us a run, and our only hit beside my three, with an inside-the-park homer that the Des Moines outfielders, worn out from chugging around the bases all afternoon, just didn't seem to have the energy to run down. Billy, who had just finished calling me a smart-assed old man but had agreed all the same to one more bet, for forty dollars this time, was standing by the water cooler shaking his head. And the kid on the mound, who could understand the stupidity that had led to the home run but couldn't understand how I had hit him three straight times, was grinding the ball in his glove and glaring at me. I was thirty-five bucks ahead and would be out only five even if I lost this time, and besides I wasn't arrogant enough to really think I could go on getting consecutive base hits forever, so I decided I would at least have a little fun. He was throwing hard but sharp and obviously wanted to get me this time, as I'm sure he had a right to. He wanted to be a major-leaguer, that was what he was peddling himself to his devil for. His first two were curve-ball strikes, and I just let them go by with no intention of swinging. I was ready on the next, but it was low and away. Then he came in with the fast ball, and 1 and 2, nine to one, forty dollars and all, I just let my bat hang out there in front of it and dropped a lovely little bunt down the third-base line and skipped on down to first while the pitcher, catcher, third baseman, and poor Billy most of all just stood there and watched it roll dead on the grass as if they'd never seen such an obscene thing in the middle of a ballfield before.

Now I wasn't at all worried about that kid pitcher, even if he did blow sky-high after my bunt and walk the next two men on eight straight pitches. He was going to be a major-league star and that was all there was to it. Fame, money, and women, and nothing short of a broken back in an automobile accident or an all-out war was likely to stop him. I even doubted if war could. He'd probably turn up 4-F in the spring and pitch three hundred innings that same season. So naturally with the bases loaded and no one out in the last of the ninth, he struck out Henry on a 3 and 2 count and got Goldburg to bounce into a double play. That kid was no different than anybody else, just a particularly obvious case.

I was more worried about Billy, who was already muttering, even as we walked off the field, about getting it back tomorrow afternoon. He was also an obvious case, in a way. I think he never really wanted to be a hitter, even though he broke in on a long-ball reputation, but mostly just wanted to be in baseball, somehow or other. So when he found out what it was like, standing up there at the plate four, five times a game, he bargained himself into a managership. Now he didn't know that was going to mean seven years at Muncie, but you deal for a managership and you get a managership; nothing guarantees

it's going to be in Detroit or San Francisco. If he'd peddled himself for Detroit he could surely have had that, but
maybe he'd have ended up there as a used-car salesman,
who knows. Also he didn't know that every time he put
a decent team together he'd be raided in the middle of
the summer by the parent club and end up finishing the
season with the same ragtag bunch that had come in 24½
games behind the year before. He didn't know he'd have
to live with things like his big dumb catcher slipping on
the dugout steps and stomping down on the toe of tomorrow's starting pitcher in the middle of today's dismal loss.
Yes, and there was that poor kid, who hadn't yet made up
his mind whether or not this was what he wanted to peddle
himself for, sitting in the locker room watching his big toe
swell up bigger and bigger. It was time for him to decide.
And poor Billy surely didn't know he'd end up the day
$75 in the hole, with $80 riding on the first inning of the
next day's game, to a 35-year-old left-fielder who was an
eleven-year veteran of a minor-league team he not only
couldn't hit his way off of, even with the leading average
in the Three-I League for eight of those years—to say
nothing of the longest stay on record at Muncie—but didn't
even seem to care about.

"Al," he said, when we were having a beer at McDougal's after the game, "when are you going to grow up and
do something with your life?"

"Billy," I told him, "I am doing something with my life.
I'm hitting .386 after today's game." He looked up at me
and emptied the pitcher that was on the table between us
into his own mug. He hadn't paid up yet, but I supposed
that as long as I was ahead, even if only on the books, I
was going to have to buy the beers, so I carried the pitcher
over to the bar for a refill. When I came back he was waiting with an empty glass.

"Look," he said, while I filled it for him, and then poured
myself one as well, "why don't you be a good boy and go
hit .386 for the Pirates, or the Yokahama Giants, if that's
what'll make you happy?"

"Billy," I told him, "I am happy." But he went right on
as if he hadn't even heard me.

"Maybe you'll have to settle for .322, or even an occasional season at .298, but you could do it, Al, I know you could. All you need's a little confidence."

"Billy," I reminded him, "I've got plenty of confidence. Didn't I already show you that today?"

"You smart-assed college kids are all alike," he muttered, finishing the pitcher off again. "You get a little lucky and right off you think you know it all." He pushed the empty pitcher across at me, so I went and got it filled again.

"Billy," I reminded him when I came back, "I'm not one of your smart-assed college kids that comes and goes here. I may have gone to college, but that was a long time ago, when I didn't know what I wanted yet, and you don't see me tripping on my degrees while I'm running the bases, do you? I'm no kid, either, Billy, I'm as old as you, or maybe a little bit older. And I didn't get lucky, as you damn well know, unless you want to say I've been lucky for the past eleven years. No, Billy, what I had was confidence that I could go up and get a hit each one of those times today, and I've got confidence I can do it first time up tomorrow, too, if you're still on, and for as long after that as you want to keep it up." I got up to leave, before I got stuck buying another pitcher.

"On," he said. Feathers and Goldburg were standing at the table by then, and when they heard that the bet was still on for tomorrow, they wanted a piece of the action too. But this was strictly between Billy and me, so when I left the two of them were sitting on either side of Billy trying to arrange a bet between just themselves. Billy, between them, had his chin in his hands and was staring at the empty beer pitcher.

I had three hits in the first four innings the next day, including a single, a double, a triple, and five RBI's before Billy pulled me out with the excuse that we were already eight runs ahead and put old Falucci in for me. Falucci had always wanted to have the strongest arm in baseball, and he probably did. He could throw strikes across the plate from anywhere in the outfield. But he couldn't hit well enough to stick on any team, and so he had spent a couple of decades bouncing around from one minor-league club to the next and never getting in enough playing time to fulfill his dream of throwing out all those runners at the plate. Meanwhile, it had become a real obsession with him: everything hit to him he fired to the plate, whether it was a bases-empty single or a fly ball with a man on first. You had to have a sharp catcher, which we didn't, to remember to be ready for a Falucci peg every time somebody banged one to left. But meanwhile, we were ahead 13–5 when I went out, I was glad to see the lefty with the swollen toe was determined to hang in there long enough to pick up the win, and I now had ten straight hits and $635 of Billy's money, though I had yet to see any of his real cash.

Thursday, when I came in from left field after the top of the first, I saw that someone had propped a chalkboard up on the bench in the dugout and was keeping a record of the progress of our running bet. It read "11–$640" and then further over on the same line it said "$1275," which was the total of what Billy would owe me if I got a hit the first time up. I did. Johnson walked leading off, Feathers drilled one to right on the hit-and-run, and I bounced one off the left-field wall, scoring both of them.

When I came up again in the third, we were ahead 3–0 on Wiltz's second-inning triple and a wild pitch, and the chalkboard read "12–$1280–$2555." I looked over at Billy from the on-deck circle and he looked grim but he shook his head up and down. They didn't give me much to hit at this time but I was determined not to take a walk, even though that wouldn't have lost the bet for me but only postponed it till my next at-bat. I got the first two pitches in the dirt and the next one behind my back. The 3 and 0 pitch was a curve spinning low and away but I went for it all the same, got underneath it just like I wanted, and lofted it high down the right-field line. It stayed up there, in the still air under dark clouds that were building up all around us, and dropped over the fence just inches inside the foul pole.

By the last of the fifth Des Moines had gone ahead 6–4, the chalkboard read "13– $2560– $5115," and when I stepped up to the plate with two out and McKay, who had singled for the pitcher, on first, the thunderstorm that had been threatening suddenly broke and sent us all scampering for the dugouts. We sat for forty-five minutes and watched the heavy downpour before the umpires called it off, and Billy, who had been deep in silent thought all the while, carefully pointed out to me that since the game had now been cancelled and wouldn't appear in the record books, my two hits were wiped out, and so were his losses for the day. I couldn't argue with him and didn't want to.

FRIDAY IT RAINED all day so Des Moines went home, and Saturday, when Fort Wayne came to town, the field was still too soggy to play on, so Saturday's game was rescheduled as part of a Sunday doubleheader. But when Billy fell suddenly quiet after standing there in the locker room Saturday afternoon telling us that, I could see just what was going through his head. Even wiping out my two hits in Thursday's rained-out game, I had ten straight and he was $635 behind. A doubleheader, if I played both games—and he didn't have another left-fielder except Falucci, whom he couldn't really justify using in my place unless we were way ahead—could mean as many as ten more times at bat for me for the day. He had already had a taste Thursday of what just a couple more hits could cost him, and even if I had to hit a couple more in place of those two that had been wiped out, he was clearly beginning to have his doubts. If I went to the plate four times in the first game, he'd be betting $5120 against that fourth hit. Ten times and the bet would be up to $327,680! Which was a good bit more than he could afford. He just stood there and looked at me where I sat on the bench in front of my locker. Everybody else was picking up to leave. I just sat and stared at the floor, not wanting to look him in the eye. I didn't know whether to pick up and go myself and let him sweat it out or to take pity on him and offer to call it off, and I was afraid I'd offend him either way, which never was my aim. All I ever wanted to do was hit .368. Not even .370. I thought that zero at the end made it sound a little too astronomical, a little arrogant. Just a nice ragged .368. It didn't make any difference to me where I hit it. None at all. The fact that there were rarely more than five hundred fans in the stands or that I wasn't getting $100,000 a season or that I didn't have my picture on trading cards, my signature on bats, and Marilyn Monroe on my arm didn't bother me in the least. It wasn't

fame or fortune I peddled myself for. It was, as I said, a
.368 average.

When I looked up Billy was gone and so was everyone
else. The locker room was empty, and damp and chilly
from two days of rain, and I felt pretty much the same way
myself. I went home and tried to watch the nationally
televised game, Senators at Boston, but both teams seemed
to be trying to set a major-league record for pop-ups, and
I couldn't stand that sort of boredom for long. Watching
someone else play was never my idea of baseball anyway.
I strolled down to McDougal's, but when I looked in the
window and saw Billy sitting at a table with half a dozen
of my teammates around him, I felt too embarrassed to go
in and join them. Instead I went back home and with
some trouble got my old Ford started—I never used it much
during the season because you can't hop around all day
and night if you want to hit .368, that's part of the price
—and went and had dinner by myself at the Country
Kitchen and then came back in to the Drive-In and sat and
ate popcorn and watched a horror movie triple-feature
until one-thirty A.M.

Sunday was bright and clear again and not too hot. We
even had a decent crowd, for a change. And Billy had a
surprise for me. Fort Wayne scored twice in the top of the
first, mostly on walks and a couple of errors. When I came
in from left field Billy was standing on the dugout steps
holding my bat out to me.

"Don't sit down," he said, "you're leading off."

"Billy?" I said. What was he trying to do, pushing it
like that? Why, leading off I might even get a couple more
at-bats in, as he had to know. The chalkboard was still
there in the dugout, but it was lying under the bench and
there was nothing written on it, as if whoever had thought
it up in the first place had realized it was a bad joke and
was now trying to ignore it. A little calculating on the way
to the plate told me that a pair of extra chances, beyond
the ten I'd already figured on for the afternoon, would get
our bet up over a million dollars. I didn't know whether to
laugh or cry.

But one way or another, I didn't wait. Their first-game
pitcher was an aging major-leaguer sent down to work out

some mid-season shoulder miseries, but from what I could see of his warm-up pitches he hadn't worked out much of anything yet. I stepped up, tugged at my cap, tried to smile over at Billy but couldn't spot him right off in the dugout shadows, and cocked my bat. The first pitch was right down the pipe and had nothing on it. I took my swing and sent it bouncing on nice even hops right out to the short-stop. Then, just to make sure, in case that damn-fool high school kid let it go through his legs without touching it, I fell down on my way to first base.

BILLY DIDN'T HAVE a great deal to say to me for the rest of the season after that. He let me stay in the number-one slot, which was all the same to me, and I finished the year, like I said, at .397. When we had our final little get-together at McDougal's after the last game and just before everybody took off, most of them to play winter ball in Mexico or the Caribbean, Billy to go back to his wife and kids in New Jersey, he seemed a little sad and distant, and not much interested in all the beer that was flowing. We hadn't been there more than an hour before he stood up and announced he had to get on his way. He said good-bye and thanked everybody and then went around the tables, shaking hands with each of us. I was last. When he came to me, I got up and walked to the door with him. At the door I shook his hand and then reached in my pocket and took out a five-dollar bill, which was what I still owed him from all those bets, and tried to give it to him, but he wouldn't take it.

"Use it to buy the boys some more beer with," he said, and then he turned and left. I did, and then I left too.

Next season we had a new manager, a red-headed wild man, and I heard that Billy was managing Amarillo in the Texas League. Red, who had been a fine catcher till arthritis had started creeping into all his broken finger bones and knuckles, had the idea that a manager's job was to manage as much as possible, so he juggled the outfield around every couple of days or so and had me batting everywhere in the lineup but ninth. I never knew from one day to the next what field I'd be playing or where I'd be hitting. Curiously enough, we weren't doing any worse than under Billy. But it was all very unsettling for me, and the result was that around mid-season I found myself in the midst of the worst year I could remember. I was hitting .306, watching a lot of fat ones go by, and settling for a hit a game, mostly singles at that. Red wasn't very happy with either my attitude or my style of play and was platooning me with a fat farm boy who had a penchant for hitting tremendous homers with the bases empty and then striking out four times in a row with men on. But what did all that have to do with what I really wanted to do? Nothing, I realized, and then took off.

It was a Fourth of July doubleheader, and when I went four for five in the first game Red let me stay in for the second. I picked up three more hits in that one and kept on going. I had the hottest three weeks anybody ever saw. By the end of July, even with that chubby strike-out king getting his chances now and then, I was over .350 and going strong, even though Red still couldn't decide whether to have me bat first, third, or fifth. We were in Peoria and had just won the last of a three-game sweep with a 9–0 shutout in which I'd walked twice and then banged out three straight doubles to the exact same spot in left center. When I came out of the shower, I found Red waiting for me next to my locker. He sat on the bench and smoked a cigar without saying a word while I dressed, then he asked me to come with him. He had driven his own car up so that he could cut over to Chicago on our off-day to visit his family, so we sat in the car in the parking lot outside the ballfield until he finished his cigar and threw it out the window. Then he turned to me and started telling me what a fine job I was doing for the club, and what a great hitter I was.

"I know," I told him. "I've been hitting like that for a good many years now."

"Al," he said then, "I talked to the general manager this morning." I knew just what was coming next: "He said they could use a boost in their batting order up there."

"Red," I told him, "forget it. I've been there before. I hit here." He had a sudden pleading look in his eyes. They must have offered him a fat bonus if he could send someone up who would have a hot bat for the next few weeks. Even an old man like me.

"Look, Al," he said, "you can do it, I know you can. I've watched you hit. All you need is a little confidence." That did it.

"Red," I asked him, "what am I hitting?" He told me without even having to look it up: .357, including today's game.

"Red," I said, "that's not what I mean. I want to know what's my lifetime average." That took him back a bit, but since he was a hot one for managing and a demon for statistics, he was carrying all the club's record books with him. He reached over and got the big cumulative team book out of the back seat, along with the current season's book and a pencil and pad of paper. Then he lit up another cigar and sat and figured and chewed on it and relit it a couple of times and finally turned back in my direction.

"Well," he said, "I've checked it and double-checked it and it keeps coming out the same. Like I said, you're a fine hitter, Al."

"Red," I asked him, "Just tell me what it is."

"Well," he said, holding the paper up close to his face, "it figures out exactly at .36802."

"Red," I said, "I quit."

IT WAS JUST that easy, for me at least. Red spluttered and argued, and I was a little taken aback myself when we got back to Muncie and I went over to watch a Wednesday afternoon game with Cedar Rapids and Red wouldn't let me in the players' entrance but made me go around through the main gate and buy a ticket. I was about the only paying customer in the stands. He started to make some noise about my contract too, until he found out that it had been a good three years since I'd had anything more formal than a letter announcing my salary for the season. In spite of how angry he was, he still wanted to keep me on. I guess he thought I was at least some sort of stabilizing force on the team, good for the rookies going up and the veterans coming down. Fact was, I'd been around so long that some of the rookies I'd once seen going up were now the veterans on their way back down. The team, for that matter, didn't seem to do much different with or without me, and the farmer was already beginning to learn something about easing off on that wild swing of his.

What now? you may ask. Well I don't know. In a way I've jumped back a dozen years or so to where I was standing with a B.A. in one hand, an M.A. in the other, five years of semi-pro ball in my bones, and a little voice in my head saying, What do you want? What do you want? I didn't know, then I knew, then I got it, now I don't know again. I only know that I didn't just quit while I was ahead, unless you consider .00002 ahead. I know I got exactly what I peddled myself for. Who doesn't, as long as he's willing to go all the way with it? And I know I didn't get much else besides. Who does? I don't know what else I know.

The Bad Trip

Maxine Kumin

THE LEOPARD frogs are chuckling in the dark.
The sky holds up a brand new zodiac
and a diesel crossing the creek sends back
its wolf cry. We are sitting in a warm room
open to the turpentine of trees.
The wine goes round, and with it go these
stick fingers of stick men—Cambodian
contraband wrapped up in paper flags,
your flag and mine. The game is turning on.

Dreaming awake, I see the shapes of things
thicken their outlines like a Rouault painting.
The centers grow so clear they self-destruct.
The hifi thumps on a vault of underthoughts.
The offbeat bursts its doors, all locks unlock
and spaces hand-to-hand attenuate.
They sting like burned skin. Distances pivot.
The time that measures words yaws like a yoyo.
Someone speaks in my mouth. I admire the trick.
We are good children! We love one another! We all go
riding the wind's back to a dear republic.

But later, alone, I've played the game too well.
My heart hammers a hole from inside out.
Sparklers from a child's July needle
my eyes, start fires, will not be blinked shut.
Four things that were my arms and legs die down.
Porous enough to float, they are old stones.
The fingers are falling from this icy leper
but the mind hangs on spinning like a hot star.

I am afraid in three languages. I am
shipwrecked in poor French, beached in bad Russian,
cast up like a grain sack. J'ai peur. Old terrors come,
not one too small or secret to take in.

I am back at the local firehouse. I watch
the dogs dragged in on skidding toenails, one
by one, for their rabies shots. The floor's awash
with Pinesol, vomit, and the urine of fear.
They know as much as I and I know nothing.
It doesn't end. The cornered dogs are here.

And then you hold me. You, outside my tunnel,
my dark drownings, the knife thrower at the fair,
the noose, the ice fall, the starved hounds in the kennel.
You, crawling my long crawl out of the nightmare.

Foreshortening Dark

Peter Cooley

I

Summer, some evenings, a man wants to lay himself out,
edges to the sky; scutter, a sail there, perpendicular
to all desire, washing the sun. Or steady his life
mythic & definite, plinth for a god.

                              All at once
his future is beginning, blooming through his head as if
she's walking down his rib, bone-dark like stars.

Already, long fields of him are off & running, compass
to every distance on his map. Grasses take up
first names under his hands: leaning, they whisper
Let us live forever: now the small birds cry
Pray for us, spokes of the sun. The oak, the turtle,
worms, line up to chant: *tender your blessings, lord,*
that we survive. What is he making at arm's length?
he asks the fable a man's life
comes down to, not his Lady, now called "Fate"

who walks out of his side one night to show
how she can open for him, still water to lie down.
What question? We pull a curtain on the scene.

II

Sometimes, the sky turning, unexpected, gray
an instant, I turn from my work & tender, mute,
the question stutters back: Why is this mine? Because
the place is not, nor am I any but a claiming of
what others had. And suddenly what I had been
afraid of, why my life had seemed like chapters
filling daily with another, one I kept
inventing out of water, a character in prose:
this & all stone wrappings fall away. I hear the sun
begin to turn through me, my hardened lock. & suddenly
the bearings spring; I walk a night of which
each instant lit is different, falling aside the man
on the horizon, continuous, a picture, where like inks,
I had deposited myself for years & just
in the interest of this other, one who is, of course,
the Foreshadower, my only answerer, who says:

And wouldn't you like to lay your body wherever
you could? And couldn't you sleep in the ghost
of your other forever?

King Kong: A Meditation

Kenneth Bernard

TARZAN AND KONG

IT IS LOGICAL that having written at some length on King Kong I should turn to Tarzan of the Apes. There are many striking parallels. For example, their native habitat is jungle. Further, Tarzan, like Kong, seems unable to find his generative organ, or, if he has found it, seems equally unable to divine its function. Hence in both cases a good deal of sublimated sexuality in the form of encounters with wild beasts. (A good question here is, how would Tarzan and Kong have gotten along? Perhaps they would have established what one critic has described as an innocent homosexual relationship. Can you imagine, for example, Kong and Tarzan floating down the Mississippi on a raft, sharing a perfect trust and understanding as well as naked moonlit swims under the stars?) But all this is really by the way, though not without a certain interest. What makes Tarzan of the Apes peculiarly interesting to me at the moment is his faculty of speech. Kong, for all his expressiveness, for all his frustrated flooding at the gates of articulation, is a dumb brute, whereas Tarzan has given utterance to several of our civilization's notable word and vowel configurations.

Take "HUNGAWA!" for example. (One is reminded, perhaps, of Eliot's "Hakagawa.") This is almost invariably the directive Tarzan gives to an elephant when a situation is critical. Miles off (down or up river), a young, frightened woman is about to be ripped into four pieces by bent saplings as lascivious sweating savages leer at her. (It is really very stupid of them, since all they can do afterwards is eat her.) But crashing through the bush on the tide of "HUNGAWA!" come Tarzan and his elephant (or sometimes elephants). She will be saved (though not won); the savages will scatter in jabbering fear as their meager huts are crushed by an elephant's foot. It would be a mistake, of course, to think that "HUNGAWA!" meant only "Hurry!" Sometimes it means "Push." And sometimes "Gather ye (elephants, beasts of the jungle, et cetera) round." On at least one occasion it was addressed to a lion and meant, roughly, "Cut it out! Behave yourself!" Upon (repeated) which, the lion slunk off. In other words, context and tone (even repetition) are everything. One constant, though, is the imperative, the exclamatory. Urgency and command are always there. It is man's Ur-*cri* for crisis—but crisis in which man still feels the power to control. There would be something laughable in the businessman rushing by taxi to catch his train shouting "HUNGAWA!" (The cab driver would fix his wagon promptly.) But how appropriate for the astronaut at blast-off to scream "HUNGAWA!" to the TV audience. What a thrilling link of old and new.

Another notable expression of Tarzan's is the discovery, "Me Tarzan, you Jane." This is the quintessential boy meets girl. With the reservation that Tarzan does not know the generative function of his penis. It is quite likely that Jane does not either; otherwise she would learn to use "HUNGAWA!" for her own end. A horrendous scene would be Jane screaming "HUNGAWA!" like a fishwife at Tarzan and Tarzan scratching his head in befuddlement, as did Kong when he held the screaming blond maiden in his fist for the first time. (Why is she screaming? What does she think I will do to her?) But Jane does not know about his penis. That is why she spends so much time swimming. But her relationship to elephants is significantly different from his. She obviously gets a different feeling from riding them than does Tarzan. It is not blatantly sexual, but quite clearly we would see nothing wrong with grape juice dripping down her chin while astride an elephant. Tarzan, on the other hand, never masturbates. He simply does not know it. Yet, contradictorily, we feel he disapproves of it (whatever it is), and speaks harshly to his household chimps when he catches them at it. Jane is probably more permissive.* This slight difference in their natures would undoubtedly have pushed them to some domestic crisis in which Tarzan could not have shouted "HUNGAWA!" There would ultimately have to be a limit to the amount of swimming Jane could take, or flowers in her hair (what a clever game, that), or pineapple stuffed in her mouth, or tandem swinging through the trees. They are saved from this crisis by the discovery of Boy in the jungle. They have fulfilled the Biblical injunction and multiplied. Yet one senses some artificiality in all this. For example, "Me Tarzan, you Jane, him Boy" clearly does not have the epic rightness of the shorter phrase. Equally clearly, some accommodation has been made. And in this accommodation we have one of those mirror instances in which we see ourselves naked, so to speak. Because it is all right with us. We are content to have them find Boy in an overgrown cabbage patch. We *want* Jane to go on swimming and Tarzan to go on fighting crocodiles and renegade lions. Just as we do not want Kong to violate that blond maiden, so too we do not want Tarzan to share carnal knowledge with Jane. Yet at the same time these are precisely what we do want. We want Kong to grow big and approach the blond maiden with bloodshot, lustful eyes. Similarly, one day when Jane has arisen dripping from her swim and is awaiting her flower in the hair, we want Tarzan to rip off her garment and shout "HUNGAWA!" The elephants would undoubtedly come running but would not necessarily be a problem. Boy, in this event, would become the jungle's first juvenile delinquent; his reversion to abandonment would be too much after reigning as Tarzan's heir apparent. Perhaps he would seek his

---

* We must also bear in mind, I think, that Jane is a barbarian American and Tarzan an Englishman, Lord Greystoke, to be precise. In whatever he does, there is a "natural outcropping of many generations of fine breeding, an hereditary instinct of graciousness which a lifetime of uncouth and savage training and environment could not eradicate" (*Tarzan of the Apes*, Chapter XX). Thus, though he may eat the raw meat of a lion he has just killed, his erections must in no way intrude, that is, rattle the teacups. There is also, perhaps, just a *schmeck* of Anglophobia in having Jane, whose breeding is, after all, only acquired, civilize the apelike English lord.

real father. Perhaps he would destroy Tarzan and Jane's first genital child. In sum, civilization would ensue. But this is not what happens. The balance is kept. Paradise is not lost. We have our cake and eat it, too, for in fantasy we penetrate the blond maiden and Jane, are ravished by the vision of innocence outrageously, stupendously lost. Tarzan or Kong with erections are unthinkable, but somewhere in the furry depth, beneath that loincloth, they *lurk*, waiting to spring to life at our call. And at that moment, civilization will destroy itself, for we could not, in our finitude, in our infantilism, stand that much joy. We would go mad with it and run raging in the streets. Kong, because in effect he *wants* his erection, must be destroyed. Tarzan, the docile one, we allow to live. "HUNGAWA!" is no fit comparison for Kong's shrieks of rage on the Empire State Building as bullets pour into him. It is the pain and anger of all men in their betrayal. Deep within us we all cry out for the blond maiden to violate, to plunge the very Empire State into her and achieve orgasm with the cosmos. But we do not, we cannot. We must content ourselves with a "HUNGAWA!" to the elephants and the lions, while Jane, sleek and wet (but ever clothed) with the lily-studded water, swims ever away, even as we join her and swim down, down into the misty depths.

HOW BIG IS KONG'S PENIS?

IN A RECENT meditation on King Kong and Tarzan of the Apes, I wrote the following: "We want Kong to grow big and approach the blond maiden with bloodshot, lustful eyes." There are several interesting problems here. For example, Fay Wray, the blond maiden, who is to say she is a maiden? (Actually, she is not even blond.) When found by the impresario Carl Denham and taken to a waterfront cafe (read *dive*), she is alone and starving. She is down on her luck. She has come upon *bad times*. Denham clearly wants someone with nothing more to lose, and when he sees her there is a flash, or burst, of recognition. The cards, we can say, are pretty heavily stacked against maidenhood. Yet, surprisingly, Fay Wray *is* a maiden, which gives this adventure much of its fairy-tale quality. We know this from a scene that is not (and could not be) in the movie but which obviously had to take place. For years the island savages have been giving maidens to Kong. They are not going to break with tradition simply because Fay Wray is white. The whiteness is merely an added spice, or sauce. She must be maiden *and* white. The scene not included in the movie is that wherein the chief, the elders, and the midwives of the tribe examine a naked Fay Wray gynecologically. As all those black fingers probe and poke Fay Wray, she must be thinking that nothing can be worse than this, just as in the waterfront cafe she had thought she could sink no lower. How wrong she was and is. This limit to her imagination makes Kong's initial appearance all the more devastating. Kong is literally *beyond her wildest imaginings.* It is worth noting that Fay's first vision of Kong is an (arch) typical bride's first night fantasy of her husband. When Kong appears, Fay Wray is severed forever from the civilization that bred her. The unspeakable has become life. If her mind has not already been sprung by the savages' examination of her virgin body, it surely is now. She will never be the same. In any event, it is clear that the savages would not have offered her to Kong had they not been assured of her maidenhood. We could also adduce as proof the evidence of the first mate's love for her: his instinct would not have failed him: no *used* woman (and he surely knew them) could have aroused him to a pure love. But this is superfluous; the anthropological inference is conclusive enough.

A second interesting point in the quotation is the oblique reference to Kong's penis in the phrase "to grow big." Exactly how big *is* Kong's penis? It is a matter of monumental cultural and psychological interest. And a great mystery: for *Kong's penis is never shown; he is no common monkey in the zoo.* (Its absence, of course, is the reason why it is dreamed about so much.) It is quite possible that Denham, before he leaves the island with Kong, emasculates him (in another unfilmed episode) ° to assure his

° Dare I suggest how admirable this scene, as well as the earlier one between Fay Wray and the savages, would be, today, in Technicolor or Vista-Vision?

docility later on. (An interesting question here is, if this is so, what did the savages do with it or them? There is quite possibly an interesting totemic myth buried here.) That might well explain Kong's interest in the Empire State Building later on. Realizing that he is without his penis or its generative power (in fact or in his mind—for his defeat and humiliation at Denham's hands may well have resulted in a psychological emasculation, a temporary impotence), and that there is something he cannot do with Fay Wray without it, he seeks to attach another penis to himself. Here his ape brain reveals itself. (Question: Does Fay Wray have any inkling of what Kong intends? Probably, though only an inkling. Kong constantly shatters the limits of her nightmares. He plunges her from one insanity into another —but who is to say that heaven itself is not awaiting her within that final, absolute, insanity?) If this is so, we might well accuse Kong of a certain immodesty. A penis (even erect) the size of the Empire State Building? But we cannot be sure, for we have never seen it. There is, however, some slight indirect evidence of size. When Kong storms the walls that separate him from the savages, seeking his stolen maiden, with what does he batter them? It is definitely a possibility. But still, not Empire State dimension, not even the upper dome. We can only put *that* gesture down to a rage beyond all reason.

Which still leaves us with the problem of Kong's penis. There is, of course, the peculiar behavior of Kong from the beginning. He obviously does not ravish Fay Wray immediately. He is not even sexually curious about her. How are we to explain his early *playfulness* with her and his later *libidinous determination?* (He has not chosen the Empire State idly.) The answer, I think, is to be found in his age. Kong, up through his island adventures with Fay, is a child. He sees her merely as a new and unusual plaything. (What has happened to his earlier playthings is problematical. As I have indicated elsewhere, I lean toward the idea that he ate them.) But, during his voyage to America (possibly even just before the voyage, if we bear the wall-battering in mind), he arrives at puberty, and in America he is a young adult—hence his altered interest in Fay. But now there is no penis or penis power with which to effect his end. Part of his problem (assuming Denham's butchery, which we need not) is that he very likely has little recollection of his penis and what its varying aspects were. (Question: *Did* Kong ever masturbate?) He is also unsettled from the sea voyage, the gas, and the total change in environment. Hence his berserk casting about for a substitute.

But *we* need not be equally at sea. A simple scientific approach will give us at least a reasonable working hypothesis. One of Kong's first destructive acts in the New World is the wrecking of an elevated train and its track. The track is about twenty feet off the ground and reaches Kong's shoulders. Kong therefore must be about twenty-four feet tall. Further, we can usually count on a six-foot man having a three-inch inert and six-inch erect penis. Assuming the validity of comparative anatomy, we can say therefore that Kong's penis would be twelve inches inert and twenty-four inches, or two feet, erect. And this is a startling fact. Because it really doesn't seem so very big. Even its fatness would not increase its shock impact, for the fatter it is, the *shorter* it would seem. Possibly it is some horrendous blue or purple, or pointed, or wickedly curved—but even these would have limited shock value. A more experienced woman than Fay might even, *momentarily and in spite of herself,* entertain the thought of what it would be like. So we are left with this fact: that the penis Kong ought to have is insufficient to cause the terror and anxiety he inspires. Therefore the penis Kong has is the one he *ought not* to have. Of course one can suggest that the horror of Kong is in his size *in general,* that is, a twenty-four-foot ape—but only to reject it. For the entire drama of Kong is not built around his general size or destructiveness but around his relationship with Fay Wray. And the entire point of this relationship is that it is male and female, and that it aspires to the condition of consummation! The only question—and it harbors an anxiety that reaches into the very depth of our civilization—is *When?* When will Kong's twenty-four-inch erect penis penetrate the white and virgin (and quivering) body of Fay Wray? And there, of course, we have the solution. It is easily conceivable that in these circumstances some people, perhaps many, would say, "Who cares?" Precisely. Twenty-four inches is not *that* awe-inspiring. But people say no such thing. *It is obvious that Kong must exceed the estimates of comparative anatomy to inspire the universal dread that he does.*

Kong's penis, therefore, is at least six feet inert and twelve feet erect (or seventy-two and one hundred and forty-four inches respectively). In a state of sexual excitement it very likely rises over his head. *That* would certainly explain the battering at the savages' wall, and it certainly explains the terror in New York City's streets: a twenty-four-foot ape with a twelve-foot erection stalking the streets for his woman. The blasé mode is simply not possible in the face of such a Kong. No experience is equal to it. There is no room for wonder, only fear. And so, in the end, when Kong, half-crazed by the bullets and frustrations he has experienced, identifies sexually with the Empire State Building, he is not, after all, being immodest. He has sought only what all true lovers seek, in the only way that he could. He has brought his love to the threshold of his love and valiantly persevered to his last desperate breath. Dazed beyond recall, so near and yet so far, he loosens his grip, his fingers slip. No longer can he guide his new-found power into her. Kong cannot live erect in the New World. And uttering a last terrifying cry from within his battered heart (who will ever forget it?), he falls, falls ever so far, perhaps momentarily remembering the lushness of his island paradise, wet from dew in the silent and foggy primeval morning, falls to his cold and concrete death. In truth, as Carl Denham mutters, Fay Wray hath killed the beast.

THE MIND AND HEART OF FAY WRAY

IT IS CLEAR to me that far too little attention has been paid to Fay Wray, the love of King Kong. Not only is her experience terrifying and transcendental (*sublime*, as Burke would have it), but it is also not lost on her. When Kong dies, Fay Wray knows that no other lover in her life will be equal to him. She may not be able to articulate the changes that have placed her beyond merely human experiences, but she has absorbed them, she is alive and (psychologically) whole: she has confronted King Kong and received his blessing. But she has in no sense *returned*. She is as a stranger among an alien breed. She will henceforth dwell among them but not be *of* them. Had she experienced sexual union with Kong, she would (also) have been omnipotent and omniscient. In this essay I should like to discuss several aspects of her psycho-psychical journey.

The Disappearing Bottom

WHEN WE FIRST encounter Fay Wray, she is the most ordinary of women, except in one respect. She has fallen down the socioeconomic ladder. Her attitude at this point is that little, if anything, worse can happen to her. She has touched bottom. What makes her different from other girls is that instead of laughing at Carl Denham's crackpot offer she eagerly accepts it. This decision is focal: all things come from it. It is a decision that reflects deeply on her character. However, this decision is also the beginning of a series of false states of mind. For at the moment Fay Wray decides in favor of Denham's proposal, she thinks that she is rising from the bottom. In fact, the bottom has just dropped, and she is falling further. She reaches the new bottom when the island savages seize her (we shall examine this in detail later). For now we can say that once more Fay Wray thinks nothing could be worse, but in fact the bottom has again dropped and she is falling. (It is part of Fay's destiny always to have her worst expectations exceeded.) She reaches a new low when, tied to the stake outside the savages' protective barrier, she hears and then sees King Kong for the first time. At this point, being down and out in a waterfront cafe must seem like heaven to her. Although she is conscious here of things being worse than they were with the savages, she knows that they are probably going to get still worse when Kong actually reaches her. Death, of course, will be the absolute bottom, and she cannot face it; she faints. When she comes to, she realizes that Kong perhaps has other ideas, and once more the bottom has dropped: she now faces a fate worse than death.* She exists in this extreme anxiety until she is rescued. Again the feeling of rising from the bottom. Then Kong returns for her (some brief anxiety), is subdued by Denham, and carried to the New World. Fay Wray has, apparently, reached *the* bottom and come back to tell the tale. Although she must undoubtedly be psychologically wary, she is relieved, she relaxes, she feels it is all over. She is about to resume her former life, but on a higher socioeconomic plane. And then the bottom drops again: Kong escapes, finds her, and takes her to the top of the Empire State Building.

Kong and the Empire State Building: the meeting of two giants. (Which one will get Fay?) Kong is on the verge of a great symbolic act. He will ram the Empire State into Fay as if it were (as in a sense it is) his very own. It is a desperate, noble, futile, tragic attempt on a par with Ahab's defiance of his finitude. But Ahab's attempt, while broadly human, is entirely personal (monomaniacal, as his first mate realizes). Kong's attempt is personal, yes, but it is also grandly humanitarian, an attempt to reunite two worlds God never meant to be separate. However, it is too late. Any progeny of such a union could be only monstrous (or totally holy, which would be monstrous). The distance is too great; time has become too irrevocable. Here Kong seems not so much apelike as he does innocent. Here we take him most to our hearts. He is, like Prometheus, Satan, and Faust, one of myth's great losers. (Or, in more recent times, winners.) For raising the specter of what has been so poignantly lost (and forgotten), he must be viciously cut down. Civilization has too much riding on its Empire State to give it up.

---

* Or, to be more correct, cf. E. R. Burroughs' *Tarzan of the Apes,* Chapter XIX, when Terkoz, the deposed ape leader, bends Jane Porter to his "awful fangs": "But ere they touched that fair skin another mood claimed the anthropoid. The tribe had kept his women. He must find others to replace them. This hairless white ape would be the first of his new household, and so he threw her roughly across his broad hairy shoulders and leaped back into the trees, bearing Jane Porter away toward *a fate a thousand times worse than death.*" [my italics]

It is entirely to Fay Wray's credit that at the end, she has an inkling on some level of the nobility of Kong (he is not called King for nothing), and of the tragedy of his fall. At any point in this odyssey Fay Wray could, of course, have gone mad. And she has that option now. I obviously do not think she exercises it. The Kong experience has, let me repeat, consistently destroyed her notions of what the worst could possibly be. Its effect has been to instill the idea that things could always be worse, that the bottom could (is) always open. For most people, the idea of an absolute bottom is necessary; the idea of a continually receding bottom is too great an anxiety. But it may well be the beginning of true wisdom. When Kong finally lies dead (Question: Will—*can*—Kong *ever* die?) on the pavement, it would be easy for Fay Wray to think, "It's over at last," and go about her business. I do not believe that is her thought. If it were, she would still be a very ordinary girl. But she is much more pensive. True, Kong is (seems) dead. It (the nightmare) is (seems) over. But she looks at him more like a lover. Not a lover in flesh any longer: a lover in spirit. Somehow, she senses, Kong's death *is* tragic. And part of its tragic quality is that Kong, in addition to being her lover, has been her teacher—but an unearthly, transcendental, metaphysical teacher. He has exploded her forever out of all possible human complacency, and there at the extreme of anxiety she has found peace, a peace that removes her from the ken of almost all other humans. Kong is dead, but Kong lives in Fay Wray. And if one does not know this, one does not know Fay Wray.

The Examination

BEFORE FAY WRAY is offered to Kong, the savages ascertain that she is a virgin and therefore worthy of being offered. This is done by an examination. The examination is conducted by the chief, the elders, and the midwives of the tribe. It is even conceivable that the entire tribe is witness. At any rate, Fay Wray is stripped and laid bare on a (bamboo?) platform in a fire-lit hut. Her legs are forced apart, and black fingers probe, pull, and manipulate her. God only knows what she imagines is going to happen. No doubt she yearns for the good old days on the waterfront. The savages are curious about her in general, and in spite of the business at hand they must be oohing and ahing over peripheral matters like her pale nipples (are they erect?), her skin, and her corn-silk pubic hairs, some of which they pluck (*why?*). Fay Wray has never been so naked, so exposed, so manhandled in her life. Being lower class she has never even had a gynecological examination. She is, in spite of herself of course, phantasmagorically titillated.

Two important things are happening here. The first is that Fay Wray is feeling totally *abandoned* by her world. She could not, at that moment, be further away from it. Nothing in her experience has prepared her for this. Dialogue, for example, is impossible. Imagine, if you will, the total inefficacy of, say, "What are you doing?" or "Please, you're hurting me." Not even the females look familiar to her or reachable. Everything is *strange*. Her thoughts, her sensations, are *new*. Needless to say, she also feels existentially abandoned, by her god. Where can God be if there are black fingers in her private parts? This aspect of her experience is to be repeated in the jungle with Kong (during, in effect, their honeymoon) when Kong battles prehistoric creatures. (How does one react to real pterydactyls trying to eat one up?) An interesting juxtaposition for her must be the occasion when Kong and her first-mate lover are present and a *Tyrannosaurus rex* attacks. How ineffective and remote must seem the strengths and values of her society then. It is Kong who saves her by killing the lizard.*

The second important function of this episode is that by deranging her from the usual and the known it is preparing her for Kong, a still further derangement. Her despair becomes manageable in part by its *gradual* escalation.

* It is interesting, by way of comparison, to note that when Tarzan rescues the prim and proper Jane Porter by killing the concupiscent ape Terkoz, she springs forward, suddenly the primeval woman, and embraces and kisses him with panting lips. (*Tarzan of the Apes*, Chapter XIX) Fay has no such reversion.

Nevertheless, one must see that in the end Fay has been *staggeringly* prepared. It is difficult to say whether Fay knows how much depends on her being a virgin. Had she been an experienced woman, the savages might simply have eaten her outright. In this one respect, her American upbringing has saved her for the greater experience of Kong. As low as she had fallen in America, she had not fallen so low as to sell the precious jewel of herself (eloquent testimony to America's higher standards of living). Poor but pure is an adequate description of the Fay that Carl Denham propositions for Kong.

Fay and Kong's Penis

FAY'S ATTITUDE toward Kong's penis is a ticklish problem. On the one hand there is the purely bestial part of it (the lesser part, we might say). On the other, there are the several metaphorical tensions. Let us take them in order. Fay the rather ordinary virgin of the masses is terrified of Kong's penis, which is huge. No normal girl wants to make love with a giant gorilla. (Yet, how often will a woman describe her lover affectionately as a "big gorilla" or a "hairy ape"?) But Fay, the woman of wisdom through nightmare, is aware that the loss of Kong's penis, although it would probably have killed her as it thrilled her, is tragic. It is a loss that will haunt her all her life. She grows from one woman into the other as she sees Kong change from monster supreme to victim supreme. Kong begins as horror and ends as martyr, and in the process his penis is humanized (tenderized). The impossible union between Fay and Kong is symbolic of mankind's fatal *impasse*, the dream of paradise lost irrevocably.* However, this particular symbolic inference is complicated by several other factors, notably the idea that Kong is the black man violating American womanhood and the idea that Kong is the emerging (and rampant) Third World nations. With the first we

* I think that somewhere in the Kong story (I am not sure where) there is a moment (but only a moment) when all *does* seem possible, even Paradise. (Cf. the double vision of America at the end of *The Great Gatsby*.)

suffer from colossal penis envy and ego collapse, for we sense Fay's attraction in spite of herself. In the latter, we have violated Kong's sanctuary and brought him back for profit and display, and now he threatens (literally) to screw us. Kong is the classic myth of racist and imperialist repression and anxiety. Carl Denham is the white entrepreneur *par excellence*. Like Rappaccini in his noxious garden, he fosters evil into being. His manipulation of Fay and Kong for side-show profit and fame is instinctive. He is also stupid. Confronted with tragedy of epic magnitude, he mutters nasally that Beauty killed the Beast. Kong's sex organ (seen, dreamed, inferred, or guessed at) is indicative of our fear of his creative energy. Our destruction of him is confession of our limited imagination. His death will weigh on us more heavily than his life, and it is part of his power that he will be continuously resurrected (by us, in fact).

Fay has come to this knowledge, and it is only in her faith in Kong and his memory that there is any hope for all of us. In these respects, we can say that Kong leaps sexually erect into New York City's streets directly from our nightmares of guilt. We have created him and can no longer awaken from him. Denham is our blundering and loud middleman. And Fay is our vulnerability in a nutshell. Her yielding to Kong, spiritually if not physically, is felt as a betrayal. But a betrayal we ourselves *will*. (We *are* ambivalent about her and Kong.) Hence a frequently suicidal madness that engulfs us. Given time, Fay in her understanding might well have come to love Kong physically, might well have accommodated herself (as the sex books tell us) to Kong's penis. But there is no time. Kong is killed and split into millions of Kongs. And they are coming at us without quarter.

The idea of Kong leading a rat charge on New York City is entirely reasonable. For Americans, rats and cockroaches and bedbugs (vermin) are the living presence of the dark-skinned hordes, the *teeming* masses which spread themselves like crud over the face of the earth. Which is why, of course, the lower we go on the socio-ethno-economic ladder, the less we worry about them (i.e., vermin): they *belong*. A recent eruption of rats on Park Avenue caused matrons to pee in their pants and call the police. The mayor of New York peed in *his* pants when it was discovered that welfare people (epi-vermin) were living in the Waldorf Astoria (something like finding a rat using your toothbrush). By the same token, our hygienic mode is an attempt to keep America safe (pure). If ever the cockroaches and their brethren get out of hand, the *others* will not be far behind. But spick-and-span as our bathrooms are, we can never lose the awareness of all that dank plumbing in the cellar. Where *do* the pipes (finally) go? What conspiracy is happening down there in the sewers? We can never totally lose our anxiety about sitting on the toilet because when the invasion comes, there is where we are vulnerable: a black hand reaching up from the toilet bowl and grabbing our testicles when we are most unprepared. Our behaviorists, meanwhile, allay our fears by telling us all rats can be taught to drink tea. They literally have rats on the brain. Behavioral psychology is the last refuge of the imperialist.

KONG AS TOAD

AND NOW WE COME to the fairy-tale aspects of the Kong legend. There is, of course, a great deal of charm in the Kong-Fay Wray romance. Consider, for example, the vapidity of Fay Wray before her discovery of Kong. She swallows Denham's tale whole and fantasizes on the purely meretricious glory that will be hers. Any girl with half a brain would have sent Denham packing. But through Kong, Fay Wray becomes a *woman* (*King Kong* is in many ways a *portrait*). She develops a depth of understanding about the nature of life that comes close to being wisdom. Her silences are no longer blank. She is *transformed*, though not at all in the way she first envisioned. We tend to lose sight of this change in her because of all the *noise* (violence) and Kong's dramatic end. But if we concentrate on other aspects of the Kong story, we can begin to see these other possibilities.

For example, his *playfulness*. Even when Kong kills, there is often an element of playfulness in it. He seems more a petulant child than a savage beast. When in the beginning he clutches a writhing Fay Wray in his fist and she is screaming, he cocks his head and looks puzzled, as if to say, "Now what the devil is the matter with this funny little mouse?" When he plucks the screaming woman from her bed and drops her to the street, he is the child who is dropping his toy because it is the wrong one. Even when he is enraged by the sperm bullets the planes shoot into him at the end, he is the child who doesn't understand *why* he is being abused, *why* he is feeling pain. There is more puzzlement than animosity in him.

What I am saying here is that there is a colossal innocence in Kong that exists ostensibly in the midst of much evil: Kong has no awarenes of doing bad things. We must learn to see and understand that. In this respect his inarticulateness is a reinforcement: Kong cannot speak because he is *too young.* But it is even more than that. The words *too young* do not mean, or say, enough. They only shadow, are emblematic. Kong is, in a sense, pre-experience; he is *prior* to experience and the consciousness that it implies. Articulation is the (deceiving) tool of civilization. Further, Kong very often seems on the *edge of articulation.* He seems often about to *tumble* into speech. But he does not. And he does not because he is *imprisoned.* With his arms, especially with his eyes, he reaches out constantly. His eyes are, in fact, the eyes of the lifelong prisoner. They plead, they cry, they scream—but they do not speak.

And the question for us is, first, who is behind those eyes? who is imprisoned within Kong? And second, what is it that will free him? (Perhaps there is a third: *should* he be freed?) The second is, I think, best answered first, because it is very easy to answer. In the familiar story, the princess kisses the frog and he becomes a handsome prince. The kiss I think we may understand to be merely symbolic. In the Kong epic, the kiss would be insignificant. Fay Wray's head would easily fit in Kong's mouth. None of the film's anxieties relate to kissing. No, what is needed to free Kong is for Fay Wray to give herself sexually to Kong out of love and trust. That alone would allow Kong to break through. That she does not do it is part of the tragedy of the story. Although Fay Wray does arrive at a deepness of womanhood at the end, it is a deepness with nowhere to go. She *understands* but now there is no application possible. She is the living memorial of the tragedy of loss. But just what would Kong have been freed into? *Who* is imprisoned within Kong?

That is a difficult question. It is obvious that no mere beast provoked such a depth of response in Fay and others, but rather the *intimations of something other,* within, something frightening, incredible, even transcendent. Otherwise we should not weep for Kong, as we do; his death would not be tragic, as it is. Perhaps Kong is twice or even thrice enchanted, that is, sexual union with Fay would only turn him into a frog, so to speak, leaving her with another ordeal, or several. (Could faith be more severely tried?) For all the change that her encounter with Kong has provoked, Fay has, in one sense, only been *prepared* for the real change, which can come only as the result of one thing. Kong's death leaves her imprisoned as well as him—but with a deep awareness of the change she can now never experience. I don't think that Kong would turn into a handsome prince as a result of union with Fay. Nor do I think that he would turn into, say, a dwarf or a pumpkin, though the ramifications are interesting. Perhaps he would just expire beautifully, or disappear, and it would all be with the seed (so large) he would leave in Fay. Jesus, son of Kong! Or something like. Fay, then, would become the bearer of mankind's redemption. A chance to regain Paradise. For surely Adam in the Garden is *not* so remote from Kong. Would not he, too, have been inarticulate with confusion and rage in the New World? Would not he, too, have been cornered atop the Empire State Building for daring to walk the streets with his penis erect? His affront to civilization would never have been tolerated. Sometimes I think that Kong should be opera. What grand arias Kong would have. But even opera is not *big* enough. Who, in voice, could project the edifice of Kong's gigantic penis? And what a stage would be needed. Alas, in our heads the drama remains. Kong *is* godlike in his unprogenitured existence. That jungle has *always* known Kong. We cannot say Kong, son of. We can only say Kong *is* and Kong *was.* And therein lie much history and sorrow.

The Heroine

Peter Davison

1.

SHE WAS one of the few I can speak of to believe
in personal destiny; the only one who swore
by holy writ that death was worth gambling on;
the meanest spirit to claim a martyrdom
since sainthood ended. What a cunning braggart
she was, a frailty who pictured herself
as a rider of skis, of waves, of men, of horses.
She lugged about a pessary in her purse
like a baloney sandwich in a lunchbox
and referred to Dylan Thomas and the sun
in the tone of voice reserved for recent lovers.
Breck hair, white scarves, clean flesh, hard muscles,
sun-worship, and a trough of molten and remorseless work.

2.

I've seen her love-letters—those she wrote
to other men while she was using me—
and her hate-letters—those she wrote
to me while she was using them—but only once
or twice her tiny writing in a different hand,
tilted across the page, wounded but credible
as the early-morning trail of half an earthworm,
speaking of her selfhood in the tiny voice
that had been hers as a child, hers once as a girl, hers, hers.
In the usual rooms she spoke in a voice more humble
than the one she wrote in, cozening her larynx
to belie the costumes of ambition, clothes
Mother had dressed her in to go to school.
In saddle-shoes and page-boy bob, disguised
as Betty Boop, inculcable, unresisting,

she set out bait for poets and professors.
She was as innocuous as Lenin in Switzerland.

3.

The passage of the years bathed her again and again
in acid. Skin thin as onions, she hugged cringing
her throbbing flesh to herself and learned to climb
the headwalls of her solitary cell.
Husband, children, poems grated on her.
Each taught her a little more of how humans do it,
until the relentless cadence began that would
transform her heart. A tiny voice struck up
its canticle of hatred for ambition—
his, hers, or anyone's—and so, snarling
and sobbing in all her voices,
she leveled the forests of ego,
whirling around her blonde head with a sneer
a sword as keen and holy as a samurai's.

Lucky Pierre and the Music Lesson

Robert Coover

There is a young girl at the door, smiling cheerfully,
dressed in a pinafore with full skirts, a crêpe de chine
buttoned blouse, and high-buttoned shoes. Over her soft
curls, she wears a lacy bonnet, tied under the chin. The
man, ramrod straight in his black tuxedo, scowls down at
her. She curtsies, her head bowed in guilt. Words appear:

YOU ARE LATE!

O MERCY, SIR! I AM ALL ALONE IN
THE WORLD! MY MUMMY AND DADDY ARE
IN HEAVEN AND I MUST CARE FOR ALL
THE LITTLE ONES! PLEASE DO NOT
BE HARSH!

He grimaces coldly, unappeased. He snaps his finger
silently, and meekly she follows him.

They enter an ornate music room with high velvet drapes
and thin patterned carpets. Daylight filters grainily through
net curtains, falling on the highly polished surface of the
grand piano. Bookcases and landscape paintings in heavy
gilt frames line the somber walls, half lost in dense shadow.
On the mantel of the tiled fireplace, reflected in the
gilded mirror over, are gleaming brass candlesticks, a
small comport encrusted with flowers and cupids, a walnut
mantel clock, a set of ivory elephants, and two china figures
of a lady and a gentleman seated on couches. Bellows and
a brass bedwarmer with a five-foot handle hang nearby.
Along the near wall: a row of cushioned chairs with fluted
legs and high scalloped backs. On two of them sit small
girls, a glitter on their young cheeks as though of tears. A
third child stands by the piano, wiping fresh tears from

her eyes. There is a metronome on the piano, an Oriental vase with dried flowers, and a polished birch rod. As the new girl enters, the girl by the piano leaves her place and joins the other two, rubbing her eyes with one hand, her bottom with the other. The new girl watches this with some amazement, glances apprehensively at her professor, at the birch rod on the piano.

He sits on the piano bench, tossing his tuxedo tails behind him. He stiffens his back and with a flourish strikes an unheard chord, then nimbly runs the gamut with long white fingers. He turns to the new girl, standing uneasily beside him, still wearing her bonnet, her hands clasped nervously at her child's breasts, and smiles perfunctorily. He strikes a key and indicates that she is to sing the note. She purses her lips into a small "o." He shakes his head, shapes his own mouth into a broad "O," doubles his chin, holds his hands, palms up, at his diaphragm, and moves them slowly up and down as though lifting some weight. Again, he strikes the key, as she attempts to sing the note more openly. He is still dissatisfied, and waggles his finger at her in admonishment. He rolls up a quarto of music, stuffs it in his mouth, slowly withdraws it, holding his lips in the rounded position fixed by the rolled quarto. She attempts to imitate this. No, no, no! He stands, motions her to open wide her mouth, pokes the rolled music into it. He shapes her cheeks around it with his fingers, as though modeling clay, ignoring her gagging. He withdraws the music carefully. Though her chin is quivering and there are tears in the corners of her eyes, she holds her lips in the molded position—but as soon as he strikes the note she is to sing, her mouth pinches reflexively into a smaller "o" once more. He leaps up, she clutches her mouth in guilt and embarrassment. He pulls her hands away, stuffs the rolled music into her mouth, withdraws it partway, thrusts it in again, out, in, out, in, finally, very carefully, out altogether. He smiles, gestures encouragingly with upraised palms, hold it, just like that, dear, sits quickly, strikes the key: success! He smiles. She smiles faintly, almost afraid to relax her mouth. He pats her hand.

He proceeds to climb the scale, note by note, twisting his mouth broadly around each of the sol/fa syllables of the heptachord, she imitating him, anxious to please, terrified to fail. On the subdominant, he claps his hands over his ears and grimaces. She shrinks away, clutching both hands at her mouth. He lowers his hands, clenched and trembling in anger, glowers at the girl, then forces a grim smile on his pale face. He commences the scale again, urging her to try harder. She takes a deep breath, and again stretches her mouth around each of the syllables, and again, on the fourth note, she offends him—he leaps up in rage and grabs the polished hickory rod. He orders her to lie down across his knees. She shakes her head, seems about to run. He smiles cruelly, repeats his order. Too frightened finally not to obey, she kneels, leans tentatively forward, keeping a suspicious eye on her voice teacher. He shoves her brusquely on across his lap, and holding her down by force, strikes her smartly across the skirts with his rod. She starts to rise, momentarily breaking free, her face showing confusion, astonishment, indignation.

Abruptly, she is across his legs again; it is as though something has been passed over. Her skirts are up now, and her bottom, receiving new blows, is protected only by a pair of woolen drawers. The man signals to the other pupils, and they come and unloose the drawers, pulling them down to her knees. Smoothing down his moustache, the man gloats unabashedly over his view of this smooth plump bum, still thrashing about rebelliously. He seems to enjoy all this movement, and wriggles about beneath it with unconcealed pleasure.

> WHAT A DELICIOUS EXPANSE OF SNOW-
> WHITE BOTTOM! HOW I LONG TO CUT
> IT INTO RIBBONS OF WEALED FLESH
> AND BLOOD!

He assumes a mock-serious face once more, and lectures the girl. Then he wets his fingers with spittle, marks a damp spot on one cheek, and brings the big birch down on it with a sharp slashing stroke.

—Ha ha! That's great, Luke! The Ceremony of Eph-phetha!

—You've got it.

The girl writhes and plunges, but there is no getting free. Again and again, he brings the rod down fiercely on her flashing buttocks, until they are darkly striped.

Again there is a break. The other girls are holding her face down over the piano stool, her legs widely spread, the drawers now abandoned altogether, her pinafore unlaced. The professor wields a long limber switch. He tests it out against her streaked posteriors, then standing by her shoulder, brings it down stingingly between her cheeks, the tip of it snapping against her bottomhole. Over and over he switches the little crack, allowing the tip of the switch to creep gradually down to the mossy vulva below.

—Look at that timing! Those were the days when you just turned the cameras on, and if anything was going to happen, it was entirely up to the actors.

—Makes you ache for a zoom lens, though, doesn't it?

There is a pronounced bulge in the man's tuxedo pants: one of the little girls unbuttons his fly and releases the throbbing instrument trapped within. The girls kiss it and nip at it with their teeth, strike at it with little switches from the bowl of dried flowers, as he administers his punishment to the girl across the bench. They push the foreskin back with rounded lips, bite at the crown, grip his scrotum between their teeth and pull. Their lips, eyes, his genitals, pants, all are dark and shadowy; only the shaft of his rod, their teeth, and the whites of their eyes are clearly visible. The welts on the horsed girl's bottom are now crossed, and her vulva is puffy and enflamed.

At the professor's signal, the girls turn the victim over on her back on the bench. She resists but feebly, exhausted with pain and fruitless struggle, though she still tries vainly to hide her pubis from view. He slaps her hand away, switches her thighs and childish mound tauntingly. Her face is streaked with tears; she seems to be wailing mournfully, tossing her head back and forth.

—It's almost tangible, isn't it? I mean, not being able to hear . . .

—Wait!

The other girls strip her of her pinafore and blouse, draw her chemise up under her armpits, pry her legs apart. Her smooth white tummy jerks spasmodically with sobs. He switches her small white breasts softly to bring the dark little nipples erect, as the girls pull his pants down, bite his hairy bottom, snap his garters. He fingers the pouting cunny, separating the labia, searching out the tiny clitoris. He pokes and pries curiously, then smiles triumphantly, nods to the other girls. He inserts the tip of his penis: a final fight—the girl rears up, kicks, strikes out at him, seems to be screaming. The others hold her down, suck her breasts, double her knees back, exposing her striped and bleeding thighs and bottom. They suck the blood, guide the man's penis, push on his buttocks, tug at his balls, kiss and finger each other excitedly. The victim's eyes roll back, her tongue lolls idiotically out of her mouth. He shoves and butts, but she is too tight. The girls reach in with their fingers, trying to create an opening. At last, with an enormous effort, he bursts through—blood spurts violently out of the girl's mouth, fountains erratically, then dribbles down her cheeks, trickling darkly into her lacy bonnet. Her eyelids flutter briefly, then cease, showing at the end only the filmy whites of her eyes. A halo seems to form around her bonnet. After a moment, there is sudden darkness, a flicker of scrawled numbers and letters, then light again as the film's tail rattles out of the projector.

—That's wonderful, Luke, how she wears her boots and bonnet right to the bloody end!

—Mmm. Those were the days, Cissy!

Cissy brings the office lights up to a soft amber, threads the film up for rewind, glancing briefly at the *ident* trailer. He rises slowly, moved by this vintage flick of his, more moved than he'd like to admit, goes to mix drinks at the bar.

—In those days, we fucked with our socks on.

—Never knew when you might have to make a quick exit . . . ?

—No. The floors were cold.

Eighteen minutes of his life: how to judge them? And how judge the eighteen minutes just spent watching them? Or these passing ones, reflecting on reflections?

—That's right, says Cissy with a light laugh. You never see people balling on the floors in these old Lucky Pierre films, they always get up on something.

—Besides, you could get splinters.

—Wasn't that Cally playing one of the other girls?

—Yes, the one biting my cock there, early on. She was just eight years old then, but already a great actress, already very beautiful. God, it was great to see it again! Where'd you find it, Cissy?

—At an auction. I couldn't resist.

He hands her her drink. Dry nostalgic scent of cellulose nitrate in the air.

—Did you like it?

—Sure, I like everything you do, Luke, she says, smiling up at him.

—Well, it's not very good, he admits, gazing down into those absorbent blue eyes. I made it before I met you.

They kiss. She sucks his tongue gently, pushes her soft breasts against him. The projector hums and flutters.

—It's beautiful, Luke. So true to life. Brought back all my own lessons at that age. And it has that something special. Integrity. It's what makes you great!

—I don't know. Something not right about the opening.

He moves to the window, away from the explosive old film, to light his pipe. The snow has stopped falling, but down in the streets it is blowing still. Is this the city that men call the perfection of beauty, the joy of the whole earth? The day is fading, and the endless streets are filled with homebound masses, butting against the wind. Distantly: a couple of fires. He scratches his chest; some itch he can't quite find.

—A lack of preparation, or something.

He suddenly feels, as he says that, that he's been here before, or knew before he'd be here, that he's making some vast impossible connection, as though the world has come sliding up behind him and picked him up. The line, Cissy will . . .

—Maybe it's the girl's line, Luke. Maybe it's a bit too much.

He smiles wryly out on the city, sips his drink. In sync. For a moment.

—Yeah, probably. But she really said that. I had to use it.

—Said it . . . ?

—In the interview before. When we were casting. I asked her why she'd answered our ad, and that's how she put it, mummy's gone to heaven, the whole routine, a whole lot more in fact I didn't use. You'd have loved it! I decided not to tell her what the film was about, she'd never heard of Lucky Pierre, probably thought it was an animal fable for kids. To tell the truth, that line is what I thought it *was* about, raping somebody like her, raping every silly thing she stood for. On the set, just before the shooting, she even prayed for success!

Cissy laughs, returning the film to its battered old can.

—Oh wow! I thought her acting was too good to believe!

—Now, today, I wouldn't put it in the dialogue like that, I'd just use the interview itself as voiceover, maybe later, during the rape.

Cissy contemplates the possibilities.

—But I don't remember seeing her in any other films, Luke. How come she didn't go ahead and make a career of it?

He looks up in surprise. But of course. She couldn't know.

—She died. She really died.

Cissy nearly drops the tin of film. She sets it on the workbench, gazing at him in amazement.

—Died! You mean—?

—Yes, in the film. That was real life.

She laughs, claps her hands.

—You're kidding—!

—No, fucked to death, I swear it, the old gokuraku-ojo, it was fantastic, I've never seen anything like it before or since! Couldn't have worked out better if we'd scripted it in!

—My god! That's really wild, Luke! But then, how was it supposed to end?

—I don't remember. I don't think we had an ending for it. We weren't sure what she'd do. I suppose we thought she'd dig it, once she'd tried it, like they all do, like we all do, and that we'd end up with some kind of orgy, maybe rape the sadistic old master to exhaustion or something, you know.

—That's wonderful! Now I'm going to have to have a

slow look at that ending on the editing table! Besides, I want to see how you got that weird halo effect at the end.

—The gloriole! Pretty spooky, isn't it? Like maybe her prayers were answered, or something. Actually, that was an accident, too. It just happened we'd got ahold of a piece of film without any anti-halation backing, and we picked up some refracted light from the whites of her eyes. Normally, we'd have thrown the film out and shot the scene again, but of course there was no plugging her up for a second try.

Cissy laughs gaily, admiring him with misty blue eyes. Sends a sweet warm flush through him. She kisses him.

—You're a genius, Luke!

—Aw, come on, my part was easy, Cissy!

—Easy! You were the one who chose the girl, weren't you? And who else was mixing documentary techniques with scripted movies in those days? Then there's that whole music lesson apposition with all the fantastic associative ironies, you were the one who set that up. I don't even mention the subtlety of your own performance, those delicate shifts of expression, the minute muscular twitches, your incredible vocabulary of eyebrow movements, your sense of command.

She nudges up against him.

—And, love, whose cock but yours could have pulled off that ending?

She gives a soft tug on it. He laughs, relights his pipe.

—And then to stay so cool through it all! No, Luke, confess: you were the reason the medium was invented!

—Well, he laughs, if you'd been on the set, you might have a different judgment about our staying cool! In fact, I wish we'd had good recording gear then! There was a kind of shocked silence, about as long as it took to get those last couple hundred frames there, and then all hell broke loose! I mean, we really flipped! Knocked over the cameras, bunged up the lights, it was real panic!

—Wow! Hey, you could have used that sound up front, you know, over the slow build, all that unfocused turmoil —it would've been really weird!

—Yeah, that's good!

—And then the interview with the girl throughout the

rape! Maybe, let's see . . . maybe an unanswered question at the end!

—Hah! And on top of it all, a panegyric on the beauty of music as pure art, scrambled and scattered through the whole track!

—Oh right! balm for the bleeding lover's wounds!

—The golden tongue! the prophet's art!

—Let fancy float on this aeolian fart!

—Ha ha! And how about a nice dry humdrum lecture on solmization and the guidonian hand as a bass continuo!

—Use that hymn to John, you know, that *ut queant laxis* thing . . .

—Yeah, and all in the key of Fuck Minor!

—Or just A Minor!

—Hah! With a heavy beat!

—Cane Sharply on Ass Flat!

—Progressions toward a dirty Deflower Seventh!

—Or even melodies made from anagrams of the scale! Like B-E-D, or D-E-E-D!

—D-E-A-D!

—B-A-B-E!

Cissy pushes a button: a panel slides away and an electric harmonium rolls into the room. She fingers the melodies they invent, working improvisations on them.

—B-E-G-G-E-D!

—B-A-G-G-E-D!

—A-D-A-G-E!

—A-G-G-A-D-A!

He drums on the edge of his tumbler with his pipestem, moves to the bar to play the bottles. A BAD DADDEE! AGED CAD! A DECADE ABED! FAGGED BAGGAGE!

Cissy programs the harmonium with a progression of automatic chord passages, flicks on flashing strobelights, pops a tape of random sound effects on a recorder, moves to a sound synthesizer at the workbench. She throws off her heavy sweater: DD cups uncupped. Her face is flushed with excitement now, there is sweat on her brow and between her breasts, loose locks of blond hair bobbing.

—B-E-A-D-E-D!

—C-E-D-E-D!

—F-E-E-D! A-G-E-E!

—And A-C-C-E-D-E, Luke! B-E!

He connects a tape deck with delayed relay to a radio with a wandering tuner, puts a videotape of the history of syllogistic music on a color receiver, sets them sounding like the drones on a bagpipe. He trains one TV camera on Cissy at the workbench, programming it with alternating black and white switching-tones, uses a second to scan a Victorian pornographic novel, which fills the holes of the first camera's tearing images with fractured histories of serial orgasms. The resultant image appears on a wall-size plasma crystal monitoring screen mounted behind the workbench, and thus in the first camera's scope, producing an infinity of diminishing illusions.

Cissy dances in front of the synthesizer, bringing their improvised melody-codes to life in an orchestra of citharas and rebecs, flügelhorns and quint-fagotts. Her tits slap softly, sweat gleams on her pale freckled back. He turns film tins into cymbals, bins into drums, sets mirrors gyrating. The music history tape is on backwards, proceeding from percussion and brass, back through winds to strings, from the twelve-tone dead-ends back through the industrial orchestra-machine to the innovations of the Italian individualists. At the synthesizer, on the wall-screen, and in a thousand whirling reflections, Cissy bounces rapturously, abbandonatamente, blending crembalums with sackbuts, psalteriums with fifes, from C to C and back again: alla camera exercises on her way out of time and tonics. While there's still any signature left at all, he yanks her culottes down, slaps her perspiring ass, her gleaming stromento da fiato, in syncopation with the wild imbroglio of percussive effects already vibrating in the exploded office. Christ! I'm alive! he thinks.

—Oh yes, Luke! Smanioso! Fuocoso!

Whoppety-clap, giving her cheek to him that smiteth it! he smacks her multitude of glistening grundbegriffe with half his hands, rips his own clothes off with the other half. ABBA! DADA! CACA! EGAD! Still plugging into the screaming circuits their diatonic messages, Cissy lowers her own membraneous reeds over his jack, his quill, his pomposo piccolo, while he, Tubal the Mighty, raps her resonant ass, discovering movement. Pucka-pucka-pucka-

pucka-pucka-pucka-*puck!* her back, belly, bridge, and ribs, anteludium and coda, bell and groove, she giving it back, a quattro mani, all of it multiplied and augmented a thousandfold, clappety-whop-whop, pucka-pucka-puck! She modulates his root, double-tonguing, while transforming, metamorphosing the pregnant themes, distorting the elemental notes, wrenching them out of their old assembly-line functions in the manufacture of progressive sound systems, destroying them as unique entities, creating a whole new sonic domain, a new geography of aural activity. Meanwhile, their ghiribizzo is counterbalanced with inverted dogma on the resolution of dissonances, the nebenthemas of newscasters, the spastic plaints of apocalyptics, and it's not the words they hear, but the click of alveolars and plosives, the hiss of fricatives.

She lifts one thigh to commence the main exposition, and he fingers her f-hole, sets her plectrum quivering, her valves hopping, her rosebud resonating. Frantic zoom shots of their duodrama surround them on six sides, infinitely mirrored and refigured, presided over by a four-gun video image of Monteverdi jacking off backwards: the broadcast semen is sucked back up his instrument and his flushed face turns pale and cold, the art of instrumentation now just a gleam in the father's refocusing eye. Cissy frets with his capostato, while he blows a jubilant blast up her pipeworks: it sets her golden belly quavering, then comes rumbling brassily down her wind-way: *poop-titty-poop-poop-WAAAHH!* Hey! he putteth his mouth in the dust; if so there may be hope! *BLAAAATT!*

Then, volti, into her a punto d'arco, probing her arrisways, third position athwart, thy breach is great like the sea, an allegro di bravura movement fully of executive difficulties, cadenza d'inganno worthy of a virtuoso, oh, he knows they're watching, knows the whole world is watching, all that pass by clap their hands at thee, knows and revels in them, *hello folks!* yes, and knows he's good enough: the master! He vibrates in her tits, her ass, her mouth, her pussy, T-A-M-P! T-A-M-P!, runs the body-gamut up and back again: TAMP! TAMP! TAMP! the ur-beat, arsis and thesis, recte et retro, ductus circum-currens, stroking her to Helicon and back! Oh god-

damn, he's blowing jism everywhere, but he's really
up, up to stay, per omnia saecula saeculorum, man!
over and over, ab initio: their canon perpetuus, their
fa plagal doxology, missa anti defunctis, oh yeah! their
canticum canticorum: he thundering out the dux in his
intrepid barbasso, I am the man that hath seen afflic-
tion by the rod of his wrath, and his love responding in
her sweet antiphonal

who can heal thee?

discant . . .

To My Mare
Harnessed to Pharaoh's Chariot
I Compare You, My Love

Roger Weingarten

Lester's wife Irene, daughter of Cletus (whom some call
Rema, daughter of Plotz) missed what I call her husband
so badly, that the minute he departed for Saigon she shaped
a paraffin statue of him and laid it in their bed. But this
was a sad comfort, and when news came of his heroic
decapitation,
she begged Christ for Lester's resurrection, if only for
three hours.
The God Jesus granted her request, muttering something
about his mother
under his heavenly breath. Michael, the warrior angel,
brought forth
the ghost of the headless Lester to animate the cold
statue lying
in his marriage bed. Talking through a tube in the neck,
provided by Christ, Lester said, "Believe me, Irene,
Chicken
Little was right." And the three hours had no sooner ended
than she choked herself to death on the silent tube.

Others say that Irene's father forced her to remarry, but
she spent her nights with Lester's statue. When one
morning
the milkman looked through a crack in the bedroom door
and saw her embracing what he took to be a corpse, he ran
across the street to Cletus, who burst into the room to
discover
the truth. Rather than have Irene torture herself with
unnatural

and fruitless longing, Cletus had the statue incinerated. But Irene
threw herself into the incinerator to perish with the melting Lester who,

according to another version, survived Saigon, and boarded a submarine
bound for the States. Not quite home, he landed at the southern tip
of Africa. However, while Lester was ashore searching for postcards,
Rema, daughter of an African queen, persuaded her handmaidens
and eunuchs to sink the submarine; and Lester, thus obliged to remain
at the tip, settled down with Rema and founded the hamlet of Thelma.
This, however, is an error: Irene, which means "just beyond the tip,"
and her entourage, sunk the submarine just beyond the African shore.
Lester did not figure among the survivors; Rema was thrown to the lions
for her political intrigues; and Thelma is an anagram of hamlet.

Survivors

UPTOWN THEY MAKE money in invisible buckets and spend it with cards. If you don't believe us you can watch it on television. Or turn on the radio and listen to the money sing. Music is a billion-dollar business. On our block? Sweet gut sounds for cooking up dog food or heroin, or falling off a roof.

When you're dangerous enough the state picks up the tab. You've got maximum security—hot meals, bars on the window in case a tiger's loose outside. They ought to lock us up. If we had a telephone we'd make threats, if we had dynamite we'd plant it, or drugs, we'd give them away to kids. But everything takes capital.

The junkies and roaches have removed our portable property. The Light, Gas and Water Gang has discontinued service. That leaves only the walls and weather, all gray. There's no news anymore, but we can imagine. When there is a knock on the door we answer it with growls.

Sometimes we fuck each other off the mattress, down the stairs, into the street, arriving at the corner where the federals hang out, hot for fresh developments. Otherwise we don't get out much, except to shit in phone booths, check the garbage. Naturally we'd like a change, we're just waiting.

The days fill up without much help from us. We listen to the crosstown surf and watch our patch of sky. Soot sifts in from unseen wars. Birds gather on the windowsill, tapping their beaks occasionally on the glass. At night the city glows. People of America are smoking dope and listening to music, lots of talk about the Revolution. Us? Everything is out of our hands now, what a relief. We tell each other stories. It's easy, our tongues are swelling with lies. We could go on forever.

WE USED TO work for the government, everybody does,

eventually. We sat at numbered desks that matched the numbered badges in our lapels. From time to time procedurals and informationals arrived. The government didn't have time for elections so we simulated them, along with the GNP and a six-game World Series.

When any group came to us we gave the same advice: randomize. Whoever won, we still had miles of underground vadnium banks where impulses leaped and chattered like dolphins. It was an easy dodge, too good to last. First they hit us with a job freeze, then they tried attrition. One day we came back from lunch and our desks were missing. We cashed our final checks and moved to the country. It looks good in pictures.

❂   ❂   ❂

YOU NEVER HEARD of the Pinetop Collective. We were just a bunch of small dope farmers, the usual lick: an old white shitbox, machinery rotting in the yard, brown rice, long days, flies.

The Summer of the generals' coup a storm blew the wires down. Nobody came up to fix them, but we didn't care. We were too busy getting in the harvest and purging ourselves of bourgeois tendencies.

It was a wet Fall, and fighting had started in the Green Mountains. On clear days the planes came over dropping leaflets or napalm. We carried our dead into the woods and buried them beside black birches, shiny in the rain.

❂   ❂   ❂

THE WOODS WERE full of roving bands. We weren't a secret, just little facts that no one noticed until Makhno brought us all together. One of us could make mud soup, another knew how to start fires in a storm, or tell good mushrooms, or navigate by stars. We taught each other.

Seasons changed without news. We moved only at night, sometimes in circles, it hardly mattered, we were ascending. Empty packs bounced on our backs. We had grown thin on cracked wheat and self-criticism. Dogs followed us everywhere, waiting for the next vomit.

We climbed through federal forest, past the last canted

pines. The sharp air turned our songs to vapor. Winter was coming and still no Revolution.

❃   ❃   ❃

WHEN THE WEATHER got worse, we went down to the hot springs. We pitched camp and waited for Makhno. Everybody was there: cadres, collectives, vanguards, movements, countercultures. A good place for recruiting, we had thought. But who were we? What was our program? Crouched in pools, we listened restlessly to questions. Waiting clogged our brains. We were always smarter in motion.

Finally Makhno rode smiling and unnoticed through their plenary sessions, up to our smokeless fires. We put on our boots and gathered around him. "I have spoken to our little brothers, the computers," Makhno said. "They have asked me, what is to be done? And I have told them, Anarchy is the mother of law and order." Then he gave the marching call.

We galloped along the New York Thruway, burning toll booths and scourging the local bureaucrats. There was a fresh wind in our faces. At night we could see the distant blur of cities and overhead Orion rising, like the masses.

❃   ❃   ❃

WE TOOK Syracuse in a fleet of rented green vans, with hardly a shot. Our big black banners flapped in the main square, while brother Makhno spoke. We went to a bar and watched him on television. The announcer called it a turning point, but the next night loyalist gunships cut us to pieces. A regular shit storm. If you made a run for it, you were picking lead out of your liver. The word came down: lie low. We had entered an urban phase.

❃   ❃   ❃

The mails and phones stopped working. Streets, names, buildings changed constantly. We would toss bombs into an armory and hear only the answering shriek of birds. Brothers and sisters just kept disappearing. They must have picked up everyone who mattered. If you were on the loose, you felt invisible, immune, rejected. At meetings only the informers had ideas. There were rumors about the camps—not so bad, they said, but we found out.

* * *

We were kept in sealed shipping containers. EarthAir-Water had the contract. They fed us kibbled meal, full of drugs—leapers, downers, freakers, all mixed together. Mostly people fucked or beat each other up in the dark. The containers were stacked and when the piles shook, it meant another transfer. Finally ours would jerk up spinning. We always sang "Bound for Bayonne." Everything shipped through Bayonne arrived missing.

* * *

We were free again. Makhno has got us out, we said, and recognized our voices. We moved effortlessly, blinking in the sudden light. At each crossroad the column swelled. All faces seemed familiar, thoughts converged.

Behind us lay the mountains, like a remote impenetrable fog. Arms linked, singing, we were millions. Who could count us? Marching through bright fields toward the sea.

* * *

WHAT HAPPENED then? We don't know anymore. We used to. You should have seen us in the beginning. We were shitting art and pissing dialectics. Now the story only gets shorter. Yesterday, a paragraph. Today, a sentence. Tomorrow—a word? Soon we'll be back to silence, nothing left, barely a memory, just time.

Who are we? It varies. With four billion people sucking on the same minute, why worry about character? We're cumulative, like dust or lead poisoning. Before the Revolution we were nothing. We listened to dead voices. We stuck needles in our arms. We ate shit and dreamed. Then the Revolution came. Suddenly each of us had power. Everything was possible. We rose and moved together.

Listen, they say Makhno is dead. Why should we believe them? True, the state has not withered away. The banks and jails are filling up again. But Makhno must be in the mountains. That's where it started last time. When we're ready, we'll join him.

Hammie and the Black Dean

Austin Clarke

You wouldn't see Hammie eating with one of them. And you wouldn't see him playing Frisbee, or touch football, or softball with them. Not in the early days anyhow. No, not one brother at Berkshire College, high up in the mountains, would think of sitting down at the same table with a white student. Not if he was really *black*. But there were a few "blacks" who reasoned that Berkshire College was not set up to make the forty black students there feel as if they were back home on some street corner in Harlem or in Roxbury. These "motherfuckers," as Hammie called them, would reason that the college was indeed a white institution, that everything about it was going to remain white in spite of Hammie's black-power rhetoric and also in spite of the fact that the college had two black professors and a black dean. Those few "jive brothers" saw this clearly, and they went on sitting and talking with the white students. They even moved into the same dormitory with the white students. The *real brothers*, the "bloods," stopped speaking to them. And they called them "niggers." "Toms" was too polite a name for these motherfuckers, Hammie said.

And what made the real brothers really mad was the hurtful fact that among these "motherfuckers," there were the only two black women on campus. One of them was passably beautiful. The other was tolerably intelligent and had a lot of money and a rich daddy. The bloods would spend long hours between hands of bid whist or Tonk or penny poker plotting the murder and rape of this sister; and in more jovial moments, they would talk about "embarrassing" her in front of the white boys. She dated only white boys. The other sister said openly that in her "honest and intellectual opinion, black men are bastards, and those who aren't bastards, are children!"

The real brothers therefore stuck close together. They talked loud in their section of the dormitory, which they baptized the Black Mosque—although they drank Boone's Farm and smoked pot every night, and on weekends slept with their friends' dates—and they called one another "niggerrrr," in loving twists of endearment; rapped and rapped about their fear and discomfort and alienation from studying at a white college in such swallowing circumstances, so close to the "motherfucking honkie"; and, although they did not know it, swam together in their romantic parody of myths about white people and myths about black inferiority, like fish in a strange current, in difficulty, in a rushing mountain stream.

And the white students, the "others," *them,* watched the brothers coming and going, envied something about the way they talked and walked, and how they told the administration to "fuck off!"; about the way they spoke at dinner, loud and happy; indeed, everything that these black students did among themselves; and still the white students failed to understand the real reason for it. So the white students puzzled a little more over it, and then decided to hate the black students in return, although they didn't tell them so to their faces. But you might hear two of them in a dormitory washroom discussing blacks in words similar to the graffiti of sentiments and sexual fantasies which wallpapered the toilets in an adolescent confusion about prowess and dreams that indicated some kind of sexual lockjaw. Perhaps this was why the black students started living and eating apart. It probably began in the dormitory toilets. "Those motherfucking white boys. Always thinking about their pricks. Shee-it! when they not thinking about their pricks, they writing about it. But they sure's hell can't do much fucking with it! The motherfuckers!" This is how Hammie, the most talkative black student, put it. Whatever it was about the white students and about practically all of the white faculty which caused this deep and obsessive hatred from the black students, they always mentioned the dormitory toilets. "They bug the hell outta me, Jim!" Hammie said, meaning either the whites at Berkshire, or the toilets, or both. And whether it was some kind of puritanical vengeance, or merely the depths to which the blacks disdained graffiti and writing hands on the walls of the dormitory, you could not find one smudge of sexual fantasy or sexual jokes on the pearly white walls of the toilets in the Black Mosque. Hammie used to yell *"damn!"* almost each time he saw a white boy with a white girl; and straightaway, because you might have been close to the circumstance, you knew he was commenting upon all those hips going to waste, and on his own ability to "outhump any white motherfucker on this mother-fucking campus, Jim!" When he saw one of the two sisters with a white boy, even in the daytime, he went wild. "Damn!" That second "damn" told you many things about Hammie.

And the situation at Berkshire continued to be divided. The whites went their way, many of them getting A's, because, as Hammie put it, the university was theirs, and they were programmed from childhood to get A's; and the blacks—except those who were integrating—roaring into the dining hall, laughing loud like there was an epidemic of forced hilarity, at things which normally back in the Black Mosque they would not laugh at, but laughing loud publicly, as if with their voices they were standing like so many cowboys rearing back on some secret inner strength they had over these white boys; and they continued to get, mainly, C's, because, as Hammie said, "all the white profs are racist bastards." But there was little open conflict. A small conspicuous group of whites was determined like National Guardsmen to fight for the system and for what was right, and eventually to enter the system at some cozy corner of its trimmed haircut of security and of middle-class living. The others just wore their hair long, and did their thing with pot and drugs. And the brothers were content to "just slide, Jim, sliiiiide!"

THEN, ALL OF A SUDDEN, something happened. No one noticed the first indications, for no one ever expected anything like it to happen at Berkshire College. Mountain people, Hammie said, are like farmers. They live off a land of hard and tough rules, like a tradition. That is what Hammie said he meant when he told one of his white professors during a seminar in political science, "Man, this place ain't nothing but a motherfucker!" And that was Hammie. He could translate the most complicated analytical statement into the basest colloquialism, into the most ordinary expletive. But whatever he said, whether you were present or you heard about it afterwards, it made you laugh. It made you laugh first, and then it made you think. And most of all, you found yourself thinking of why he so often, among his wise sayings, so blatantly said such deprecating things about himself. "I'm only a nigger from Roxbury ghetto, Jim!" was a favorite saying of his, spoken with fierce conviction, at the top of his voice, in the presence of white students even. Hammie would spit the words out, not so much as a testament to the source of his fierce militant blackness, but rather as an embarrassment to those few black students, who, Hammie reasoned, had forgotten in one of those pitiful moments of their integration, that being a college student at Berkshire was not the same thing as being white. So that, after all, if the truth was going to be faced, these "misguided" blacks had to be reminded with the pain of embarrassment, through Hammie's voice, that they were nothing more than "motherfucking niggers, too, Jim, so dig it!"

So that in this circumstance of place and in these strengths of vibrations, as Hammie liked to say, the bloods at Berkshire College came and went, went and came, carefree in their posturing, walking through the snowbound and unshoveled walks of the campus, pretending that they belonged here in the mountains; late for lectures, when they did decide to go; late for breakfast, raucous and starved by dinnertime, but leaving the uncooked, badly seasoned roast beef on the edges of their plastic trays. And no white student dared open his mouth to reproach Jack or Jim or Hammie. The bloods, the real brothers, sat by themselves, with their Afros or with Afro-hair braided in pigtails, and demonic defiance of whatever thought and suspicion and chip they might have placed upon their own worth, before and during their time at this exclusive college in the mountains. And they cut their style with combs and cake-cutters jutting from their stubborn hip pockets.

But all of a sudden, something happened. One detected the first signs when the weather became better. The bloods started to walk through the campus in sweat shirts, leaving their evil-fitting winter coats behind. They had bought them anyhow in disregard of the care and the style which they normally used for buying clothes—purple, green, or black silk trousers—as if they had all lived their lives in the deep, winterless South. At first, the change might have been seen as, and called, more of an aberration of behavior and of attitude than a change. Many had come to think of the attitude of the bloods to the white students as something fixed in the stars of their births. Anything like a change in this feeling was bound to be unthinkable. But a change it was. The bloods began sitting at tables with white students: at breakfast, at lunch, and at dinner. Those other blacks who had always done so were petrified. And the two sisters did not know what to do.

The change came first during breakfast. And it looked as if the first few bloods to sit with the whites were doing so because not many of the real brothers, and certainly not Hammie, who never awoke before midday, would see them so early in the morning. Nobody would ever see those "jive bourgeois black motherfuckers *in-tee-gratin'*, Jack!" The Black Dean happened to have got up early one morning, for some kind of administration business, and he decided to have breakfast in the students' dining hall. He saw a few bloods sitting with some white students, eating breakfast and talking. He couldn't believe his eyes. He hurriedly ate his cornflakes and french toast, having forgotten to take the five glasses of orange juice which he liked; and he rushed over to Baxter Building to meditate on the phenomenon. He was so worried about it that he took into his confidence the Dean of the college, a sallow-faced young man, with blond hair and badly fitting suits. "The black students are beginning to exploit the facilities of the college at last," he told his colleague in administration, in a whisper, in confidence. Getting the black students, the militants and the middle-class ones, to exploit the facilities of the college to the full had been the Black Dean's aim for the two long years he was Dean of Minority Groups. During that time, he had worried about being a radical dean. Should he be a *black* dean, or a member of the administration, like the other white college employees?

The bloods had, on more than one occasion, embarrassed him through small reminders that after all, not only had they made his appointment possible, but that he was just a "jive motherfucker!" Everyone, black or white, who met the enmity of these bloods, was a "jive motherfucker!" Hammie had been the mouthpiece of this ironical reassurance. "You ain't nothing but a nigger, Jim! Brother Malcolm was hip to your ass, Jack!"

But after talking to his colleague, the Black Dean, with a bit of the mission of the television white knight attached to his pride, was beginning to feel that his tough position with the bloods was the correct one: black students, whatever their social origin, in ghetto or in suburbs, should have *one* motivation and *one* mission at a place like Berkshire College: "to get the best goddamn sheepskin possible. Stop the shitting around about black nationalism. Remember that they're really white-blackmen, as the Indian chief said in the movie. And be cool. Shit, those niggers're more *white* than me, and I'm on the goddamn administration! Can you deal with that?"

The *in-tee-grating* beginning at breakfast was apparent right up until lunch, when most of the students were wide awake enough to notice the metamorphosis taking place. Word about it came to the President of the college, who made a note in his confidential file, reserved for ATTITUDES AND ETHNICAL DIFFERENCES OF BLACK STUDENTS AT BERKSHIRE. *TOP SECRET*. The President had become something of a figure in the Northeast by being misquoted once at a meeting of his faculty, and he made a point of writing this note himself.

What he had actually said at that meeting was, *"There is no intellectual room at Berkshire for the encouragement of black studies. We already have two black professors on faculty, one has tenure. And there is a black dean. To encourage racial viewpoints is not within the interpretation of the charter of this college."* His secretary had made the mistake—perhaps through fatigue, for it was approaching the end of the fall semester—of leaving out the negatives in the first and last sentences. When the speech appeared in the Alumni Bulletin, the trustees drafted a letter of protest, and sent it to the President; but they kept a sealed envelope demanding his resignation, waiting to see how the alumni and the press would treat what the spokesman for the trustees termed, "this remarkable lack of prudence."

Then things begin to happen. Some black students took up arms on another Eastern campus. The demonstrations spread and their demands for more black students and faculty and courses were reflected in the nation's headlines. All of which had nothing to do with the President's remarks at the faculty meeting. But, as if by magic, they were picked up and publicized as a notable example of academic realism and courage, and the President of this small exclusive college, tucked away in the forgotten mountains, became suddenly a national celebrity. "The most liberal and intelligent college president in the nation"— that was how the most influential newspaper in the country summed him up. The trustees suggested new ways and means for recruiting more black students to Berkshire, and they voted him a small increase in his salary. So this was why the President wrote this confidential note himself. He also called up the Black Dean, and asked him to have lunch with him in the Faculty Club that afternoon.

The Black Dean would get these invitations out of the blue, and at first they puzzled him. But it did not take him long to realize that there was a connection between each invitation and some variation in the attitudes of the college toward the black students and the faculty. All the employees of Berkshire College were white except for the two black professors, the Black Dean, and a cook for one of the fraternity houses. The Black Dean accepted the invitation in high spirits. He felt sure now he was on the right track. Only a few minutes ago the Dean of the college had assured him, "You're doing a great job," giving him the credit for this historical change. "Keep it up."

The Black Dean even was a bit disappointed that this was all the Dean could think of saying; but he had always felt that the Dean was not a very bright man. He knew he could make a much better Dean of the college. "Shit, man, I would whup those niggers' ass into such shape!" he used to tell his wife, just before they fell asleep after the Channel Seven eleven o'clock news. "Baby, those niggers' ass would be so whupped, that . . ." And he would dream of sitting in the College Dean's chair, in his office and with his private secretary; and of inviting the Assistant Dean, *and his wife,* to cocktail parties in his university-loaned house. "Shit, baby, just sit tight. For one more year! One o' these afternoons when I come home for lunch, I'll be telling you that from next month, I'll be the new . . ." The President was smiling as the Black Dean approached his table in the Faculty Club. Soon the President was talking about playing golf, that it was a shame the Black Dean didn't make use of the facilities on the campus. "You don't mind if I call you Burt, do you? we're informal here at Berkshire, you know, and I hope you'll drop the Mr. President title you've been using to address me by, and remember always that I'm Cliff to you, that the time has come for you and me to have a little rap session, heh-heh-heh! . . ." And afterward, they walked back to the President's office. "Sit down, sit down, Burt . . ." Burt told the story to his wife that night as they pulled the blanket over their naked bodies, just after the weather. . . . "When I really dug what that motherfucker was into, I freaked out. Siddown, siddown, Burt, he says, and shit, baby, the only chair *I* could see, the only motherfucking chair I could see that he was pointing me to, was *his* chair . . . the President's chair. Ain't that a bitch? And then comes the bomb! Baby, when that bomb dropped, I thought I was in Japan. Hiroshima! The son of a bitch made me sit down, siddown Burt, made me sit down in his chair, and then he pulled this Polaroid camera from a drawer and took a picture of me sitting in *his* fucking chair! Then he took another one. Gave me one. Look! And kept one for him! Ain't that a bitch, though? . . ." And when he was deep into the trough of his first sleep that night, he saw Hammie appearing from behind a fence as you climb the slight grade from the students' dining hall, going up the slippery path beside the house where the football coach lives with his shaggy-haired dog which runs out at you, barking—there Hammie appeared wearing a pair of red-white-and-black trousers, red-white-and-black shirt, white tie as dazzling as the snow on the path, black socks which the Black Dean could see, because the trousers were worn high on the waist, a black jacket like an Edwardian undertaker's, and a black felt hat left over from Zorro and the days in the wild cowboy West, and pulled wickedly down to a corner of his dark shades. And he could smell the grass Hammie was smoking, and could see it, at his lips. "Nigger, you smoking shit? In my motherfucking presence, nig-gerrr? 'Amma going see that your ass is kicked out of this college . . ."; and when that dream faded, the Black Dean was riding the horse of his wife's buxom thighs.

The weather turned warm. The bloods appeared on the field, on the first fine warm evening after dinner, to play touch football. Nobody had organized it. It just occurred. Hammie was naturally the quarterback, the "general" as he called it. He quarterbacked for the juniors against the sophomores. But the sophomores were stronger and keener and they hit hard and professionally, as if they knew that the white coach was watching them from his verandah with his shaggy-haired dog. The sophomores hit so hard that they caused Hammie to yell, "Do you motherfuckers think we's *white boys?* Shee-it! This is only a *game,* Jack!" But the sophomores had seen the coach in their dreams of greatness, and having a few overgrown jock-strap-full freshmen in their lineup, continued to hit hard; and once they made Hammie bend over for two minutes writhing in silent pain. "Smoking grass and playing touch football is a bitch, Jim"; and the white students on the same field, but in their own corner of the world, playing a girls' game of volleyball, stopped slapping the ball over the makeshift net and rolled on the ground in laughter. "Those motherfucking white boys!" Hammie hissed, and continued to evade the hard tackles of the misdirected, misguided but very conscientious sophomores, big as professional linebackers. That was the last game ever played on the Berkshire College campus in which all blacks or all whites played.

The very next evening the game was integrated. It began at dinner, which was veal cutlets with something on them like sawdust mixed in tomato sauce, and Hammie, always able to see the pleasanter side of college meals, roared, "This motherfucker *got* to be digested!" Leaving his dinner untouched, Hammie went on telling a joke about a white professor who had the best grass on the campus, but who was still "not cool," and was a motherfucking racist, Jim! and then asked each of the bloods for a cigarette. No one had a cigarette for Hammie. Hammie then went on saying something about the "motherfucking white students who are more racist than the faculty, although they come on strong as hippies, Yippies, and shit like that," and all of a sudden, without a reason or rhyme, he got up and went to the next table where all whites were sitting, eating the veal cutlets, and said to a long-haired white student, "Gimme a cigarette!" The white boy stopped eating, dropped his knife and fork on the plate, kept the chewed veal cutlet in his mouth, some sauce dripping through his front teeth which had gaps between them, pushed his hand into the breast pocket of his green army fatigue jacket and took out a package of Kools. Before he had got the cigarettes out, each of the seven other white students sitting with him had theirs out too, and were offering them to Hammie. Hammie smiled. The white boys smiled. He took the package from the hand of the first white boy, who was now fumbling with his gold Dunhill lighter, chose one cigarette, smoothed the edge of the pack, handed it back, took one cigarette from each of the seven other white boys, put them in the pocket of his dashiki, and then held his lips squeezed tight around the first cigarette up to the hand of the white boy holding the lighter. The white boy's hand held the lighter firmly. He looked into Hammie's eyes. Hammie squinted his eyes, closed his hands over the white boy's, and said, "Thanks, Charlie." The boy's name was actually Charles. When Hammie walked back to his own table, the other bloods said, "Did ya get for us, too?" Hammie piled the glasses and the un-eaten veal cutlets onto his plastic tray, got up, squeezed his lips more tightly over the cigarette, squinted his eyes in a half-smile, and said low to the table, "Cop for yourselves, niggers!" And the whole table exploded in laughter. The white boys nearby, inclined as always toward black humor, laughed also. They had not quite heard what was said, but they felt that the release in the laughter of the bloods meant it was groovy, and they themselves felt more relaxed.

Everybody on the campus was feeling more relaxed these days. The Black Dean met a black and very militant student the next afternoon in the hallway outside the office of Loans and Bursaries, and thinking that this student would, in these circumstances, and since he was alone, be more reasonable and open to less radical opinions, and thinking also of the change in the bloods, said to him, "I knew I was right, don't you think so, Brother?" The black student nodded his head, skinned a smile, and said, "Yeah, man! Yeah, you copped!" and hastily left. When the student got out of Baxter Building, where he had been to ask for a loan to pay for his long-distance telephone bill, and also to see whether the college would give him some money for his plane fare to California for the summer vacation, he wondered what the hell the Black Dean was talking about. Hammie loomed up somewhere on the campus, and when he heard about it, he said, "I *told* you that motherfucker's freaking out, Jim!" But Hammie knew what the Black Dean was talking about, and he added, "Ain't that a bitch?" The bloods were no longer seen sitting on the short wall near the dining hall where they would watch the white students of Erin House playing softball with a child's beach ball; and they were no longer standing by making ethnical and racial remarks when the whites played Frisbee, something which the bloods never did, which led Hammie to conclude that it must have been a white man's game. They were no longer onlookers and spectators of these games. "Right into that shit! In-tee-gratin', Jack!" was the way Hammie put it, and he and the other bloods got down and did their thing with a panache and a style, as if they were eating Southern fried chicken and ribs and playing bid whist, which was *their* black thing over in the Black Mosque.

The bloods were changing. Those who had integrated before the change continued to be confused. At breakfast, which was served from seven-thirty until eight-thirty, the bloods were all there. Sitting all over the dining hall. Sitting with whichever white student they might have been in the line with, and no longer separated in a corner of the dining hall nearest to the kitchen, and occupying the three tables which they had claimed as theirs. And when not a single one of them had turned up for one of the three meals, these tables would remain empty. But the change was now like the change in the weather. In-tee-gratin', Jack! Like a bitch! Even at their games of boredom and ritual, bid whist and Tonk, you could see the bloods and white students sitting down around the low tables, smoking each other's cigarettes, but mostly the white boys', not that they were necessarily more generous, but because they were wealthier. Touch football had become an inte-grated sport, like the television version on Sunday after-noons. The bloods even got up in time for their eight-thirty classes. And some whites professors had to call the Dean of the college and inquire whether So-and-so, *a black student,* was actually registered because, "I'm sorry if I cause some feeling here, Dean, but I haven't seen that student in my class before, not even on the first day of classes, you under-stand of course, that I'm not implying that . . ." And the Dean of the college smiled into his voice which went over the telephone and then he called Burt. Everybody in ad-ministration was now calling him Burt. He called Burt through the thin eaves-dropping partition between their offices, and laughed with him, and made two coffees from the nearby machine, and sat down in his chair, while Burt, who was the most popular member of the administration these days, sat on the Dean's desk. The Dean of the college said, "Things are happening. We've even got the black students to go to classes at last." The Black Dean sipped his coffee hot and black, as he himself was black and now feeling beautiful, and he said, "Right on!" To himself he added, Those niggers're copping!

One afternoon soon after that, the black professor of history, a neatly dressed, moustached-cropped, short-haired middle-aged man, stopped Burt as he was getting into his car, and he said, holding onto the top of Burt's opened car door, "Could you tell me, man, I'm not sure myself, because naturally I haven't done any research on the topic in question, but it seems to me that the black students are going through some attitudinal metamorphosis, which as far as I can deduce, I mean, one couldn't conclude from this evidence that . . ." Burt cut him short happily. "Right on!" he said. But the black professor of history went on talking, ". . . now, I know, that a few days ago I personally had to take a stand with the black students in respect to their attitude toward my course . . . because some of them mistake rapping for discussing, and even although I am black like them, still I want them to understand that I am not going to give them A's in my African History course *merely because* they're black, and by the same token, I'm not going to give a white student a C because he's white. As far as I'm concerned, I'm black like them, but as an intellectual, I'm more concerned with their scholarly evaluation of the historical material . . ." "Right on," said Burt, and drove away.

The white professors spread the word throughout the campus: the black students are coming, the black students are coming. And indeed they did come: lectures were full again, the white professors saw for the first time the number of black students on campus, and their first reaction was, "Where are they coming from?" Some said, "I didn't know *we* had so many black students in this place!"; and others said, "I wonder whether we have a disproportionate number of them, to put the student population out of its national racial perspective?" One bearded white professor, known as the radical on the faculty, was worried by the relative numbers and the significance of those numbers in situations which made small numbers look like extraordinarily large and frightening numbers.

For instance, one morning, at seven-thirty, all of a sudden, all the bloods, through some luck of electronics, for some strange reason or other, turned their stereos high, almost as high as they could go, and the campus swung with "Oh Happy Day!" It was a beautiful day, a typical and beautiful New England day in spring, as many residents would describe this kind of a day to you, a day without the feeling of oppression which the bloods said they got every day of their lives at Berkshire College. Perhaps there was even a bird, which nobody saw of course, singing somewhere in some tree. And when the bloods blared this weather forecast into song, and the

Edwin Hawkins Singers were happy as the birds, the four campus policemen came down on the doors and the halls in the Black Mosque, and in the black entryways over in the Freshman Dorms (although no music came from there), like thick slabby grimy hands slapping a cricket dead. One of the campus cops grew emotional and said, "Turn that fucking savage music off! You're disturbing the goddamn peace!" Hammie's record player was playing the loudest. "Dig it! the motherfucker *said*, check it out! he *said*, you niggers're disturbing the peace. *Not* the white students, he didn't say you're disturbing the white students, but *the peace*, Jack! Law and fucking order!" So they turned off their stereos, and the campus, already awake because the students were studying for exams, filed happily into the dining room for breakfast. The campus cops didn't know that the white students, those who were being disturbed, had really liked the idea of being disturbed by "Oh Happy Day!" first thing in the morning, after a hard night of studying.

With nothing else to do, since it was so early, all the bloods arranged to go to breakfast, all of them, all forty out of an enrollment of fourteen hundred, all one thirty-fifth of the student body, all three percent and a little extra bit, this "large number of blacks" lined up outside the dining hall this morning, and havoc reigned. The student at the head of the stairs as you come up into the dining hall dropped his pencil and notebook in which he checked and counted and saw to it that no student ate who shouldn't; he ran into the dining hall office at the rear of the meat cleavers and the large aluminum pots hanging like trophies, to ask the dietitian, "How many blacks registered to eat here?" She didn't know. But he made her look at the line of "cruel-looking blacks," and she changed her color. She immediately got on the telephone to check it out with somebody over in Baxter Building. The bloods kept on coming. When the first one was checking his eating credentials with the frightened student, the last one was still outside the dining hall building by the metal sculpture of something or somebody which nobody could determine. Some white students who were in the line further up ahead moved back and allowed the bloods behind them to move up in the line. The bloods were coming, and somebody called the President to ask him if he knew that there were so many black students registered here, because no one had ever seen so many of them together at one time. The President said he must check into it. "What's going on, Burt?" he demanded of the Black Dean on the telephone, even before the Black Dean had left home. When the telephone rang, the Black Dean was still lying on top of his wife; and on the radio, which came on automatically at seven, Roberta Flack was singing "Reverend Lee." The Black Dean smiled into the telephone in his hand, and said, "Mr. President, I can't tell you that." He looked at the telephone in his hand, as one would look at a ticklish problem, and afterwards he turned back to his wife and said, "White folks sure *is* crazy!"

Something had happened to their communications, but it wasn't anything which couldn't be patched up later that day, at luncheon at the Faculty Club, for instance. Or on the next day, Friday, when they now went trap-shooting together, a new experience for Burt, which he indulged in, through his love of guns and with the President's encouragement. Both he and his wife realized that something special had happened to his social prestige in the white academic community. The other two black wives on the campus heard about it. "Burt can't make it, I don't think, because as you know, Fridays is when he and the President leave to go trap-shooting," his wife would say, excusing him from a party. So the rupture in communications was nothing that could not be mended. Only last week, when news came to the President that the black students were taking part in seminar discussions and had actually started going to almost all their lectures, for the first time in the history of Berkshire College, the President had ordered a bottle of champagne from King's Liquor Store down on River Street, to decorate both the otherwise bare table in the club and to put a bouquet upon the breast of the President's "right hand man," as the President himself begin to refer to the Black Dean.

When the cork in the bottle went off, it sounded like a rifle shot in the peaceful dining rooms of this old sedate Faculty Club so high up in the mountains.

"What's going on, Burt?" he asked later that morning, when they were together in his office. His secretary was present and, for some reason which the Black Dean couldn't understand, was taking notes. He was standing facing the President, and the questions being fired at him. "What's really going on? What *are* they organizing?" The questions contained slight variations, but they pointed to the same implication, that the Black Dean was doing something awful behind the President's back. Into the President's mind flashed a picture of Burt and himself, walking through the wet grass, half-hidden in the fog and mist, and Burt with a gun walking behind. . . . "Burt, you can tell me what's going on, surely?" The Black Dean began to think of his wife lying under him, and of the words Roberta Flack had been saying at the very moment when the President had called; *do it to me!* . . . and he wanted to smile, but this was no time for smiling. After all, he was standing and the President was sitting in the President's chair, and Burt who was, at heart, in spite of whatever impression he made upon others, a very ambitious man, and had seen himself more than once in his imagination sitting in the President's chair, with his official capacity making it legal—Burt wanted to smile now as he was standing watching the President's chair. The President asked the secretary to leave them alone; he wanted to say something confidential to the Black Dean. "I feel as if you have betrayed me, Burt," he said, the moment the door was closed. "We have been close, you and me, we have always discussed things, like men, like brothers, as you people say. You and I. Brothers, Burt. What's going on now, therefore, all of a sudden? I have been fair to you, haven't I? You can't deny that. I have suggested your name for membership in my Country Club. I know, I know! you don't have to tell me . . . I know it's nothing like the things which still aren't done in this country or even around here. But it's a start. I know that. You are on the waiting list, and in a few more months, if everything does well, you'll be *the first black member of this college* ever to eat his dinners at the Country Club, not that this is any great honor, as I said, but we're still in this damn country, aren't we? And I'll be there at your side! I've also nominated you to the Berkshire Gun and Rifle Club, so that you can keep your guns. Legal, you know. And you and me have been trap-shooting several times, when there were only two of us in the woods, with loaded guns, and I never *for one moment* ever thought . . . I even took your advice and built a gun panel and rack in my office, to give the place a little urbanity, as you suggested. Who did I come to? You! Your word, urbanity . . . bringing the suburbs back into the inner city, you told me that, and I did it, because it was a damn good idea. You told me that. And I did it, Burt. Because I had faith in you, because I could see that one day, not too far in the distant future, you'd be sitting right here where I am sitting now, talking to you, but you have . . ."

He left the rest of the sentiment dangling, and without any warning, he went over to the panel behind his desk and pressed a button. Part of the wall slid back and there was a gun rack with six double-barrelled shotguns and two beautifully wrought rifles. All of a sudden, it occurred to Burt that the President's building the gun rack in his office was like building an extension onto a house—it suggested permanency. The President threw one of the rifles, an M-16, at Burt. "I've never regretted taking your advice in acquiring this one. Try it out. It's your suggestion. Go on, try it out, take aim at something. Go on. Take aim at something, goddammit. You make me nervous just by the way you stand there being so goddamn cool. Burt, take aim at something . . ."

They didn't have luncheon together that day. The secretary told Burt that the President had a heavy schedule for the whole day. Burt walked over to the students' dining hall, crossing the grass lot in front of Baxter Building, which he had seen through the scope of the powerful and accurate rifle from the President's office a few minutes ago. Now from this position, he was seeing in the lens of his imagination the President's face mapped out against the rich black leather of his chair. "*Take aim at something, go on! Go on, take aim at something!"* The instructions hit against his head as he walked along the gravel path between the snack bar and the college theater building. *"Take aim at something, go on!"* But what was he going to take aim at? There was nothing he wanted to kill: hunting didn't please him all that much; no one he disliked so much that he wanted to kill him—or her: he thought, all of a sudden, of his wife, and their five children she had borne him in just under six years of their marriage, and he wondered why she couldn't go on the Pill, like any other ordinary middle-class wife. No, she believed in naturalism. Naturalism. Shee-it, I could take a shot at naturalism, right now! *"Go on, Burt, take aim at something, anything!"* He was holding the powerful weapon; and into his sights came Hammie. Yeah! Sometimes, he felt as if he could kill Hammie. Even with his bare hands. Yeah! he would like to "off" Hammie sometime. Yes! get his ass kicked and kicked out of this college, for Hammie was a pain in the ass these days: organizing the black students, organizing a back-to-lecture campaign without first having discussed the strategy with him, and he was *the* Black Dean, shee-it, who that motherfucker think he is, anyhow? He trotted down the last of the gravel incline before the parking space of the dining hall, his mind full of the meeting with the President, and he almost walked right into a pale green station wagon. He recovered from his thoughts quickly, and his disgust for Hammie shot into his mind like a bullet; and he had actually shaped the words with which he wanted to reproach Hammie, but as he was about to explode *"motherfuckerrrrrrr!"* Hammie leaned his head and shoulders out of the window on the driver's side, and smiled. "How you *doing*, Dean?" All the Black Dean could see were the nicotine-stained teeth grinning at him, like a large derision. "Motherfucker," he said, not quite as harshly as he had intended. "The college should take away those cars, if y'all don't know how to drive the motherfuckers!" And he went into the dining hall, hearing Hammie's broad laugh behind just before the tires screeched.

He went in, trembling and frustrated, to have his lunch. Boston beans, wieners, bread, cole slaw, three glasses of milk, two glasses of orange juice, and a slab of cherry pie with a block of vanilla ice cream. His plastic tray was loaded down. He deliberately walked in the opposite direction from the "black tables"—although there was no such thing lately—*ain't messing with no niggers today!* He didn't look around too much as he put down his tray. So when he spread his napkin and looked up, he was slightly surprised that he was sitting at a table with white students. Suddenly, he felt relaxed: he didn't have to talk, he didn't have to rap about blackness and about the legitimacy of black students at a white college, which he found himself drawn into each time he sat with the bloods at a table. With these white students, he could just sit there and eat. This afternoon was his own. He was going to sit down and try to eat the bad food which the college dining hall served, and afterwards, he would even take a walk along the highway, past the two motels, turn right, walk up the hill behind the dormitories and the dining hall, and return to his office. He didn't know what he was going to do when he got back to his office: the two secretaries in the outer office would look up at him as he entered, in that way which said they knew something was going wrong, something which involved him. So these two middle-aged and not very attractive ladies, he felt, would look at him and feel sorry for him. And the woman in the next office, the one in charge of the girls at the college (there were only about ten of them), well, this woman too would come out of her office with her coffee cup in her hand, her lipstick painted onto the white porcelain, and would find some common ground for opening a conversation with the two secretaries, which was bound to focus on the Black Dean. And he could expect that neither of the other two deans would be coming into his office this afternoon for coffee. They already would certainly know that something was wrong, because almost every day he had found some time between work and the President's invitation, to go with them to the gymnasium to play handball; and they would kid him about going trap-shooting with the President on weekends. He didn't know what he would do this afternoon. There were so many things he had to do, and none he could think of wanting to do. He couldn't even take aim when someone said, Take aim. He wondered whether he was wise in having taken this job as Dean in the first place. What was he aiming for in life? He had often looked through the lens of his conversations in bed with his wife, and he had seen himself sitting in the President's chair; and sometimes, when it seemed that just being on the campus had taken away even that ability to dream about a future, he would see Hammie in his lens and he would pull the trigger of his discontent and fire a few bullets into Hammie's body, just to show himself that he still had some guts left, and because, too, of what Hammie was doing to the less militant black students. But still he would not feel satisfied. He knew that he should not have recommended Hammie's admission three years ago, after the college had become morally bound to admit "black disadvantaged kids from the inner city." But there was one victory he did have over Hammie and all the other Hammies on the campus: not another one of them who showed any sign of becoming another Hammie, not one nigger like that would he ever again waste a word on, suggesting that he was suitable for admission to Berkshire College. "This is no place for ghetto blacks, just because they are deprived," he would reason with himself, and sometimes with his wife. This college, Berkshire, was for middle-class blacks, decent people from decent homes . . . he himself had graduated from Berkshire in the days when there were only two black faces on the campus, and he didn't occupy administration buildings! . . . from decent families who could appreciate and "exploit" the facilities of Berkshire College, people with whom he would want to drink tea on Sunday afternoons, talk with at meals when he went to the dining hall to eat; people with whom he might even drink a gin-and-tonic at one of the few cocktail parties he had to give in his rented house.

He was walking now, aimlessly, to his office, and he was thinking that he should have put his hand in the money. In the petty cash, in the funds for black students' entertainment, in some fund for the *ABC* program at the college, and buy the Jaguar XKE he had had his mind on for so long. But he was too honest. "You're too goddamn honest to be a nigger!" his wife screamed at him one night. "An honest nigger? And working for those racist bastards over in Baxter Building, shee-it, Burt, you're something else altogether!" And this is what his wife had come to say to him, and to regard him as, over and over. If he had only put his hand in the money, if he had put his hand in his wife's ass more often, if he had done this and done that, he told himself, he would not now be walking back to his office without aim, as if he was a black freshman again on an all-white campus.

He entered the door of Baxter Building, and he climbed the stairs to his office. This afternoon the marble steps pounded against the leather in his soles like a bad thought against his mind.

He reached the door of his office the same time that Hammie, a half-mile across campus, was coming down the stairs of the Black Mosque. Hammie was talking to two other bloods. They were on their way to a class in Social and Environmental Psychology. It would meet only twice more that semester, and no blood had yet attended Miss Vanderdikeman's classes, which were very popular with the white students. Hammie had instructed the bloods that for them to attend a class in Social and Environmental Psychology taught by a woman from South Africa was tantamount to offering themselves as guinea pigs for "that motherfucking racist bitch, a *rabbit*, Jack!" And of course, the entire body of bloods agreed that "Social and Environmental Psychology was not *relevant*, right on!"—all the black students boycotted Miss Vanderdikeman's class, except for the two black girls, whom no blood on the campus regarded as redeemable or black. They attended religiously. And they got good grades in it, too. Something had happened, therefore, for Hammie to be going with two other bloods to Miss Vanderdikeman's class! But the whole shit was changing, Jack! That's how Hammie had been putting things recently: the whole motherfucking shit's changing, Jim! Jim and Jack were now going to all their classes, and the administration was more and more confused about the change in the bloods, although the administration had previously criticized the black students for not going to classes.

This afternoon was still a beautiful one. Some white

students who were not hippies suddenly grew brave and walked about without shoes; and a few bloods wore waistcoats next to their skin. The grass was warm enough to sit on. There was a dryness in the air sufficient for Hammie and two bloods to enjoy a can of soda; and you could see them walking lazily across the campus, each man with a bright can of soda in his hand. And then one other *baaaad* mother came by with a paper bag in his hand and put it to his mouth, as if he was drinking something other than soda. As he joined Hammie, he passed the dripping paper bag from hand to hand, from mouth to mouth, in a perfect example of brotherhood, and then they all four began grooving and laughing and looking baaaadd and so cool.

And so Hammie and the three bloods decided to remain outside the classroom and enjoy the day and the cans and the paper bag.

When they came to the path leading diagonally across to their lecture room, just beyond the Baxter Building, they stopped, just stopped like tired men, to catch their breath. When they first stopped, there were only four of them. When they first stopped, the President was in the middle of dictating a letter to his secretary about the Black Dean's application to the Berkshire Gun and Rifle Club. When they stopped and stood, as if on their haunches, rearing back like the black cowboys they had admired, tall in their hips, the Black Dean was puzzling over an admissions statistic that had to do with the projected increase of black students spanning the next two years, and the aims of the college concerning the coloring of the student body; and he was thinking of Hammie. When they first stopped, Miss Vanderdikeman was clearing her throat of the harshness from the mentholated cigarettes she smoked in too great numbers, like links on a long chain. Hammie was breaking up the bloods with a story about a friend of his from Roxbury, this baaad mother: "motherfucker's slick, Jim," and they roared, the four of them roared and the noise traveled all through the business corridors of the administration building. A woman secretary looked out, and what she saw was four black students misbehaving themselves. The bloods roared because it was a good story. It was a story of a mother who was bad,

a man who remained in the ghetto and copped, that's how
Hammie put it. "That motherfucker *copped!* that motherfucker copped, Jim! He don't have no BA from no Ivy
League college, but he's making twenty-five grand . . ."
The bloods roared. They liked this story because it showed
them that a man could be black and rich and remain in
the ghetto, that he could be bad and remain in the ghetto.
". . . motherfucker drives a *hog*, Jim! russet-brown and
gold!" Another blood, smelling out the rapping and hearing
the laughter, joined the group below the President's window, in time to hear the word, "gold," and he screamed,
"Check it out! check it out!" The bloods roared. Hammie was
rearing back on his heels like a cowboy idol of his, and he
was talking and acting and moving with his body in a total
embodiment, in a complete involvement with the story
and with the innumerable shades and nuances of the story.
The bloods followed his movements with movements of
their own, with harmony and rhythm. ". . . motherfucker
wears only five-hundred-dollar suits, drinks Chivas Regal
straaaaaaight, Jim! and lives in a ten-foot-square room
with a fountain!—and colored lights flickering! Now, ain't
that nigger the baddest? . . . can you dig it?" "Shee-it!"
the bloods screamed at the top of their lungs: for there was
not one blood among them who could look forward to this
kind of living even after his graduation from Berkshire
College, even after having been on the Dean's List for
eight straight semesters; and they all wondered in their
heart of hearts, while they laughed, whether it was worth
making it through college for a diploma and recommen-
dations and shit like that, when "this mother was so
baaad," when a blood on the block was wiser, and was
making it with more style than they could imagine. And
their laughter had a strange ring in it, something like
nostalgia, and still something like emulation, and something
too like ridicule both for their position in the college and
for their presence so near now to Baxter Building; and they
thought, each one of them, at different times in the story,
of their respective experiences walking through the corridors of Baxter Building, hat in hand in some symbolic
time and circumstance, asking the Dean or the Provost for
a break so that they might "slide through the course in

political science one more time, sir," or for "some bread to clear my motherfucking head with some wine, Jim! this place is a motherfucker, and I gotta get me some wine and some grass *this* fucking weekend!"; and some of them thought of going mad in a place like Berkshire; and some of them saw only the burnished hog parked beside a tenement, with the blood coming out, and getting into it, and the foxes sitting beside him, and he didn't have to crack a fucking book studying a lot of shit like political science and social anthropology and sociology and social psychology, when his own psychology hadn't been conceived of yet in the textbooks and in the minds of the nation's educators; it was better to be a motherfucking hustler, Jim! and just sliiiide, than to be a black student at this Ivy League institution and have to ask a white professor to *permit* you to slide! Sliding was sliding, Hammie added, and if you was gonna slide, you had to slide *with* style. And here was a mother who was sooooo baaaaad, who lived in style, Jim! In style! "And a nigger ain't a nigger 'cept he got *style!* Style, style, style, style . . . you see that motherfucker dressed! cashmere coat draped over his shoulders like if he is Superman, Jim. Dig it! or Zorro the Black . . ." And they laughed even harder at this.

A white secretary looked out of a window on the second floor and saw ten noisy niggers in the words of her heart, but in her report to the Provost, she said there were "some black students talking, sir." Upstairs, in his office, the President was sitting in his deep black leather chair, rearing back, listening to classical music on the campus radio station. It was his habit. He liked Wagner. And he was listening to Wagner now. Somebody on the students' announcing committee had found out the President's tastes, and every afternoon, timed for the President's return from the Faculty Club, this enterprising student would put on his heaviest Wagner and lull the President into raptures of relaxation and of power and of health and vigor. The small transistor radio was on the desk and the President was listening, with his eyes closed and his muscles completely relaxed. The gun rack was locked. His windows were slightly ajar.

Meanwhile more bloods were coming to hear Hammie.

Hammie was three floors below, on the grass, telling his audience about this "baaaad nigger who started his fortune with a half-pound of heroin and a Greyhound bus ticket, and who got busted once while *in transit* with the stuff," and who took the two Italian cops to his golden hog and said, "Here! here!" giving each cop a couple hundred eagles, Jim! 'cause my man was baaaaad! The bloods exploded like a volley of bullets: this was the supreme existentialist black man, able to deal with the motherfucking materialist white man, Hammie said, quoting from somewhere. Their voices reached a crescendo, and the President, just as Wagner closed his overture, just as the rolling timpani came to a peaceful end after the explosion of musical and intellectual torment and exertion. At the second roar, the voices of the bloods frightened him out of his reverie. He rushed to the window, and he saw all those blacks down there . . .

In a minute the Black Dean was summoned to his office. "What's going on?" His voice was like the clarinets in the music he had been listening to. The Black Dean looked down and saw Hammie. He saw Hammie using his arms, his mouth wide open, his brown teeth parted in a grimace of dramatization. The Black Dean didn't know the context of the grimace. "What's going on?" The President ordered Burt to tell him. Burt looked down again, and there were, all of a sudden, the forty black students gathered. The bloods and the others. To talk about the "large" number of black students on the campus was one thing: to see them gathered under the President's window was something else! Burt thought then of the students' demonstrations taking place in the country: Yale, Brandeis, Cornell, Columbia. But those were big schools and far away from the peace of the Berkshire hills. Then he thought again, or rather had the thought pushed into his head by the insistence of the President's voice behind him: yes! there was also Dartmouth and Amherst and Wesleyan, even Smith had had some black rumblings recently. And when this thought really registered, and when he realized how close he was living to the black students on campus and how far they had kept him from their deliberations, he panicked. *"What's going on?"* The President's question seemed to be a demand to know the reason, a demand that was repeating itself loudly, like a record stuck in its grooves.

The blacks were demonstrating, sir, he thought of telling the President. He even thought of exploiting his role as consultant. The President had called *him* first. The President had not called the Provost. Not the Dean of the college. Not even the campus police. Not the press. Him! He! The Black Dean! Burt looked at the President and saw only the large black leather chair in which he was sitting like some small frightened animal accustomed to being petted and being loved when it was disturbed. Burt saw the President's chair. Just then, a roar came up from the throats of the forty bloods three windows below. "What are we going to do about this, Burt?" The President got up from the chair and stood beside Burt. He was agitated. "What would you advise, Burt, in an emergency of this nature?" Burt waited. He didn't know what to advise. He didn't even know whether it was an emergency. The President walked the miles of nervousness from the door back to the window. Burt waited. Then he took up the telephone. His first thought was to call the town police. *If ever I had power on this motherfucking campus, I would've whupped these niggers' ass!* He remembered saying it, many times: he even remembered how his body became tense whenever he said it. He imagined how he would whup them; and he imagined himself cradling the telephone between his head and his shoulders, lighting a cigarette at the same time, and he waited in his mind for the answer at the other end; and as he waited, he actually walked round the desk and sat in the President's chair. The bloods were carrying on down below. "This is the President of Berkshire!" he imagined himself telling the police chief. He was talking to himself, as he swiveled in arcs, in the chair. Burt knew the chief personally. Only a few days ago he had been to the police station to get the chief to fix a parking ticket; and while he had waited, he saw a chart on the board showing the "Rise in Town Crime: a correlation between the increase in blacks at Berkshire College Campus and Local Crime." The chief didn't see him reading the chart. "Any time, Burt, boy!" the chief had said, fixing the ticket. Burt imagined the chief responding to his call to come and get the black students; and he could hear the chief's voice, *"Sure, Burt! sure! any time!"* Burt imagined the police coming. The police were coming. The police were coming. The campus cops, all four, were coming, too.

The bloods were coming to a climax in their appreciation of Hammie's supreme rapping performance. ". . . and one night, Jim, in Boston, in Roxbury, two cops came face to face with my man, and single-handed, my man *stomped their ass!"* Another blow for not attending the Man's institutions, but instead, "copping for yourself," as one of the black students, from Harlem, shouted. They were coming to the end of their entertainment, and Hammie had interposed in his narrative something about having a party later tonight at the Afro-Am House. The President heard only the words: *later tonight at the Afro-Am House.* And some of the bloods were going to go down the hill to King's Liquor Store to buy some wine, Boone's Farm Strawberry Wine and Bali H'ai, because some Smith College sisters were coming up. The sisters from Smith were coming. Burt got up from the President's chair and looked down at the bloods and focused his eyes on Hammie: "motherfucker! I could shoot your ass right now, I could take one automatic handle . . ." he said to himself, as Hammie jumped up in the air, overcome by his own glee. Motherfucker, I could take your ass right now! he was thinking, and he was imagining himself holding the President's M-16, and the police coming: *the town police were arriving stealthily; yes, they were coming through the back door, through the basement, actually, the door where supplies for the stockroom were taken in on the elevator, and he saw them mounting the marble steps as if they were wearing rubbers, and they had guns in their hands, and he imagined the campus police driving up in their campus stationwagon; yes! they drove up and parked beside the building on the other side from the bloods, and he could see them, like four thieves, which he had always called them, climb the silent stairs, and one of them would stop and drink a mouthful of water from the fountain, as he always did before climbing the stairs.*

Burt saw all this, lived all this, as he saw two bloods move off in the direction of the liquor store. The others remained laughing. A secretary from the office of admissions looked out and saw "all those blacks! oh my God, there must be hundreds of them!" and she called her unemployed husband in a neighboring town, and her husband told her it was a goddamn shame, that he was going to call the police and get them up there for those goddamn radicals. Hammie, down below, was saying, ". . . and the only thing I've learned at this motherfucking place in three years, is *three* words: *slide, rabbit,* and *psychoexistentialism.* Ain't that a bitch? And I could have copped them words in Roxbury! *Shhheeeee-it!*" Niggers jumped for joy! They jumped up in the air, some of them ran to the steps of Baxter Building to sit down and recover from the exertion of laughing, and ran back; and some just jumped. And in the midst of their excitement, Hammie looked up and saw the Black Dean at the window of the President's office. He saw the Black Dean. And the Black Dean saw him. *Motherfucker, I could take your ass right now! right now!* The other bloods saw the M-16 in the Black Dean's hands. *"Crack-crack-crack-crack-crack! Crack-crack-crack!"* Somebody was screaming. *"Crack-crack-crack!"* The Black Dean held the weapon firmly in his hands, rammed into his shoulder, and screamed and screamed until he saw each one of the bloods fall to the ground. Hammie was the last one to fall. It took two rounds to put Hammie down. *Motherfucker, I got your ass, at last!* It was a happy scream, something like a hysterical laugh, something like the explosion of relief at the climax of an orgasm. The secretary on the floor of the admissions office had seen the black students jumping and laughing when she telephoned her husband, but when she came back to check, she saw them as they touched the grass, all of them, and then lie flat. She thought they were dancing. The President was at his window looking down. Burt was beside him, holding the high-powered semiautomatic weapon. He was like a man after a long-distance run: he was shaking from the exertion of his movements and emotions. *I got the motherfuckers at last,* he was saying to himself. The President looked at the gun and all he knew, all he was aware of, was that it was the same gun he had thrown at Burt that afternoon, demanding that he take aim at something. He was so far from the present, so far from the fact of the black students below, that he could not tell whether the noise he had heard as he watched Burt from his desk was really the noise of firing or the noise of Burt's voice. They both waited to see what the bloods would do next. "What's going on, Burt?" he asked Burt. "What are they going to do next?" Burt waited. "What's going on?" Burt put the weapon on the chair again and left the President's office. The President waited in his office window and watched, waiting for the bodies to move, and he watched and watched until it brought fuzziness and water to his vision, and in time he thought he saw blood oozing from various parts of the black students' bodies lying on the ground. But it couldn't be blood, could it? What would blood be doing down there? What was he thinking? There were only black students down there.

The two bloods came running back across the grass with four large paper bags. They had brought the wine. One of them held a bottle in his hand, and just before he reached the group, he put it to his lips. The President expected every man to jump up when they saw that. But they remained still. And just before these two bloods reached the others, they put down the paper bags, and while getting up, they happened to see the President looking down at them. He had his Polaroid camera, aiming at them. For a while they remained locked in their stares, and then they walked on to hand the wine over to the other bloods lying so still on the grass. "*Shee-it!*" one of them said, "are you niggers serious?"

Hammie lifted his head from the grass, gasped, and as though with the last breath in his body, in a dying man's voice, said, "*Playing* dead? Shit, we *be* dead! The Black Dean offed our ass from the President's office . . ." And just then, Hammie jumped up and shouted, at the top of his voice, "Motherfuckerrrrrrrrrs!" The Black Dean had appeared on the steps of the administration building, and he faced, alone, the full venom of Hammie's curse.

(*Continued from page 10*)

Sardonic, rueful, wistful, bored, proud, tender, he stands in relation to his experience rather like a man after a full orgasm: his one desire now is not to be taken in by any of these feelings, neither to trivialize nor exaggerate what has happened to him. So he writes in terse anecdotes and aphorisms, as though only the tightest controls on expression will keep him from lying, while at the same time distrusting his memories as "retroactive fantasies" and his aphorisms as "the mark of a promiscuous mind." Meanwhile, his intelligence goes about its business of analyzing and relating, now focusing on a married woman who begged him to desist and then a few days later begged him to continue ("But why laugh? She wanted intensely to remain chaste and she wanted intensely to succumb"), now retelling the Adam and Eve myth as a paradigm of sexual realpolitik, now being skeptical of his own processes of skepticism. The result is a portrait of a rare thing, an ego without a blind spot, as well as the most tonic writing about the contingencies and ambivalences of sexuality that has come our way.

Robert Coover's "Lucky Pierre and the Music Lesson" is something else again. It begins as an elegant take-off on Victorian pornography—a silent film that carries the rape of maidenhood, propriety, and piety to its ultimate *frisson* of actual murder. But that is only half the story, for after the filmmaker, Pierre, who is also the rapist and murderer in the film, has finished viewing it, he and his girlfriend move on to their own delectations, accompanied by the latest in multi-media technology and orchestrated by all of the music of the ages. There is a sheer verbal energy in the story that makes any one reading of it pretty uncertain, but it seems clear enough that at least three modes of pursuing utterness are being brought together: the violation of innocence; the voyeurism provided by the bluest movie of all; and the derangement of the senses induced electronically—a kind of McLuhanesque holocaust in which to burn. And is there a kind of doom running through this progression of modes? Well, read it for yourself. There's much more to the story than first meets the eye, one of the things that separates art from pornography.

Finally, a few words on "King Kong: A Meditation"—an exuberant inquiry into the barely submerged sexuality of that inadvertently Jungian movie. Like Reid and Coover, Kenneth Bernard has a many-sided sensibility, so much so that it is sometimes hard to tell just how seriously he wants the reader to take his ruminations on, say, the family life of Tarzan and Jane, or the size of Kong's penis, or the mind and heart of Fay Wray. His shrewd insights into the ways urban man remembers, screens, and distorts the jungle take on a kind of idiot savant intensity—partly satirical but also partly straight—as though Bernard is not sure himself where to stop, so overwhelming is the mythic content of "King Kong" once you open the lid. The freedom he enjoys to report and speculate on these matters is conferred by the permissiveness of the age; but the intelligence that nurtures his fun, the wit that colors and points it, and the control that keeps it from running off the rails are all qualities that literature, like sex, has never been able for long to do without.

TS

IF HE IS NOT actually upbraided in the matter of *experimental form*, the poetry editor of NAR is pretty often laced into; so that it is with regard to my stance or at least my leaning toward the experimental that I should like to continue here the remarks I made in NAR *12,* a kind of brief gloss on that dialogue between two interlocutors who never speak, their pretext being, quite literally, the poems submitted to the magazine in all their thousands on the one hand, and their text being the poems printed there on the other. Well, so one hand does wash the other then, and it is precisely the quality—soapy? abrasive?—of such laundry which I want to examine in public. Is there such a thing as an experimental form in poetry? And if there should be, if it were to turn up or bed down among all that "new" writing which is merely an echo (the resonance momentarily sustained of the "old" modernism), how does the poetry editor set about recognizing it—is he gingerly or merely rueful? Or are there no spices in order here at all, if there is no constituted order to sweeten or sharpen, but merely, O merely! to seek? For it is my conviction that *because* poetry operates by means of conventions, is governed by techniques, that it can become the instrument not only of expression but of significance. Where *everything* is possible and nothing unexpected (even if that expectation is only to be flouted), communication must break down.

What then might experimental poetry be; what is an experimental form? In the earliest sense the word has in our language, the sense it has had since 1570 (when Ascham's *Scholemaster* was published), as "based on or derived from experience, founded on experience only," *experimental poetry* is either a tautology or a teratism, a necessity or nonsense. For of course poetry is based on or derived from experience; but it is just insofar as poetry escapes from its derivation, its source, that it becomes poetry and not merely a tryst, a joust, a grope, a broken engagement, or a *mésalliance*. For it is just to the degree that poetry is confided to language, to culture, that it escapes from nature and becomes, instead of something tentative, approximate, something we recognize, something we can identify and acknowledge as part of the order of our experience, even if it is the order of our experience of chaos. A poem is a victory over experience arrived at (and often fled from) by submitting to it, and the terms of that victory and that submission are the terms of experimental form.

And I do recognize (such recognition having the same look of realpolitik about it as the "recognition" of Peking by the UN) experimental forms among the welter and dither of prefabrication on hand. Let me exemplify one inflection of achieved resource as sighted from this vantage point (duck blind or conning tower, it all depends). One experimental form I recognize is the poem which is *an answer* in terms of some extra-poetical convention, some way of *getting across* from the private life to the public image by means, for once, of the media, the very forms which so promiscuously surround when they do not seduce or smother us—take Cynthia Macdonald's slide-show lecture in this issue, or David Petteys' blue movie in *NAR* 12.

Poems have been, and will be, submitted, and published, which do not *look* like "poems," but they have the form of themselves, a response to what is not themselves, sometimes the answer to a questionnaire, a multiple-choice market-research sheet, an obituary, you name it. For that is the point: the poet names it, and by so doing constitutes the identity of experience and experiment which is an identity indeed—the calling into being, not into doubt, of the made thing (the *poem*, the *fiction*—the words mean the same) which is the true vocation, the mouth, the myth, of the poet.

RH

CONTRIBUTORS

Kenneth Bernard has worked for several years with the Playhouse of the Ridiculous in New York. His work has been performed at La MaMa and elsewhere, and his fiction and poetry have appeared in various periodicals. "King Kong: A Meditation" is adapted from a longer work, "The Kong Series."

George Blecher is co-editor of *Survival Prose* and is working on a novel. He's written for *The Village Voice* and *New York Element* and teaches at Lehman College in New York City.

Austin Clarke was born in Barbados and lives in Canada. A visiting professor in the Black Studies program at Duke this year, he's also taught at Williams, Brandeis, and Yale. He's currently working on a book, *God and Mammon at Yale,* based on his experiences there.

Peter Cooley, assistant professor at the University of Wisconsin at Green Bay, is poetry review editor for the *North American Review* and a contributor to *Poetry Northwest, Crazy Horse, The Seneca Review,* and other periodicals.

Robert Coover, a frequent contributor to *NAR,* is the author of *The Origin of the Brunists, The Universal Baseball Association,* and most recently, *Pricksongs and Descants.* "Lucky Pierre and the Music Lesson" is part of a work in progress.

Peter Davison is presently on leave from his position as director of The Atlantic Monthly Press. His most recent collection of poems, *Pretending to Be Asleep,* was published by Atheneum in 1970.

Alvin Greenberg's novel *Going Nowhere* was published last summer. Editor of *The Minnesota Review,* he's coĩ tributed stories, poems, and essays to *NAR* (#8, 10, 11), *Transatlantic Review, December,* and other publications.

Pamela Hadas is a graduate student in English at Washington University in St. Louis. She plans to visit New Jersey some day.

Daryl Hine, editor of *Poetry,* is presently completing a metrical translation of the minor Homeric hymns.

James (Mike) Kempton was perhaps the most original of the young radical writers who have come our way. His story "Dare to Struggle, Dare to Win," a brilliant satire on student activism, appeared in *NAR 11;* this story, along with the present one, were to be part of a longer work. Mr. Kempton and his wife, the writer Jean Goldschmidt, died in an automobile accident last fall.

Maxine Kumin's novel, *The Abduction,* was brought out last fall by Harper & Row. Her poems have appeared in *Harper's, The New Yorker, Poetry,* and other periodicals.

Doris Lessing's fiction includes *The Golden Notebook, The Four-Gated City,* and most recently, *Briefing for a Descent into Hell* (Knopf).

Meyer Liben's collection of stories, *Justice Hunger,* was published in 1967. He's appeared in *New Directions, Commentary, Epoch,* and other magazines.

Cynthia Macdonald, a former opera singer, teaches writing at Sarah Lawrence College. She's published in *New American Review* (#11), *Prism International, Envoi,* and other periodicals.

James Merrill won the National Book Award for Poetry in 1967. Atheneum will issue a new collection, *Braving the Elements,* in the fall.

Donald M. Monroe taught at the University of Oregon (Eugene), and is presently looking for a teaching job. He previously published a story in the *Northwest Review*.

Howard Moss is poetry editor of *The New Yorker*. *Selected Poems* was published by Atheneum last year.

Steven Orlen's poems have appeared in *The Nation, The Massachusetts Review, The Iowa Review,* and other magazines. He teaches at the University of Arizona (Tucson).

Reynolds Price's first novel, *A Long and Happy Life,* was published ten years ago. "For Ernest Hemingway" will appear in a collection of his essays, *Things Themselves,* which Atheneum will publish later this spring.

Randall Reid lives in Desert Springs, California, near the Nevada border, where he is dean of Desert Springs College. His book on *The Fiction of Nathanael West* was issued by University of Chicago Press in 1968. "Detritus" is his first published story.

Peter Steinfels is associate editor of *Commonweal* magazine. He is completing a study of French intellectuals in the 1930's.

Roger Weingarten's first book of poems, *What Are Birds Worth,* will be issued by Cummington Press in the near future. He teaches at Western Michigan University in Kalamazoo.

James Welch is presently working on a novel. His first book of poems, *Riding the Earth Boy 40,* was published by World last year.

Thomas Williams is the author of five novels, most recently *Whipple's Castle* (Random House). He teaches English at the University of New Hampshire.

Complete Your Set of NAR

☐ NAR #1   William H. Gass *In the Heart of the Heart of the Country*, Philip Roth *The Jewish Blues*, William Mathes *Swan Feast*, Stanley Kauffmann *Drama on The Times*, Benjamin DeMott *"But He's a Homo-Sexual . . . ,"* Grace Paley *Faith: In a Tree* . . .

☐ NAR #2   Alan Friedman *Willy-Nilly*, John Barth *Autobiography*, Nat Hentoff *Reflections on Black Power*, Arlene Heyman *Strains of Iris*, Günter Grass *Four Poems* . . .

☐ NAR #3   George Dennison *The First Street School*, Donald Barthelme *Robert Kennedy Saved from Drowning*, Paul West *A Passion to Learn*, Philip Roth *Civilization and Its Discontents*, Albert Goldman *The Emergence of Rock* . . .

☐ NAR #4   Robert Coover *The Cat in the Hat for President*, C. C. O'Brien *Politics as Drama as Politics*, Mordecai Richler *A Sense of the Ridiculous*, Alan Lelchuk *Of Our Time*, Richard Gilman, *The True and Only Crisis of the Theatre* . . .

☐ NAR #5   Pat Watters *"Keep on A-Walkin', Children,"* Wilfrid Sheed *Eugene McCarthy*, Eric Bentley *The Unliberated University*, Jay Neugeboren *Reflections at Thirty*, Jules Siegel *The Man Who Believed in Christmas Trees* . . .

☐ NAR #6   Jane Jacobs *Why Cities Stagnate*, Ellen Willis *Lessons of Chicago*, Robert Stone *Porque No Tiene* . . . , William H. Gass *We Have Not Lived the Right Life*, Eric Salzman *The Revolution in Music* . . .

☐ NAR #7   Kate Millett *Sexual Politics*, Rosalyn Drexler *Like* . . . , Michael Herr *Illumination Rounds*, L. Woiwode *Don't You Wish You Were Dead* . . .

☐ NAR #8   John H. Schaar *Reflections on Authority*, George Dennison *On Being a Son*, Eric Bentley *Theater and Therapy*, Theodore Solotaroff *Silence, Exile, and Cunning*, Ernest Callenbach *The Death of the Movie Aesthetic* . . .

☐ NAR #9   Alfred Chester *The Foot*, Theodore Roszak *The Artificial Environment*, Samuel R. Delany *The Unicorn Tapestry*, Richard Gilman *Jerzy Grotowski*, *Symposium: The Writer's Situation I* . . .

☐ NAR #10   Philip Roth *On the Air*, William H. Gass *In Terms of the Toenail: Fiction and the Figures of Life*, Arno Karlen *The Guardian*, Jules Siegel *Family Secrets*, *Symposium: The Writer's Situation II* . . .

☐ NAR #11   M. F. Beal *Gold*, Paul West *The Season of the Single Women*, Michael Rossman *The Day We Named Our Child*, Robert Coover *The Last Quixote*, Nicholas von Hoffman *Nixon*, Norman Martien *Getting Out of Schools*, *Symposium: The Writer's Situation III* . . .

☐ NAR #12   A. Alvarez *Sylvia Plath: A Memoir*, Norman Mailer *A Course in Film-Making*, Robert Coover *Love Scene*, Michael Rossman *Introduction to Dome-Building: A Geodesic Meditation*, Donald Barthelme *Alexandria and Henrietta*, Richard Brautigan *The World War I LA Airplane* . . .

New American Review
Subscription Dept., Simon & Schuster, Inc.
1 West 39th Street, New York, N.Y. 10018

Please send me the copies of *New American Review* checked above.

Enclosed is my check for $_____, calculated at $.75 per copy.

Name _____*PB-04596_____

Address _____5-13_____
                    C
City _____ State _____ Zip Code _____

Please allow at least three weeks for delivery.
Foreign orders: add $.50 per copy for postage.